# A Mischievous Saint

(Photo Portrait by Sam and Carolyn Johnston)

ULYSSES SHORT GORDON, D.D., D.Hu.L

# Preacher Gordon:
# A Mischievous Saint

*by*

LESTER L. HALE

*Assisted by Perry A. Foote, Jr.*

*The Christian charisma of
a man called Preacher*

MAY, 1982
GAINESVILLE, FLORIDA

*Memorial Edition*

LIBRARY OF CONGRESS No. 82-81358
ISBN No. 0-9608-0820-5

COPYRIGHT © 1982 BY LESTER L. HALE
10112 NORTH MAGNA CARTA
BATON ROUGE, LOUISIANA 70815

PRINTED BY
STORTER PRINTING COMPANY, INC.
GAINESVILLE, FLORIDA

Dedicated to my wife
MINNIELEE GORDON HALE
without whom this book
could not have been written

# CONTENTS

FOREWORD .................................. ix

ACKNOWLEDGEMENTS ..................... xi

INTRODUCTION ............................. xiii

PREFACE .................................... xvii

PART I. JUST PREACHER
    Chapter 1. A Man Sent from Sardis ........ 2
    Chapter 2. A Home in Florida ............. 10
    Chapter 3. Charisma Plus ................. 22
    Chapter 4. Going to the Dogs ............. 30
    Chapter 5. Blessed Buckeyes .............. 46

PART II. BELOVED PASTOR
    Chapter 6. A Pulpit Preacher ............. 54
    Chapter 7. Mikesville's Church Mouse ...... 67
    Chapter 8. Don't Forget Prayer Meeting! ... 73
    Chapter 9. Cutting Through Red Tape ..... 82

PART III. SPIRITUAL ADVISOR
    Chapter 10. Comfort Ye His People ........ 92
    Chapter 11. The Candy Man .............. 104
    Chapter 12. "She's Stolen My Teeth" ....... 112
    Chapter 13. "Be Ye Steadfast" ............. 117

## PART IV. BOUNDLESS FRIENDSHIPS

Chapter 14. Muscle Deacons . . . . . . . . . . . . . . 130
Chapter 15. A Fisher of Men . . . . . . . . . . . . . . 149
Chapter 16. Play a Good Game . . . . . . . . . . . 161
Chapter 17. Walk Humbly . . . . . . . . . . . . . . . 168
Chapter 18. Breaking Bread Together . . . . . . 176

## PART V. A MISCHIEVOUS SAINT

Chapter 19. Tempered Wit . . . . . . . . . . . . . . 188
Chapter 20. "Blest Be the Tie" . . . . . . . . . . . 197
Chapter 21. "A Man's Shadow" . . . . . . . . . . 206
Chapter 22. Still the Life of the Party . . . . . . 214

## APPENDIX

A. Biographical Sketch . . . . . . . . . . . . . . . . . 219
B. Sermons and Prayers . . . . . . . . . . . . . . . . 221
C. Tributes and Citations . . . . . . . . . . . . . . . 233

# FOREWORD

This happy story about the life of Preacher Gordon brings forth for me a flood of marvelous memories as it will for all who knew him. It amplifies the appreciation I have for the good force he exerted on my life and all the many he touched so gently but firmly. For those who did not have the heart warming and mind expanding privilege of sharing a part of this unique and human preacher, this gives them that opportunity to listen to, walk with, and enjoy him.

It is difficult, if not impossible, to capture in printed or spoken words the contributions, the character, the moving Christian spirit, the humanness, and the events which reflect the life and work of any man—more so, that of one who was a central figure in the lives of so many. But, Les Hale has come as close as any writer could. Only one who had sat at the feet of the teacher, had shared intimate moments, had been touched and motivated by his Christian charisma, and wept unashamedly at his joining his Maker could do so.

True, the book does not tell all the story of despair which every man of God experiences in his ministry—the pain and suffering, the tugging on the heart strings, the defeats, the times when his Lord may seem to have turned a deaf ear to prayer, or a parishioner had ignored his teachings, those sad events and inner feelings. Preacher must have suffered these, too, but he rarely showed them, and in consequence, they are not revealed in this volume.

Reflection of the troubles and problems of life is not

the purpose of this book; it is, rather, a presentation of Preacher Gordon in the effervescent, always optimistic, pleasant and uplifting way he walked through his life of service to his God and to his "most fay-vor-rite" men or women who were all those around him.

I knew Preacher well for over 40 years. I played handball with him, and although I didn't attend his church, I was one of his "bed-shakers" in the Alpha Tau Omega fraternity house with the charge to awake his student parishioners on Sunday morning. It was my privilege to walk and talk with him, to benefit from his wisdom, enjoy his incomparable wit, and in later years on occasion to share with him a little bourbon and branch water for "medicinal purposes," of course.

Writing this book was a major undertaking. That it was performed as a labor of love by Les Hale is obvious in its every word. All the multitudes who loved and learned from Preacher owe to the author, and those who assisted him, our gratitude and our praise for a superb work about a truly exemplary human being who served his God and influenced his "neighbors" so indelibly as few others have.

STEPHEN C. O'CONNELL<br>
President Emeritus,<br>
University of Florida

# ACKNOWLEDGMENTS

The author wishes to make special acknowledgment of the sizable grant to Suwannee Presbytery by the Edna S. Williams Foundation as a memorial gift ear-marked for the publication of this Memorial Edition. Charles J. and Edna Williams were long time friends of Preacher; they had made extensive donations at Preacher's asking for such purposes as the Presbyterian Student Center and Highlands Presbyterian Church property, as well as for countless other causes. They had great love and admiration for Preacher, and their country place near Fairfield, Florida, at one time provided a kennel for as many as eleven of Preacher's hunting dogs. They gave him the key to the house and he was to understand he could come and go as he pleased, using it as his own retreat.

Appreciation is also expressed to the two nieces, Helen Bridger Gordon and Minnielee Gordon Hale, and to the nephew, William (Billy) Bradshaw Gordon, Jr., for releasing the portrait negative for use in printing the frontispiece. The original portrait was given for permanent hanging in the Gordon Memorial Hall of First Presbyterian Church of Gainesville, Florida.

Many references in the book are from the memory of these next of kin to whom the author is deeply indebted, not only for their contributions of material, but for their careful reading, excellent suggestions, and enthusiastic encouragement in the composition of the manuscript. Their assistance in capturing the character of Preacher has been indispensable to the writing of the book.

The author wishes also to thank Dr. Samuel Proctor and the Oral History Project of the University of Florida for material quoted from the interviews with Dr. Gordon recorded not long before his death.

It is impossible to mention the names of all who answered requests for stories about Preacher because material came to the author in varied and sundry ways and forms—some written, some verbal—and much from his own memory.

Others to whom the author is indebted include:

- Dr. Stephen C. O'Connell for the Foreword;
- Dr. Perry A. Foote, Jr. for the Introduction which is self-explanatory of his dedicated involvement in the initiation of this book;
- Dr. Douglas Taylor for professional editorial assistance;
- The Rev. William Shea for review of portions of the manuscript;
- The Rev. Sherrard Rice for helpful suggestions;
- David Beard for coordination with the printer including proofreading and other special services;
- Richard Stoop for design of the dust cover;
- Alachua General Hospital for color photos of the Preacher Gordon Memorial Chapel;
- Gayle Taylor, Debra Paterson, and Doris Little for typing;
- Morris Storter who, because of his own love for Preacher, gave his personal attention to printing of the book;
- Marinus Latour, electronics engineer, who collaborated with the author in producing broadcasts from the new church, and in taping the worship in the old and new sanctuaries from which much of the material in Appendix B was transcribed.

# INTRODUCTION

During the general outpouring of grief following the death of Preacher Gordon, hundreds urged that his anecdotes and the stories about him be preserved while they were fresh in mind and could be recorded for posterity.

In order to get something underway, I sent a letter to friends of Preacher and made other contacts by telephone and in person to exhort individuals to send in their written memories as contributions for a possible book.

Letters began pouring in, and Les Hale and I met together to exchange ideas on how such a book could become a reality. After several sessions during which we read the letters and had preliminary conversations, Les agreed to write the book and I agreed to assist by submitting short stories and my own memories of significant events. It was my happy task to aid in gathering Preacher's prayers, sermons, and pictures, and to review and offer suggestions on the completed manuscript.

My parents came to Gainesville in 1928, the same year Preacher arrived, and they promptly joined his flock. I was born eight years later and for the next forty years, he was "my pastor, my Preacher, my pal." My earliest recollection of Preacher Gordon was at the age of five when he told me, "I want to see you on the front pew Sunday morning." Dutifully, every Sunday as a small boy, I would sit on the first row of the sanctuary with Preacher's eyes on me throughout the services; somehow I knew and believed that I belonged there. Thus began a very deep and profound relationship which lasted until his death. My rearing as a child was greatly influenced by the nurturing and gentle admonitions of my lifelong "spiritual father." He referred to me as his "baptized child."

Preacher was present at all the milestone events in the life of the Foote family—baptisms, marriages, and funerals. In our joys and in our sorrows, he was always there to share, rejoice, sustain, strengthen, and guide us. When he was present, you just knew everything would be all right . . . for everything about him . . . his stature, his style, his convictions, his spirit, conveyed enduring strength. He baptized me as an infant, along with my brother and my sister, and almost thirty-five years later, baptized our first child, Karin. Preacher graciously journeyed to Pennsylvania to marry Judy and me; he also officiated at the marriages of my brother, Roger, and sister, Mary. He conducted the funeral of my dear mother and later remarried my father.

When I was fourteen years old, I began to accompany Preacher every other Sunday to a local road prison camp where chapel services were held for the inmates. A group of us would play musical instruments as accompaniment for the singing of hymns. We would gather at his home for an early morning breakfast and then depart for the prison. I continued with him in this ministry for almost ten years.

For some twenty years, it was my privilege to eat breakfast with Preacher every Saturday and/or Sunday. Those were happy times in my life. We would dine, pray, meditate, laugh, reflect, grieve, and sing together. Scriptures were read . . . religion, philosophy, world and social problems were discussed. Many an hour was spent together fishing, exploring the woods, playing gin rummy. Frequently, we took his dogs for runs in the country. During his latter years, I drove and was his companion at meetings, installation ceremonies, and parties. The last few years of his life, it was my privilege to fill the pulpit at the Archer Bethlehem Presbyterian Church when he was too ill to lead the services.

I was devoted to Preacher and followed him as he led me to love the Lord. I loved him as much as one could possibly love another fellow being. The breadth and depth of his influence on my life cannot be measured. He was a man in Christ, God's man, one of the great men of the church and of our day. We were privileged to know him and we are all better people because we journeyed with him. May this book give you a vision of the truth that is in Jesus Christ Our Lord, as it was revealed and found in the life of this remarkable man of God.

PERRY A. FOOTE, JR., M.D.<br>
Gainesville, Florida<br>
1982

Preacher Gordon Memorial Chapel
Alachua General Hospital, Gainesville, Florida

# PREFACE

This book is a story of how the Christian charisma of Preacher Gordon gladdened the hearts of the multitude that surrounded him.

Those who knew him best, and whose lives were touched by his, need no book of tales to deepen the imprint he made on them. Indeed, neither nostalgia nor legend alone would have prompted the compilation of these stories as a memorial to such a mischievous saint as was Preacher Gordon.

Much more important is the fact that when a Christian giant has fallen, it is incumbent upon someone to make his quality of life known to all generations. Just as he gave a lift in his lifetime to all with whom he walked, it is hoped he will live within these pages and lift up your hearts as you read about this eminent, well-educated, and influential man of God.

Preacher was not only my beloved pastor and spiritual advisor, he was my most treasured, faithful friend and confidant. In fact, through the years, we developed a veritable father-son relationship.

One incident, years ago, typifies the unusual bond that existed between us. I had asked Preacher to go with me to a neighboring city where I was to give a commencement address in a coliseum. When we arrived at the large arena, we noticed that the seats were roped off for the graduates and their families in such a way that there was no place for Preacher to sit near the front. I told him I would take him down and introduce him to the major domo so he could sit as a member of my family right in the front row.

We walked around until I could find the man in charge of the arrangements. When I found him, I told him I had brought my "father" with me, for indeed Preacher was my surrogate father, and needed to be seated somewhere near the rostrum so he could see and hear. Preacher had caught up with me by that time, and I introduced him as my father. It hadn't occurred to me that the stranger would have no reason to doubt my veracity much less know that Preacher was at that time a bachelor.

He put out his hand in greetings to Preacher and said quite naturally, "How do you do, Mr. Hale. We are so glad to have you with us."

Preacher pulled himself up to his full six-foot, one-inch height, tapped his cane on the concrete floor for emphasis and replied, "Well, my name's not Hale; it's Gordon. He's my son by a former marriage!"

Preacher regarded himself as a member of my family; and, of course, my wife, Evelyn, and our three children claimed him. He was present with us at every celebration and in every sorrow, and we shared our blood kin with each other. No matter where he might go on New Year's Eve, as midnight approached, he always made his way to our house and joined us and the children who were reveling in the "rumpus room."

Preacher knew I had harbored from childhood the desire to become an ordained minister. As a believer in a strong laity, Preacher convinced me that I should remain active in all facets of the church and give my testimony of faith through my career at the University of Florida. When I became the Dean of Men and later the Vice President for Student Affairs, he reinforced his contention: "Where else can you get a church of 30,000 members with a turn-over every four years?" He had made his point!

When he asked Evelyn and me to teach Sunday School, we did. When he needed a scoutmaster and a choir director, I was it. Later, I was elected deacon and ultimately an elder. I always felt one of my most important contributions was to set the clock in the rear of the sanctuary by Western Union time on Sunday mornings so Preacher would not worry about letting church out promptly. Together, we did radio broadcasts, obtained and played carillon bells, made tape-recordings of services of worship, and supplied the needs of country churches. He was my mentor; I was his arms and legs!

In due season, he concurred in my desire to retire from the University and urged me then to seek candidacy and ordination as a Presbyterian minister.

He preached my ordination sermon and contributed immeasurably to my ministry at Silver Springs Shores, southeast of Ocala, Florida, where I was the organizing pastor of an emerging mission congregation. He shared with me in many services of worship and was a frequent visitor at my travel-trailer which I named MOBILE MANSE of the PRESBYTERIAN CHURCH, U.S.

On many occasions, he called me when he needed to be taken to the hospital. When his or our relatives were in town, our table was bountifully set to include them all, especially Preacher. On Sunday nights after he had called his nephew in Mississippi and his two nieces in Tennessee and Louisiana, he would call us to share in the news of them. It was almost axiomatic that the night before he entered the hospital for the last time, he should have had dinner and spent the evening with Evelyn and me in our home.

At the hospital, I sat by his side and held his hand as he winced in pain and finally gave way to disorientation. He kept looking at his hospital bracelet and asking me what time his watch said.

"My goodness, let's call it a day," he reacted when I told him, "we've been here long enough." Then he would try to get out of bed and I would have to hold him back.

"Preacher," I said, "you can't get up. You've got too many tubes in you. You've got everything but an inner tube."

"Lesterbell," he squirmed, "you're right. I've got too many tubes. Tell them to take them out and give them to the poor and needy." Always thinking of someone else! Always trying to find the twinkle of laughter in the tear of tragedy.

At his funeral, my tribute began: A Christian giant has fallen! Nay, has been lifted up and glorified by the Holy Spirit of Christ, our Lord . . .

Preacher was not alive when it came time to share my greatest sorrow. Four months after he died, my wife suddenly and unexpectedly became ill and passed away quickly and quietly. After a long year of bewilderment, a miracle happened to me. One of Preacher's nieces came as an answer to my prayers for God's direction in my life. Minnielee is now my wife, and Preacher is now my uncle. Still another dimension has been added to my understanding and love of Preacher. I don't yet feel comfortable referring to him as "Unkie," but I am proud to be able to write about my spiritual father.

This book is organized to follow the remarks that rolled spontaneously from my heart at the funeral.

Why did we love him? Let me count the ways:

> Because he was natural and had a deep down reverance, was revered but had no superficial piety. He was just "Preacher."

> \* \* \* \* \*

> Because he loved the church and served the body of believers whether they were in or out of the sanctuary.

> \* \* \* \* \*

> Because he had the divine gift to be our "spiritual advisor."

Because he was good, but not too good, and people could identify with him: rich men, poor men, beggar men, thieves, doctors, lawyers, merchants, chiefs.

* * * * *

Because he met you where you were and walked with you to help carry the load.

* * * * *

Because he could walk with kings and not lose the common touch; his influence reached from the low places of life to the leadership of state and nation.

* * * * *

Because his friendship knew no bounds of church, denomination, status, race, or creed.

* * * * *

Because he understood people's weaknesses and forgave them, found some good in everyone, revealed the mischief in himself, was empathic with those in trouble and could become emotionally involved without losing his composure.

* * * * *

Because he could break tensions and "cut the fool" with wit tempered by good will and a profound human kindness.

* * * * *

Had the tremendous task of retelling the life of such an extraordinary man as Preacher Gordon been undertaken immediately after his death the result might well have been more sentimental than uplifting. It is hoped that this book will refresh the memories of those who experienced life with Preacher, as I did, and will inspire hope in others who need a Christian giant with whom to identify.

Preacher was a happy man who loved people, loved a good time, and loved his Lord. May the story of my pal, Preacher, lift up your hearts, quicken your steps, and lead you to a deeper understanding of God's love.

LESTER L. HALE, PH.D.<br>
Gainesville, Florida<br>
1982

# PART I

## JUST PREACHER

"... *Because he was natural and had a deep down reverence, was revered but had no superficial piety. He was just 'Preacher.'* "

# 1

## A MAN SENT FROM SARDIS

**M**ANY CITIES AND PEOPLE have been named for places and persons in the Bible so there was nothing unusual about naming a farm community in northern Mississippi, *Sardis*. What is of importance is that from this small town emerged a young man by the name of Ulysses Short Gordon who later became widely known as "Preacher."

In the third chapter of Revelation, the Spirit writes to the angel of the Sardis church in the ancient province of Asia Minor:

> I know your deeds; you have a reputation of being alive, but you are dead. Wake up! . . . Yet you have a few people in Sardis who have not soiled their clothes. They will walk with me, dressed in white, for they are worthy. He who overcomes will, like them, be dressed in white. I will never erase his name from the book of life, but will acknowledge his name before my Father and his angels. He who has an ear, let him hear what the Spirit says to the churches.
>
> *from New International Version*

Like the fulfillment of an ancient prophecy, a man was sent from Sardis, Mississippi, whose name will "never be erased from the book of life but will be acknowledged before his Father and his angels." That man was Preacher

Gordon, and, beginning with his ordination on June 3, 1917 in the Presbyterian Church at Sardis where he had been baptized and reared, he was to serve his Lord for the next fifty-eight years.

He was an outgoing and friendly man, a special kind of person for whom the name, *Preacher,* symbolized his closeness to a kaleidoscope of kith and kin. No one persisted in identifying him as Dr. Gordon, for his new acquaintances soon became more comfortable referring to him as just Preacher. Even in the cut and dried formality of platform introductions most speakers could not resist a more familiar style.

"To give the Invocation at this Commencement, is the Reverend Dr. U. S. Gordon, more affectionately known as Preacher. May I present Preacher Gordon!"

To Preacher Gordon, no man was a stranger!

While the name, *Preacher,* better suited the man, he was proud of his given name and of the heritage it represented. "I was named for a Confederate soldier, Ulysses Short, who was a cavalryman with General Bedford Forrest," Preacher told Dr. Sam Proctor, who taped a conference with him for the University Oral History Project. (*See Acknowledgements*)

He added, "I often have to explain that my initials, U. S., do not indicate I was named for Ulysses S. Grant, though I think he was a very worthy and magnanimous man in his treatment of Lee at Appomattox. But I was named for a brave, young cavalryman serving under Forrest whose courageous exploits are well known to the older people of West Tennessee, North Alabama and North Mississippi."

Preacher's heritage included a long line of illustrious national and southern heroes that began prior to the American Revolution and included two outstanding generals of the Civil War: General James B. Gordon of North Carolina and General John B. Gordon of Georgia. Preacher's pride in his lineage was expressed in the Oral History interview in this way:

"My father's name was Charles Law Gordon, a native of Maury County, Tennessee, near Columbia, where his father, a Confederate officer, was located in the 1840's. In turn, *his* father was a Revolutionary soldier, Chapman Gordon, who fought in the battle of King's Mountain, later married Charity King, and is my great grandfather who is buried under the Presbyterian Church at North Wilkesboro, North Carolina."

Even as a child, his pride and interest in his country was apparent and should gladden the heart of all who are saddened by the literal and figurative flag burnings of our day. At the age of nine, he made a patriotic scrapbook that included pictures of George Washington, the Flag of the United States, poems, hymns and other material which were descriptive of dedication to country. After his death, when his personal papers were being sorted by his survivors, this scrapbook was found—dog-eared and scarred, but carefully preserved among his most cherished possessions.

His idealism was translated into action immediately following his ordination during World War I. "I had been called to the church in Charleston, Mississippi, in Tallahassee County, and had gone down there to preach. All the young men there were in the army. I felt that I was in the wrong spot if I were not doing the same thing. I was able-bodied, healthy, and had no encumberances so I felt that I should enlist. I had serious scruples against using my calling as a dugout to protect me from army duties. The church in Charleston understood my position so I waived exemption and immediately went into the army.

"We were placed in an infantry outfit and those with college training were given the option of going to officer training school or taking a course to prepare us for being surgical assistants in field hospitals. I was one of twenty selected to Mayo's hospital in Rochester, Minnesota, where we spent several months in training to assist in field surgery. I was at Fort Snelling getting ready to go

## A Historic Cameo.
### By MARY INGE HOSKINS.

Not long since while watching a magnificent steamer churn the blue waters of the sunny Tennessee to a white foam two traveling men, with every evidence of culture and refinement, read the name painted on its white side with this remark:

"'Sam Davis.' I suppose that's the name of the man who owns the boat, but I never heard of him before."

I then thought what is fame? What was the use of dying the brave heroic death that young Sam Davis did, if within the confines of his native State there were men who had never heard of how and why he gave up his beautiful young life?

Forty years ago all this section known as the "Dimple of the Universe," or the middle Basin of Tennessee, was a scene of carnage and bloodshed. Gen. Bragg, who was located at Missionary Ridge, selected a young beardless boy of 20, with four other scouts to find out if the Federal army was moving from Nashville to Corinth to reinforce Chattanooga. Young Davis secured valuable papers, with a complete map of every fortification, found out the full strength and position of every regiment located in Tennessee. Now, let us drop the veil of forty years and look back into the unforgotten past. On November 27, 1863, when the crimson flush of a —ving day deepened into burnished gold, when the first lances of sunlight struck the treetops, shivered into a million scintillant points and fell like a glittering heap of glory into the lap of old mother earth; a group of stalwart men with saddened hearts choked back the rising sobs as they entered the guard house at Pulaski, Tenn. When they emerged one more was added to the group, a noble specimen of strong young manhood, where gifts of inheritance and environment had combined to form a perfect man, only twenty glad summers had taught him how beautiful it was to live, and as he walked out into God's sunshine that tragic morning the very birds hushed their joyous matins; the star-eyed gentian gave back to the skies its bit of blue and dropped its dewy head to the earth as if in mortal anguish; the majestic old hills of Tennessee stood with the silent grandeur of ages surrounding their sun-crowned heads to witness this day that which would be commemorated in history as long as Southern men live to —" the story of Southern chivalry. These same old hills had witnessed solemn love vows as Sam Davis, with boyish ardor, bade good-bye to the sweet mountain maiden who had pledged her troth to him under the great white harvest moon. How sweet was life to Sam Davis! Did not the same old hills watch Lieut. Spalding creep with stealthy tread of an experienced soldier into one of their secluded coverts and capture this brave boy while he was resting from the chase of life and death, and now they must silently witness the last scene in the vivid life drama. Young Davis was handcuffed, seated upon his own coffin, and driven to East Hill, a suburb of Pulaski, Tenn., where everything was in readiness for the sad execution of this brave boy. He was not to die at the battle front, with the wild excitement of overcoming shot and bomb of shell to deaden the love of life, or fear of death. No, his was death of deliberate choosing —with a calmness born of desperate resolve he was to die rather than imperil his honor or betray a friend—and yet life was as sweet to him. At any time he could have told the Achan in the camp and been free—free to have gone back to the old homestead and mother—free to pledge anew the untroubled vow at the old trysting place. When he was first captured Gen. Dodge, the Federal general in command at Pulaski, finding that the very papers hidden in the saddle seat of young Davis were taken from his own table at headquarters, knew that some member of his staff had been untrue to himself, his country and his God, he offered young Davis absolute unconditional freedom if he would tell the name of the man who had stolen the papers, and revealed official secrets. This he refused to do. Upon being told that he would be court-martialed, convicted and executed as a spy, there was no chance for him unless he told the name of the traitor, he replied: "I know I will have to die, but no power on earth can make me tell a lie. You are doing your duty as a soldier and I am doing mine. I would rather die than break my word. You may hang me if you will, but I will never betray the trust reposed in me." The Federal general ordered a court-martial, and after Davis was sentenced he was so impressed with the boy's bravery and high sense of honor that he sent a lady friend of his mother's to urge him to reveal the name and go free—free. Life was sweet to Sam Davis, but honor was sweeter. When this friend counted the joyous beads in the rosary of his life if he would only breathe the name of the traitor, his fight against the fierce temptation was sharp, but victorious—life was very, very sweet to young Sam Davis at this time. He wept bitterly as he told her that life held everything that was dear and holy to him, but life without honor was but a tarnished toy. So he was driven that morning—forty years ago today—over to East Hill. Gen. Dodge thought that when placed on the scaffold and he realized that death was inevitable, his courage would vanish, but the eagle has never yet been fed on carrion. Gen. Dodge plead with him, after the rope was adjusted, to tell the name of the man who gave him the papers; he offered to return his side arms, his horse and give him a safe escort into the Confederate lines. Davis replied: "If I had a thousand lives, I would lose them all before I would betray a friend, or the confidence of my informer. I am ready. Do your duty, men."

The hills smiled back a farewell smile,
The breeze sobbed on his hair awhile,
The birds broke out in glad refrain.
The sunbeams kissed his cheek again,
Then, gathering up their blazing bars,
They shook his name among the stars.
Oh, stars that now his brothers are!
Oh, suns his sire in truth and light,
Go tell the listening worlds afar
Of him who died for truth and right.
For martyr of all martyrs he
Who dies to save an enemy.

BALBOA TAKING POSSESSION OF THE PACIFIC OCEAN.

JEFFERSON DAVIS.

GEORGE WASHINGTON.

CROSSING THE DELAWARE.

BOMBARDMENT OF FORT SUMTER.

overseas when the war ended and the Armistice was signed."

Preacher was a great patriot and believed in loyalty to and defense of his country. He volunteered for service again in World War II but was rejected. This spurred him to buy as many war bonds as he could possibly afford. He never redeemed them; they were found in his bank box after his death.

When turned down as a volunteer, he said to a deacon who was on the draft board, "There are so many German submarines off the coast of Florida, it is fearsome. Do you think there is anything I can do with my old shotgun?"

His lineage and love of country made him very knowledgeable of American history and especially of the War Between the States. He often said that the northern and southern branches of the Presbyterian Church had been divided less over theological or regional disputes than by the fact that commissioners from the local churches and presbyteries could not cross the battle lines to get to the meetings of the General Assembly (highest governing body of the Presbyterian Church).

No such national division exists today to keep Presbyterians apart. Christian love transcends all forms of denominational barriers, and Preacher always emphasized our unity in Christ rather than our differences with each other.

His good nature and good voice often helped to create a sense of camaraderie and brotherhood at Rotary Club meetings, public picnics, or other occasions when a mixture of faiths and denominations might be present. Family night dinners at the Presbyterian Church always included visitors who felt close to Preacher but who might be members of other churches or of no church at all. He loved to lean back in his chair after the coffee-soaked table cloths had been rolled up and taken out of sight, and in pure fun and fellowship "heist" one of his favorite spirited songs.

Of all the religions I profess
Of all the religions I profess
Of all the religions I profess
The Pres-bye-ter-ians is the bess(t)
No hidin' place down here.

CHORUS
No hidin' place down here, Hallelujah!
No hidin' place down here.
Oh, I went to the rock to hide my face,
The rock cried out: No hidin' place;
No hiding place down here.

But Preacher's boasting about Presbyterians was not prejudice; it was only chiding. His Christian love knew no denominational bounds. His horizontal love for his fellow man was infinite; his vertical love was steadfast and fixed on his Lord and Master.

Such devotion did not come upon him suddenly nor through a flaming vision; it took hold of him at an early age and became a directing force in his life. Throughout his early childhood there were strong evidences of his uncommon interest in Sunday School, his church, and memorization of Scripture.

When he told his parents that he wanted to go to seminary, his mother, Alice Short Gordon, said to her husband, "Sir Charles, I am not at all surprised—only grateful."

The religious training he and his two brothers, Will and Charles, experienced amplified the nurture, care and loving atmosphere that existed in their warm Christian home.

"My father was a great hunter," he explained to the interviewer. "We fished and played baseball; there were lots of horses to ride. My forebears came from Tennessee in the 1840's bringing their slaves with them and settling in Panola County, west of this little town of Sardis. That land is still in the family! My father was a planter; he was not a rich man, but he always paid his debts. He was an elder in the Presbyterian Church, and they were church-going people. We were devoted to our parents and looked up to them with great affection and respect."

As a child, he liked to play make-believe, or to conduct funeral ceremonies for a pet or an imaginary playmate. This is not an uncommon thing for children to do. However, more than play-acting seemed to be involved in the boyhood funeral that the young preacher helped to conduct. A young, black cook in the Gordon household had given birth to a baby which lived only a few days. The old white-haired grandfather of the dead infant walked in the middle of the street through downtown Sardis with a small pine box on his left shoulder and a spade in his right hand. People long remembered how there followed close on his heels a seven year old, barefoot boy wearing a straw hat and carrying in his hand a bouquet of wild flowers—Luther, the black grandfather, and Ulysses, his young friend, on their way to the graveyard.

The little boy grew into stalwart manhood, still playing at sports and carrying wild flowers to "God's green acres." He was all boy and became all man. When he decided to go off to seminary, it became apparent that his dynamic character, good humor, and love of people, fun, and games were just some of the talents he would be carrying with him to offer to the Lord's work. He graduated from Louisville Presbyterian Seminary in 1915.

It is said that he was seriously courting a girl at the time he decided to go into the ministry. She had apparently declared that she could not, or would not, wait until he finished seminary to marry him, and that she did not want to be a preacher's wife anyway. Whether this was so or not will never be known, because Preacher wouldn't talk about her.

While his unique Christian calling was enhanced by his singular marital status, it was everyone's hope that he would eventually marry.

When asked by a stranger, "Where is your wife?" he would reply demurely with his characteristic twinkle that no one will ever forget, "She is with her mother."

He was the most eligible bachelor in every town he went. When an attractive widow would approach him as he was greeting people after worship and whisper expectantly in his ear, "You don't remember me, or do you?" he had a ready answer.

In a loud, roguish voice, unmistakably intended for all around him to hear, he would reply, "No'm, I can't say that I do; you see, I had to forget you so I could go on with my work."

And so, this mischievous man, who had been predestined to be God's boy and ordained as God's servant called into the pastoral ministry of the Presbyterian Church, U. S., became just Preacher to a multitude whose hearts he lifted out of distress into the light of love. While his merriment kept him human and loved by all, his unselfish dedication to service for the Lord gave him qualities of a saint.

His name will never be erased from the book of life and he has been acknowledged before God, the Father in Heaven, and his angels as "a worthy man sent from Sardis."

# 2

## A HOME IN FLORIDA

AFTER THE WAR, Preacher went back to the little church in Charleston, Mississippi, where he had first been called after his ordination. He stayed there from 1918 until 1922 happily ministering, not only to that church, but to the other country churches associated with it at New Hope, Sardinis, and Phillips.

What made him, an athletic young scholar with vision and energy, choose the life of a country preacher? The pastoral ministry was so natural a pursuit for Preacher that he simply answered, "I felt called to do so! I never had any beatific vision with a hand rising in the sky saying 'go preach.' I was from a Christian home where the Bible was read, we sang hymns around the organ, where we had family prayers. We went to church and felt the influence of the preachers. Then, when I went to college, I belonged to Pi Kappa Alpha fraternity where most of the boys were studying for the ministry; that, too, had a great influence."

Fraternity brothers searching the Oral History project at the University of Florida to find this quotation from their national chaplain may realize the tremendous value true brotherhood, as opposed to true pranksterhood, can be in the fraternal orders of colleges and universities today.

This young man, fresh out of seminary with only a tour of army duty intervening, became the first minister of record at the Charleston church. Fires and other setbacks had destroyed the previous records of the church. By the time Preacher left Charleston for Starkville, Mississippi, the membership had doubled and the young people's work and Christian endeavor had been started and stabilized.

This first congregation has many fond memories of Preacher. One pertains to his late return from a fishing trip. He was so late he barely had time to get ready for prayer meeting. He rolled up his pants and washed his feet under the pump; but not having fresh socks with him, he asked his fishing partner's wife to run up town and buy him a pair so he could go on to church.

Another time, during a sermon in Charleston, a lady wearing a veil and nose spectacles got the glasses caught in the veil and couldn't disentangle them. Preacher stopped his sermon and told her grandson to help her get loose, and the boy took out his knife and cut the spectacles free. The sermon continued, but the veil was rent.

He is still a legend there as second and third generation Charlestonians remember him as a perfect pastor—loved

First Presbyterian Church, Charleston, Miss.

by all. Several Jewish friends gave pews to the church and one referred to himself as a Presbyterian Jew. This is indicative of how Preacher was remembered in Charleston not only by Presbyterians but by the entire community.

While there, he bought a Model T Ford but on his meagre $600 per year salary he could hardly pay for it, and he couldn't learn to drive it, so he sold it. Consequently, most of his visiting was done on horse, mule, or foot.

A member of the Charleston church, who was only nine years old when Preacher was there, says his mother liked to recall, "He ate with us whenever he was invited and came at any other time he wanted to."

He seemed to be a successful and much loved pastor from the beginning. This statement in the oral history interview gives the clue: "As a country preacher you visited the people and tried to get them into active work and worship in the church. You did what any pastor does," said Preacher. "You get to know people and be with them in their troubles and their happiness—in their vicissitudes and ups and downs. You find some wonderful friends, the best that anyone could have." This compassion and sensitivity as a young minister set him off on the right foot from which he never swerved as he matured.

When he went to the university town of Starkville, Mississippi, he carried this philosophy with him and immediately became a favorite of students. Here he made pioneer efforts to bring pastoral benefits to students of Mississippi A & M (now Mississippi State University). In fact, his ministry to students here was one of the original religious ministries on state school campuses. He became such a popular "man on campus" that he was often called to the local constabulary office to vouch for young men who proudly gave his name in reference as a personal friend.

As a young man, his outgoing personality, youthful appearance, and friendly exuberance quickly made him a favorite with students. Walking on campus or in town, he would wave a full arm greeting and hail them from across the street. Preacher always left his key in his car for use by any of his student friends he called his "bull yearlings." His only stipulation was that they leave him with enough gas to get to a filling station.

A resident of Starkville recalls that she was a teenager when Preacher first came to be the Presbyterian pastor. He was not there long until all members of the church, young and old, fell in love with him.

First Presbyterian Church, Starkville, Miss.

In fact, the saga of his search for a wife was almost fulfilled in Starkville. The story is told of his desire to marry one of the Sunday School teachers. She was lovely and everyone thought her to be just right for Preacher and that they would soon marry. He was dating her and may well have been engaged to be married when she became critically ill and died. This great misfortune not only was tragic for Preacher, but it saddened the whole community.

In Starkville he established an enviable reputation as a pastor to students, according to one long-time resident. "He was a good preacher, friendly, handsome, and willing to listen to your problems. Through his kindness, patience, and understanding of young people, he won their love and admiration."

Preacher befriended one such down-and-out student by giving him fifty cents to buy a meal. The two became close friends, and soon Preacher was calling the young man his "assistant pastor" because of the many chores he performed for the church. Some time later, Preacher, having had a hand in getting Presbyterian Southwestern University moved from Clarksville to Memphis, Tennessee, urged his "assistant pastor" to continue his education in Memphis. This he did and ultimately obtained his degree at Southwestern at Memphis while serving at the same time as head track coach and recruiter for the Athletic Department.

This coach and quasi-pastor went on to become a very successful businessman and illustrious alumnus of Southwestern at Memphis. He became a trustee of that university, an elder in his Presbyterian church, and such a successful man in many businesses that he was named to the board of the Chamber of Commerce of the United States. He was faithful to Preacher 'til the end and was a chief mourner at the funeral services in Sardis over fifty years later.

In 1926, Preacher was called to the Second Presbyterian Church in Memphis to be the assistant pastor. He was asked to corral and work with the young people as well as to alternate with the beloved Dr. A. B. Curry in preaching the Word.

An elder in the Second Presbyterian Church of Memphis, Tennessee, wrote in his history of that church: "Preacher Gordon had a dynamic and most pleasing personality, was a man of great physical energy and spiritual purpose, and during the period he was with us the church membership grew rapidly. To quote Dr. Curry, 'His wide acquaintance, his attractive personality, his capacity for friendship, his genial spirit, coupled with his earnest preaching and untiring zeal for his Lord, and all this crowned with the blessing of the Holy Spirit, could not fail to bear fruit in the winning of men.' . . . It was not long before he was known as

Preacher Gordon
Second Presbyterian Church, Memphis, Tenn.

one of the leading ministers of our denomination, as he remains to this day. Second Church feels pride in having had a part in his training and experience."

In Memphis, as elsewhere, tales still circulate about Preacher. One of the most appealing concerns his invitation to Dr. Curry to go fishing. He told Dr. Curry that in order to catch fish he had to chew tobacco and use some of the tobacco juice as bait. Some members of the congregation were horrified to think of the angelic Dr. Curry chewing tobacco.

Preacher continued to be a magnet to all the women of the church, married, unmarried, spinsters, and widows. They decided to decorate his room by purchasing a five-foot square, black satin wall hanging on which they each embroidered their names in diverse, brilliant yarn. This touching memento from the women of Second Church adorned his guest room wall in Gainesville until his death.

In the middle of August, 1928, he received from the Presbyterian Church in Gainesville a call signed by a large committee asking that he come to be considered as their minister.

"Florida might just as well have been a foreign country as far as I was concerned. I had never dreamed of being anywhere else but in the Mississippi Valley. But," Preacher continued, "if there were people calling me sight unseen without a visitation or a trial sermon, I felt this was the leading of the Spirit."

A university professor, who was to be Clerk of the Session during most of the early years of Preacher's pastorate in Gainesville, kept a diary. From notations in this book, church and community were clearly in need of the invigorating enthusiasm of a new minister. On November 6, 1928, he entered into his diary, "Not a thing worth recording. This is a low ebb." He was not even impressed by his visit to the Florida Theater to hear "vitaphone," which he added had not been worth the effort, but he was considering "investing in a radio."

However, interest picked up on September seventh, because he went to a University of Florida alumni banquet at the Whitehouse Hotel to meet Dr. Tigert, the new president of the university. He wrote, "U. S. Gordon, who had arrived in town the same day as Dr. Tigert, was also present. A very good meeting." The next day the Clerk went with Preacher to Silver Springs and told his diary, "I think Gordon is the right man for us."

The following day was Sunday and the preacher-prospect gave the morning and evening sermons. The Clerk wrote: "Gordon preached a good sermon in morning. Heard Gordon again at night. A very eloquent talker. There was a love feast after church for him. Everyone much in favor of him. Hate to see him leave in the morning for Memphis." The following Wednesday the Men of the Church sent a telegram to U. S. Gordon to encourage him to decide in favor of accepting the call, and on September fifteenth the diary reports that he had done so. Preacher's first Sunday as pastor was on November 11, and the Clerk's diary revealed "the situation looks brighter." He was installed on December 2, 1928, the day before his 35th birthday and ten years after beginning his first pastorate.

For forty years, Preacher Gordon was to lead this body of believers through good times and bad. He would become the bellwether not only for the congregation but for the city and, through the students and faculty of the university, the state and the nation. One outstanding local attorney, not a member of the Presbyterian church has written of him:

> My own memories of Preacher are quite sobering, but extremely respectful.
>
> If I had to say what I think Preacher meant to the community, I would say he constituted the community's collective attitudes. Of all the people who have been known to me in Gainesville, I don't think anyone could lay claim to the public's conscience except Preacher Gordon. I have seen many well-meaning and influential people who could only be qualified as barometers or wind socks. Preacher constituted the weather and the wind. Never a gauge to reflect what others were doing. . . .
>
> I never felt Preacher changed his attitude to conform, but in truth the community changed its attitude to conform with his. This to me is the mark of Preacher's greatness and his lasting contribution to our town.

The new president of the University and the new Presbyterian preacher started off together and hit it off right from the start. They met at the Whitehouse Hotel where the church had put Preacher up for the night and where the alumni banquet was being held to introduce

President John J. Tigert. Preacher wasted no time taking advantage of the situation and accepted an invitation from Dr. Tigert to attend. From the outset these two men were destined to make their imprint in Florida sand.

"My admiration for Dr. Tigert approaches an extravagant attitude of respect. I came to know him well. I think in many ways he was one of the greatest men we've ever had in this community." Preacher, himself, became a University personality and twenty-five years later an article in *The Florida Alumnus* was entitled, "He's Loved by thousands, Respected by Everyone — Just Plain 'Preacher.'"

Students of the University of Florida who were troubled in mind or soul have gone a few blocks from the campus and talked with a tall man who had a Mississippi drawl and tempered his advice with subtle wit. Sometimes they received their counsel over the handball court, and sometimes in the quiet beside a lake well-filled with fish.

An athlete in his own right, Gordon and members of the University athletic teams became close friends. In 1939 he was even handball champion of the campus and took on all comers.

So close has Gordon grown to his congregation that in 1948, when he celebrated his 20th anniversary in Gainesville, he was given a summer in Scotland and England by the congregation. "As the 7th generation of a Presbyterian family in this country, I sure like seeing the home of the church," he said.

Now, to celebrate his 25th anniversary, plans are being made for a giant reunion of all the young men — some not so young anymore — who have known and loved Preacher. They will meet to reminisce a little in the new Presbyterian student house, just off the campus of the University, after the Florida-Tennessee football game on November 14.

All Muscle Deacons, Student Deacons and Elders, whether they still sit on the front pew or have moved to the Amen Corner are expected to return for one more encounter with the "champ."

So, Preacher found a home in Florida.

First Presbyterian Church, Gainesville, Florida, *circa* 1928

He was instantly drawn into the glory of the old, red brick church with its steeple bell on the busy downtown corner of University Avenue. Someone had told Preacher that there had been an historic battle of the Civil War fought on North Main Street and that the bell in the church tower had been used to sound the alarm. This information, of course, intensified his love for this historic bell.

Years later, when continued growth forced this flock to build new and larger facilities, at Preacher's insistence, the new steeple was designed around the bell. Everyone hated to leave the old sanctuary for a new structure, especially Preacher. However, there was no way to expand or save the old building. For example, a deacon had to pour water on the leaking pine tar from the timbers under Preacher's feet in the pulpit on cold Sunday mornings. The furnace got so hot the tar dripped out of the beam onto the top of

Present Structure. First Presbyterian Church, Gainesville, Florida

the furnace and would have set the place on fire. Some folks said the smoke came from his preaching, but it was probably that smouldering beam.

An old house behind the church that served for a nursery and church offices actually did burn down before the church moved to new facilities. Many believed the fire started in Preacher's sermon notes, but he insisted he kept them in his roll top desk in the manse.

After forty years as pastor of the First Presbyterian Church in Gainesville, the rule of the church forced his retirement at the age of seventy-five. But until his death, Preacher became the official supply pastor of the Presbyterian church at Archer, Florida, which he served with vigor. People from all over the state took turns worshipping there on Sunday mornings, and the place was always packed. This was testimony to their love of Preacher and to the love of their Lord whom Preacher had led them to know. It was fitting that on the Sunday before his death on Friday he should finish his preaching there in a picturesque country church not unlike the place where he had begun. Dr. U. S. Gordon (B.P., S.A.) lifted up the hearts of Floridians for forty-eight years. He got "sand in his shoes" and never could be enticed to leave the state for other positions. He felt continually called to stay right where he was.

When he came into the Gainesville pastorate, the good fishing and good hunting were as much an attraction as the good people. The fishing and especially the hunting "played out" but never the people. Florida was home!

# 3

## CHARISMA PLUS

D<small>R</small>. U. S. G<small>ORDON</small>, B.P., S.A., was a person of unusual talent and magnetic character. He was a strong, handsome, six-foot hulk of a man with appealing countenance. Men, women, and children of all conditions and stations of life found it easy to identify with him. He looked and acted like a commonplace, solid citizen whom people loved and respected. His outgoing, disarming personality was cheerful and charming, and yet there was a sufficient mystique about him to give balance to his mischief and everyday wit. He was some kind of a man!

To this warm likeable person was added a dimension stemming solely from his Christian faith and experience. He was completely dedicated to his Lord and Master whom he served effectively. He had a deep-down kind of reverence that surfaced with no display of artificial piety. All his relationships were natural, normal, passionate, and expansive. He was a hero to many, a humanitarian to others, a respected friend and pal to countless followers whom he loved. The singular human individualism combined with his profound and spirited glorification of God and celebration of man to give him charisma plus: *Christian charisma.*

"If you don't love people, you have missed the boat," Preacher often admonished. "I don't mean romantic love necessarily, nor sick love, nor pollyanna-ishness; I mean *good will.* You've got to have good will and compassion for people or you can't grow up spiritually."

He suggested that it might be a great weakness in himself but that he tried not to exasperate people. "If I couldn't get them to come and do things for the church by exercising good will towards them, I would not try to get them by driving them. I don't want anybody driving me, and I don't want to drive anybody else."

When Preacher found a home in Florida, he not only found it in field and stream, but in the corridors of academia. He had a tremendous vocabulary and capability to turn a phrase into dramatic prose and poetic beauty. He had a great command of the English language that enabled him to give impromptu prayers and public statements that were immaculate and inspiring. His letter-writing was superb in its beauty, and he always said just the right thing at the right time.

To his own improvisation, he added a wealth of literature he had committed to memory. He knew all of the best loved psalms by heart and could render long passages of the Bible without prompting. When most people could remember only the first line of a hymn, Preacher was not at loss to recall — all five stanzas. None of this storehouse of memory ever was recited for the sake of pride in ownership, but it was always on the ready when the right moment came to augment his point with Biblical reference. Shakespeare, Milton, Bunyan, Longfellow, Keats and others were a part of the repertoire that enhanced his eloquence. He knew by heart the Presbyterian *Shorter Catechism* together with the *Book of Common Worship* and the Episcopal *Book of Common Prayer.* The intellectual academician did not come away from worship under Preacher's leadership without being fed in his own language.

But the church Preacher served was an amalgam of many subcultures. It contained farmers, businessmen, professional people of all kinds and ages. To appeal to the complete social spectrum, he not only was, but perforce had to be, well educated, unpretentious, practical and skillful in all levels and styles of life.

He found humor in almost every kind of situation and was a master at displaying the lighter side of life to others through his story-telling and repartee. More often than not, he used the vernacular and dialect of cronies from the fishing ramps and hunting grounds rather than the classrooms of higher learning. He loved the native, natural idiom and frequently intentionally used words like *ain't, cain't, gonna,* and *wouldja* in his storytelling. He was a skillful raconteur.

Much is lost in the translation of poetry and prose written in a foreign language; so it is with folk stories. They lose much in the telling if the colloquial is omitted in favor of correct grammar and dialect. Cajun jokes are pointless when told in impeccable English; so are Georgia and Florida cracker anecdotes. Preacher was a perfect imitator of the idiomatic, ungrammatical, colloquial folk-language.

The raconteur

In fact, using the colloquial came so natural to him, often it carried over to his own conversational speech.

One reason he was so well liked was because he was such a good story teller. People loved his antics, shocking style, and use of substandarisms to dislodge the complacent or sophisticated perfectionist. Those who heard him for the first time did not always understand how a man with such education could sound so provincial.

But, Preacher's natural style, overwhelmingly an asset, was perceived by some to be overdrawn and therefore an occasional liability. One time he was told that a certain man had not liked his speech mannerisms in the pulpit on a given Sunday morning. Preacher delighted his dinner guests when this criticism was leveled at him by retorting, "His disapproval of me is my best recommendation."

There were never any hidden barbs in his funny business. He wouldn't think of hurting anyone just to get a laugh — and he never did! His was not a cutting wit aimed sarcastically to belittle anyone or anything. He was often at his best when he was making jokes at his own expense. Typical is this story which has made the rounds in many forms but which Preacher told this way:

"My brother, Charles, one time went hunting with a friend, Ben Anderson. They were waiting for a little train back in the woods of Mississippi where they had killed a few squirrels. A man drove up out of the woods cussing and swearing at his oxen and the logs they were dragging. Finally, in complete exhaustion, the man came up and sat by Ben and my brother and asked them what they did for a living. Charles only turned the question back on the stranger, who replied, "Well, you see me down there with that team and you think I'm a logger, but as little as you might think of it, I used to preach; if this depression don't break, I ain't too damn good to preach again!"

To Preacher, being in the ministry was more than a profession; it was a calling. It was something he felt the Lord had called him to do for His people. Many churches, including the Presbyterian, refer to the invitation they give to a prospective pastor as a call. Preacher was very adamant on this point of being called to preach.

"If a man in the ministry looks upon what he does as a *job*, he will be disappointed, but if he looks upon it as a calling and a commitment, he will get infinite joy out of it. The thing that grieves many of us older pastors today is to see some young bucks looking upon the ministry as a profession — a structured job — which they are ready and quick to leave when they find out they can better themselves at something else."

Preacher could have done well in many other occupations, but he felt called into the ministry. His education had provided the cornerstone for his theology. Personality and charisma was his drawing card, but love of his Lord was his trump.

But, mischief could also be apparent in his voice and in his body-language as his eyes fairly danced with delight when he told a story. They sorrowed in compassion as he empathized with someone in grief, but when he got ready to give a buckeye, to chide, or to express in some form a "Preacherism," he would throw back his head at a saucy angle and stroke his chin or run his hand over his head. His mouth would twist into a characteristic smile, and he wrinkled his nose and slid into the punchline.

Despite his authoritative composure, Preacher was basically a humble person. One seldom guessed he was a minister by his demeanor. Many a stranger wished he could retract earlier blasphemous and indiscrete remarks when he found he was in the presence of a "man of the cloth." Just as quickly, the stranger might try to cover his embarrassment by picking a quarrel over religion. Preacher never let such a man engage him. He felt, as Corrie Ten Boom expressed it, that this man's argument was not with him but with the Lord!

Preacher was especially attractive when he was dressed in his Sunday best. Pictures nor paintings could ever do him complete justice because his face was so animated and his motions so deft. In earlier days, when worship was held in less formal surroundings, he felt it was not appropriate for him to wear clerical regalia. He wore conservative, but not drab, suits spruced up with a colorful tie, usually red, with matching silk pocket handkerchief.

A good, factory-made suit seldom had to be altered to fit his well proportioned body. He was strong featured as well as strong bodied. As he grew older, he became thinner and weaker but never bowed-down. He remained erect with his characteristic smile perpetually on his face as he walked with a cane to aid his failing eyes and strength. He called the cane his "sympathy stick."

Only such an unaffected, uninhibited man—hale, hearty, and handsome—would dare ignore blemishes in his appearance and be completely natural. When his eyesight deteriorated, he couldn't see the grey smudges on his lapel or pants that came from the long ash that dropped from his cigar. Friends just brushed these off for him and said nothing; somehow, they were just part of the man they loved. If his suits were overdue at the cleaners, someone would pick them up, have them cleaned, and then unobtrusively replace them in his closet. Often, he did not know they had been removed; his thoughts were on people, not things.

If he were less than particular about the cigar smudges on his lapel, he was more than meticulous about oral hygiene. He brushed his teeth regularly, often, and always just before going into the pulpit. Then he used a mouthwash, followed by a stick of gum. Not long after he first arrived in Gainesville, he went through that ritual before worship one Sunday morning and forgot to get rid of the gum until after he was seated in the beautiful, Gothic armchair behind the old pulpit. Not knowing how to dispose of the gum, he rolled it into a little ball and carefully placed it behind his left ear. This worked so well, he did it several times again until one of the women in the choir mentioned to him after church that she had not known he had such a large, uncomfortable-looking mole behind his ear. From then on, for several months, he kept up the practice just to keep her looking at him with rapt attention during the sermon.

In the days before air conditioning, during the hot, Florida, summer months, he would not wear a jacket at less formal functions, such as Wednesday night prayer meeting. In order to keep his shirt well contained in his trousers and not hiking up in the back, he tucked his shirt neatly inside his underwear trunks using the elastic band to hold the shirt in place. This felt comfortable to him and it didn't matter that it was not the conventional way to dress. Unfortunately, his pants often slipped down a little and exposed the underwear. Most people paid no attention, for again they appreciated the naturalness of the man together with his eccentricities.

One old busy-body, of course, had to tell the Preacher how to dress. There was always someone who tried to make him be something other than what he was. Fortunately, they always failed, and he remained the constant, lovable person he had always been.

This sister told him one day, "Preacher, you shouldn't stuff your shirt down inside your underwear; it doesn't look good." Quick as a flash he turned to her with a sober but tender look and charged, "Sis-tah, you tend to your pants and I'll tend to mine!"

In the new sanctuary and at all appropriate public functions, Preacher wore his doctoral gown with its three red arm-stripes and panelled front. He never wore a clerical collar but always left the top of the gown open sufficiently to reveal his red tie as if it symbolized his own mortality and the blood of his immortal Lord. Often the robe flowed half-open as he walked quickly around the communion table during worship sending waves of warmth and compassion to the hungry worshippers.

Preacher held two academic doctoral degrees, an

Charisma Plus    29

honorary Doctor of Divinity from Southwestern at Memphis and an honorary Doctor of Humane Letters from the University of Florida. But he was even more proud of two non-academic degrees often attached to his name with the letters "B.P." and "S.A." These were unofficial and conveyed only by popular acclaim. They stood for "Beloved Pastor" and "Spiritual Advisor." His different degrees typified his dual preparation as a preacher of the gospel, a man well-grounded in the liberal arts, and a man of deep concern for the welfare of his fellow man.

Yes, he had a deep-down reverence, no superficial piety, but a practical good will towards all people that gave him *Charisma Plus.*

# 4

## GOING TO THE DOGS

"Quail used to come up and feed at my back door in those earlier years in Gainesville. That gives you an idea of how things were: the university and streets connecting it with the shopping center of the city were surrounded by fields and woods—a beautiful place to live and as near to Paradise as one would want to find."

Preacher soon became not only an integral part of the religious, academic, and civic life of his community but a part of its landscape! His sidewalk was often the scene of animated conversation between him and college students or church members who frequently went out of their way to pass by his house at the time of morning they expected him to be on his front screened porch.

Or Preacher himself would be out exercising and "walking his dogs." What a vivid memory it is, and how it gladdens one's heart to recall the picture of Preacher walking to and from the campus, the hospital, or the post office. Although these walks were mostly for the benefit of the dogs, a welcome by-product was the many friendly chats with people he met on the street. The only alteration in this scenario through the forty-eight years was the change in the quickness of his step and the size, shape, and color of his dogs.

It pricked many people's feelings that he didn't like cats and would say so from the pulpit. He once had a black cat that someone gave him—he named it Satan! Of course, he really didn't have anything against cats because, like other animals, they are God's creatures. But, it seemed difficult for him to accept the fact that cats "ate the birds," and he would rush to the back porch and run off any cat that was slinking up on a covey of birds or had jumped to the trunk of a tree intending to claw its way up to a nest.

At different times in his life his whole house seemed to be "going to the dogs" because one or two always lived inside with him and were an important part of his personal happiness. They were his constant companions when people weren't available and sometimes when they were. He loved to show them off and to have them do their tricks. This often resulted in misplaced rugs or torn cushions. Each dog had his favorite spot on a sofa or chair to curl up and sleep on or to use as an outpost while awaiting the master's return.

As one would expect, their most fay-vor-ite spots, as Preacher would pronounce it, were on the bed with him. One never asked him whether he was lonely living by himself without running into the instant reply, "I'm not alone; I have my dogs!" In addition, he had his friends and his omnipresent Lord.

Rarely did he eat breakfast alone, for someone most surely came in unexpectedly just as he was sitting down in the breakfast nook which was always set for at least two people. And the dogs? They were there, too, patiently waiting for a love portion to be slipped off the table. Preacher had been admonished by many not to feed the dogs table food, so he had developed quick moves to create "accidents" that gave his four-legged friends all he had planned to share with them, and more.

If he were alone, or with male companions that he knew would understand, he would be more deliberate with feeding them from his own plate. The dogs, politely

pleading from an alert sitting position, looked at Preacher with doleful but hopeful eyes as they watched his every move. Almost inaudible crying sounds would emit from their half closed jaws. In later years, these pitiful, high pitched sounds were more noticeable to the guests than heard by Preacher's less acute ears. Finally Preacher would turn to the dogs and say, "Give me a Christian word!" The dogs replied in unison, "woof." Then he continued to quiz them, "Make a theological statement." "Woof, woof," responded the well-schooled canines. The examination completed, he would share with them the last of his scrambled eggs or even *all* of his breakfast if the notion struck him. As a reward to the patient creatures, he would then put his plate down and let them lick it clean. He took great delight in shocking his guests with this performance and then looking up to say as if he meant it, "Now we won't have to wash the dishes."

The dogs seldom followed the African Queen back into her kitchen, but would be at Preacher's heels as he dashed from the breakfast room through the dining room and living room, still chewing on his last bite of breakfast, to answer the front door. Before he could get the door open, he was calling with dynamic demand, "Come on in, podnah." The dogs echoed his invitation but could not top his enthusiastic query, "Ain't that my pal—my most main and fay-vor-ite . . .?" He often left the sentence open-ended because the greeting had already been bounced back with the retort, "Ain't that my most fay-vor-ite Preacher?" Besides, someone had suggested to him that he shouldn't single out a favorite person. But his closeness was of a kind that made each person feel "special," whether pal, sis-tah, or elder. One might be his special bell-ringer or clock-watcher, bed-shaker, tooth-doctor, or Queen of 22nd Street. All were distinctive persons to Preacher and he loved them; he was just as unique and precious to them.

"Come forward to the first pew," he continued as he led the visitor into the inner sanctum of his abode. The front room was reserved for formal conversation, ceremonial occasions, and as outposts for the dogs. When Preacher headed for his den, the dogs jumped from their turrets on living room chairs and were waiting for him in the recliner lounge before the fireplace in his personal quarters or study.

Had Preacher and his guests sat down in the living room, their interest would have been completely distracted by the gifts and tokens of affection that formed a veritable admiration gallery on the walls and shelves. Pictures that had been taken of Preacher marrying a couple or baptizing a baby had been given him and were here on the mantle of the front room. Photographer's portraits hung on the wall in frames, with miscellaneous snapshots sticking out of each corner. Arranged on the narrow book shelves was a motley collection of picture greetings, cards, wood replicas of camels from Israel, a Florentine head of Michaelangelo, and a hand-carved miniature pointer dog with his broken tail repaired but glued at a ridiculous angle. Crosses and other religious symbols were also conspicuous on the cabinet partitions between the two rooms.

But, despite the dust under the chairs, the sand under the rug, the dog hair, the worn places on the couch, or the frayed rugs, every visitor immediately felt right at home in Preacher's house. The dearly beloved pastor, settling down in a chair opposite his visitor, gave him his undivided attention. When could anyone feel more comfortable or "at home" than at those precious moments with this man who would always give a lift to your heart and a new lilt to your walk?

But to feel really at home with Preacher, you had to go on back to his study. It was like entering into his very being, with your world becoming his world, your thoughts his thoughts, and your cares his cares. Many a decision to "press forward to the greater goal," or to "reach for the rock that is higher than I" was made in that intimate place.

It had its own enticing odor of cigar, coal ashe, pine oil, deer tongue, and dogs. The importance of this aromatic den is surpassed only by the memory of it. On the wall opposite the entrance door was his rolltop desk. To understate it simply as a rolltop desk would be unforgivable. It was the largest, most beautiful, most cluttered, most pigeon-holed, most unforgettable desk ever seen. It was specially built for him by a friend in Mississippi, and it was used as a depository for all kinds of papers—important and unimportant. Seldom was Preacher ever seen sitting at it. When he did, it was to pull out the writing board to scratch his signature on a baptismal or marriage certificate or greeting cards which were sent by the thousands. The rolltop was never closed until his nephew, Billy, disassembled the massive desk to take it back to Sardis.

Before the desk stood a high-backed, green, naugahyde, executive-style desk-chair he had worn out with years of use at the old church office. The spring that once held the

back upright was broken, and if anyone sat down too quickly in it, the back flipped and knocked the chair out from under him. Preacher had learned how to sneak up on it and settle quietly in before the spring could react, but a strange rider needed to approach the chair warily and with respect.

In rows on top of the desk and along the wall were the pictures of longtime friends. There were many, more of distinguished men, who felt it was an honor to have their pictures hanging in Preacher's study. Above the alcove into which the desk was squeezed, were tinted transome windows that cast a soft light across the room. On each side wall was a single bed, and on cold winter nights Preacher could sleep in this den warmed by the glowing coals of the fireplace. From this position he could see an additional array of mementos over his fireplace: letters, buckeyes, trinkets, candy, gum, telephone numbers (some were scribbled on the paint above the wall phone), New Testaments, old notebooks, and perhaps yesterday's, or last year's, church bulletin. Recessed on either side of the fireplace were bookcases filled with books dealing with a variety of subjects from Calvin to modern mystery stories. Some were new, but others were yellow, dog-eared and loose-paged—the result of service as constant references. These books were also his hiding place for folding money. Some of Preacher's closest companions were shown in which book they could find a twenty dollar bill "in case you ever have need for it."

Five feet to the side of the fireplace was a beautiful, antique, two-drawer, drop-leaf, cherry table that had been his grandmother's sewing chest. But for Preacher it had a more utilitarian purpose. He loved its beauty and heirloom memories, but he liked it best because it held his favorite treasures: the extension phone someone had given him, his can of tobacco, box of cigars, daily newspaper or weekly magazine, pipe cleaners, Bible, and a recent historical novel or autobiography. He was both well read and well bred!

Adjacent to the table and in the middle of the room was his recliner chair that faced the fireplace and the television set. From this throne he pursued his theological studies and his quest for more knowledge and better understanding of world events and history and their relation to Christian doctrine. He would read until sleepy and push back in the recliner, place a rumpled handkerchief over his eyes and take a nap. Invariably, the phone rang just as his jaw

dropped as a prelude to his first good snore. He would push himself straight forward and grab the instrument from its cradle as if he had been eagerly awaiting the call and then give his familiar "hell-aw. Ain't that my most main and principal deacon? No, I wasn't asleep. I was right here with Old Joe reading about . . . What's that? He did! I'll be right over." The conversation ended abruptly, and he was on his way to someone in distress.

There was a rocker and overstuffed leather lounge chair and footstool for the "podnah" who couldn't possibly overstay his welcome, but often did remain long after his business had been completed. Termination of a visit was hard for anyone who needed the comfort and strength which came merely from being at Preacher's side. In the absence of conversation, playing gin rummy, or just plain sitting, gave mutual pleasure. Preacher took his gin rummy almost as seriously as he did his dogs — and he was good at it, winning most of the time. Gin served less to pass the time than to provide relaxation, and to rekindle affection between friends.

A walk-in closet housed hunting and fishing clothes, guns, boots, paddles, and paraphernalia of all kinds. One was on a veritable treasure hunt whenever he went into the closet on an errand for Preacher.

Beyond this den of warmth, security, and caring was his bedroom, filled with family antiques and an iron bed. Few, save doctors, close friends, and attendants, ventured into this intimate retreat. Of course, the African Queen straightened the bed and made a weekly pass at cleaning the room, but when Preacher went out of town, a special church committee or a pal would have the house scoured by professional cleaners. The pictures could not be found displaced or the clean-up would displease Preacher.

But the house really never gave the impression of "going to the dogs." His dogs helped Preacher make it "home away from home" for countless itinerant friends, returnees, and prospective brides and grooms. The guest room might be occupied for as long as a year at one time by his niece and her law-student husband, or by Preacher's first assistant and his bride, or by many others. This was the manse! More importantly, it was his home and a part and parcel of Preacher.

His dogs are an institution all their own. Only his hunting friends were on speaking terms with Molly, the setter who never made a mistake. When she died of heart worms, she was buried in the back yard. There was also Mrs. Smith, a female dog given that name because she gave birth to so many puppies. She was a good hunter that never ranged far from the gun unless the men were in a jeep.

Deacon and Elder were his two most famous dogs. They were cocker spaniels, as were Noah and Nicodemus, their offspring. According to Preacher, all four were fine hunters.

"Contrary to what some hunters might speculate about them, I used to hunt quail with them. They were fine retrievers and you never lost a bird with them and you never lost a crippled bird. They were fun to hunt with."

Deacon and Elder were little black dogs who were mirror images of each other and many a home proudly displayed the picture of Preacher and these Christian mascots. However, it was Noah and Nicodemus who, along with Preacher, were painted by a Japanese artist. Copies of this painting were sent during the war as Christmas cards to about 250 members of the church who were in foreign fields of service.

His first cocker spaniels, Deacon and Elder, were his most popular pair. They accompanied him everywhere and were usually seen with their heads sticking out of the rear windows of his car. One time they were separated from

Preacher, Noah and Nicodemus

Preacher and got lost. The alarm went out over radio stations. A good, black man called the police station to say he had just seen the dogs on the loose down in the "quarters." They eventually made it home through the help of many people who recognized them and helped retrieve them. They were certainly good "retrievers"—everyone knew the dogs as well as Preacher.

The Catholic priest, a good friend of Preacher, purchased a female cocker and asked Preacher if she could be bred to one of his dogs. "Of course," said Preacher, "but only on the condition that the puppies be raised as Protestants—Presbyterians!"

Preacher thought the cocker spaniel was the sweetest dog of all the canine family and his were admitted to some of the finest homes in Gainesville. On one occasion, they were even found under the table in a local restaurant.

He also raised a large weimaraner he called Joseph. Again, contrary to the prevalent belief that this breed was just a show dog, "Ole Joe" was also a good hunter that never missed a trick nor made a mistake. He had been whelped in Bavaria and was a big, gentle animal particularly close to his master's heart. Preacher used to say, "He is the clumsiest, funniest dog I ever saw—like an adolescent boy." As big as Joe was, Preacher would still throw a ball through the door of the den, under the dining table and into the living room and Ole Joe would retrieve it with great care. The rugs were all that he ever disturbed.

One day a little lady looked up at Joe poised on the porch and exclaimed, "What kind of a dog is that?" After coaxing the lady to safety through the old and flimsy screen door, Preacher picked up on her question. "You ask what kind of a dog this is. Well, ma'm, this is a carpenter dog."

"A carpenter dog! I've never heard of a carpenter dog before."

"Yes'm, he does odd jobs around the house."

Preacher probably talked to Ole Joe more than to any other canine companion. He particularly enjoyed showing

him off to visitors. During a conversation, Joe would force himself to his feet and lumber over to Preacher looking at him with that quizzical curiosity for which he was well known, and Preacher would stop, turn to the questioning animal and ask, "What's the good word?" Joe always barked once in reply. "Is that the Word from the Good Book, Joe?" Woof, woof, he would reply intelligently.

After Ole Joe died, Preacher said he wasn't going to have any more dogs, but he was lonesome without one, and a local funeral director knew it. Preacher frequently engaged in light-hearted conversation in the offices of the funeral home before a service to relieve his own tension and that of others. His good friend detected that something was wrong. Preacher had lost his sparkle.

Shortly thereafter, on Christmas Eve, a tiny chihuahua puppy was left on Preacher's screen porch. It could have been left in the living room just as well where it would have been out of the weather, but there was more romance in leaving the foundling on the porch. Preacher always locked his front door, but told everyone that the key was on the screen porch under the cushion of the old church pew just to the left of the door. When Preacher found the tiny bundle on the bench late one afternoon, he couldn't resist having some fun. He called up the long-time church sis-tah with whom he was to dine that night.

"Somebody has left a little baby on my porch!" he told in hushed dismay.

"Preacher! What are you going to do?"

"Nothin' *to* do but try to raise it."

"You can't do that, Preacher, by yourself."

"Yes, I can, too. I love children and once took care of my nephew, and I have the African Queen here who can help; we'll get along all right."

"Where do you have it now?"

"All bundled up here by this coal fire. We will be just fine. I just wanted to let you know in case I was a few minutes late getting to your house, but I'll be there as soon as I can."

Preacher named the little fellow after the friend he knew had left him on the porch—"Dicky." After Ole Joe, Dicky seemed so tiny that Preacher said he was only a "make-believe dog", and he went on to spoil him more than any of his predecessors.

Dicky was a good watch dog because his bark was so shrill and persistent. When he barked with joy at his master's return, Preacher would hold him in the palm of his hand and lovingly say, "You poor little imitation of a dog. Why, you ain't no dog at all. Here, put your nose in my pocket and see what I brought you."

At night, Dicky always slept with Preacher, starting out on the foot of the big, double bed, but always turning up the next morning on Preacher's pillow. Poor little pitiful fellow!

Preacher was often heard to say that the never ending and unfailing devotion a dog has for its master is similar to the love we should have for our Maker and Creator. He believed, too, that if a dog sleeps with his master, he knows to whom he really belongs. After Preacher's death, Dicky was lovingly placed in a foundling home where two women, who had cared for Dicky when Preacher went to Sardis and Memphis, gave the grieving dog devoted care. One of the ladies habitually took Dicky, who was "an old man" by then, for his daily walks, while the other sis-tah fed him and slept with him.

The benefactor who had given the dog to Preacher repeated what he had heard Preacher say so often about Dicky when he had previously left him with the ladies.

"I know he loves them both equally well, but I would rather have a woman to feed me and sleep with me than one who would just take me to the bathroom."

Preacher was noted everywhere for his dogs and especially for Dicky who was left behind to grieve. He had always brought a doggie-bag home for him from a restaurant or someone's dinner party. If a bag wasn't available, he would just stuff something into his pocket.

Many a hostess has been distressed to see Preacher, when served a steak, first cut the tenderest portion of the meat and wrap it in the paper or finest linen dinner napkin to take home to Dicky. But it was heartwarming to see that steak disappear, even naked, into his pocket as a provision for the poor, little, "make-believe" dog.

On Preacher's casket, across the corner and away from the floral blanket, there was laid a lonely, red rose "from Dicky."

Preacher and Dicky

# 5

## BLESSED BUCKEYES

There is no way of knowing how many people still carry Preacher's buckeyes out of reverence and love for him and in his memory. Many others have put theirs carefully away in a drawer with other sacred memorabilia.

No one really knows how the custom began, but Preacher always had a pocket full of buckeyes (horse chestnuts) which he blessed for any good purpose and gave out as a talisman. He kept them by the crocker sack in his pantry along side the dog food. They were sent to him from all over by people who knew he needed them in great supply—the demand for them was inexhaustible. Preacher gave them to friends and strangers alike and avowed that if you carried a buckeye, and rubbed it every day, then it would be a tremendous help for whatever ailed you.

He delighted in presenting one buckeye each to the bride and groom during a wedding rehearsal, telling the couple that they were most effective as a fertility blessing and were so potent, that they had been known to counteract "the pill." Many a baby owes its start to a Preacher buckeye!

Lest the reader think this practice was just a mischievous prank, one should know that some of the medical doctors in town carried buckeyes.

One time the Gainesville Kiwanis Club was recognizing two of the most outstanding men in the city: Dr. W. C. Thomas, a physician, and Dr. U. S. Gordon, a pastor. The room was packed and jammed at the luncheon due to the popularity of these two great servants of mercy who worked almost as a team: Dr. Thomas looked after the body and Preacher Gordon looked after the soul. They had great admiration for each other; both knew the importance of spiritual well-being in matters of health and physical well-being in matters of the spirit. The Preacher Gordon Memorial Chapel is in the W. C. Thomas Tower of the Alachua General Hospital. (See Appendix C.)

Well, the person making the presentation for Preacher Gordon could not avoid mentioning the buckeye talisman. He told of the miraculous "healing" powers of the buckeye when carried by someone who loved Preacher and wanted always to be reminded of his goodness, his friendship, and his love for his Lord. Before the speaker could finish the tale of the buckeye, lawyers, judges, doctors, merchants, salesmen, professors, and chiefs of all kinds in the club that day began squirming in their seats and fishing in their pockets until the speaker said, "Okay, every one of you who has his buckeye with him get it out and hold it high in the air." Three-fourths of the business and professional men in the room—including Dr. Thomas—displayed their well rubbed, glossy buckeyes.

Another time, an older man asked Preacher for a buckeye that was blessed to help hemorrhoids. Preacher gave him one with the assurance that he would get along much better if he carried it religiously. Some weeks later the man told Preacher he had never had such relief. However, in another month Preacher visited the poor, old fellow in the hospital. With a pain in his face, the man told Preacher, "You know, right after I saw you the last time, somehow I lost that buckeye, but I takened a little, new, Irish potato in my pocket and I fooled them hemorrhoids for two weeks!"

Preacher was not one to believe in magic nor in quack medicine of any kind. He would do anything that anyone suggested, however, to obtain relief from his own rheumatism. He often said, "Now, there are two kinds of ailments: one is rheumatism and the other is arthritis. Only rich folks have arthritis. Now me, I don't have arthritis—only rheumatism."

One helpful, Florida cracker claimed that if he would wear a copper bracelet that Preacher could get relief from his rheumatism. So Preacher purchased one and wore it for quite a while. He got no relief from it, but he had gained a friend and much additional attention from those who were curious about the bracelet.

He was well aware there were no magical qualities in a buckeye—but he claimed it did possess mystical powers. "There ain't no magic in this nut," Preacher would say, "but if you carry it and believe in the love it stands for, it sure cain't hurt you—and it might help!"

However, one young woman returned hers! She said that right after Preacher had given it to her, her luck changed all right—but for the worse. She had flunked an exam, gotten hit by a bicycle, caught the flu, and been arrested for speeding. Preacher told her that she better keep on carrying it because, as he put it, "There ain't no tellin' how much worse it might have been if you hadn't had that buckeye in your purse."

He was so famous for his buckeyes that two buckeye trees were planted in the landscaping of the Gordon Glen Manor, a retirement home named for him. Not only that, but some individuals who had buckeyes to spare planted them, and several of them were known to grow and produce nuts. These could be called grandbaby buckeyes, but being one generation removed, their powers were less potent.

Preacher loved to give buckeyes to his friends who were devoted members of other denominations to "offset their disadvantage" in not being Presbyterians. "Sure, you can probably get to heaven in that church," he would chuckle,

Blessed Buckeyes    49

"but why *chance* it? Here, take this buckeye; it may help you when your time comes."

As many Episcopalians carried buckeyes as did Presbyterians, for he loved these people almost as much as he did those of his own parish. His nickname for them was, *Episco-lopians*. When he encountered one, he immediately and automatically recited in rapid-fire:

"Well, you know—
 Episcopalians are
  the best fed,
   the best dressed,
    the best drilled,
     hardest drinking regiment in God's army
      never to have taken a shot at the devil!"

He reeled-off that blank verse in the presence of his lifelong Episcopalian friends—including the priests and bishops.

But, the Episcopalians, too, had their turn at repartee with Preacher. They liked to tell how he had visited a poor woman who hadn't been to his church in over a year because she couldn't afford suitable clothes for herself and her family. Preacher had set about to rectify that regrettable situation by going out and buying an entire wardrobe for her, her three children, and her husband. When they still did not show up at the Presbyterian church, he waited patiently for several weeks and then went back to visit the lady.

"Why haven't you been at church? Surely, it couldn't be because of your clothes because we outfitted your whole family."

"No," said the mother with a pride that made even Preacher do a double-take. "When we all got dressed up in those duds, we felt so high-falutin' we went to the Episcopal church."

The Baptists carried buckeyes, too. A Baptist pastor of earlier years recalled walking to town one day with one of his deacons when they met Preacher. His friend immediately told Preacher, "The day after you gave me that buckeye, I caught the worst cold I ever had."

Not a bit dismayed, Preacher replied, "Why, man, if I hadn't given you that buckeye, you would have taken pneumonia and died."

There was a sequel to that story that the Baptist pastor remembered with great vividness:

> I last saw Preacher during Holy week in 1975. He came to the First Baptist Church to worship when I was the guest speaker for the week's services. When I saw Preacher in the congregation, I told the story about how Preacher claimed the buckeye had saved the man from dying of pneumonia. In his usual, uninhibited manner, Preacher got up in the congregation, scrambled out of the crowded pew and came down the aisle to the pulpit, saying as he walked, "You're absolutely right: that's the way it happened. These buckeyes are helpful for all kinds of ailments, from the common cold to creeping chillblains. Here's another buckeye for *you*, Brother."

Preacher was so highly regarded as a member of the Baptist family that no one hesitated to call upon him to house a delegate or two when the Southern Baptist Convention was held in Gainesville. When Preacher was telephoned to see if he could accommodate a visitor, he told the caller, "Why certainly; I'll take seven men."

"Preacher, I know you only have one extra bed in your guest room. How in the world can you take care of seven delegates?"

"You said they were Baptists, didn't you?" Preacher asked the caller. "You know you Baptists are so narrow you can put seven of them in a bed any night." He wound up having two Baptist preachers as guests to whom he not only gave lodging but an evening of enthusiastic conversation. After a good night's rest, each was given a big breakfast and a big, shiny buckeye.

Preacher was right; there was no magic in a buckeye, but

there was much mystical communication of love, fun, and happiness inherent in the act of giving it and much joy, hope, and merriment accrued in the carrying of it. Part of the Christian charisma is giving a tangible token of love to help one remember the Gift of God's love. To remember Christ's love and sacrifice, we wear a cross; to be reminded of the vows of marriage, we wear the seal of a wedding band; to remember Preacher and all of his kindness and good humor, many a person carries a buckeye.

One should look in his box of memories to see if he can find some trinket being kept only for its sentimental value; it may turn out to be one's most prized possession, whether it is a doll or a dollar. There may be no magic in it, but there is the making of magic in it, for it will remind you of a father, mother, sister, uncle, or preacher who has enriched your life and motivated you to enrich the life of someone else.

Therein lies the magic of the buckeye. If one has a buckeye or some other talisman, he should keep it; "there is no telling how bad things could get without it!"

# PART II

## BELOVED PASTOR

*". . . Because he loved the church and served the body of believers whether they were in or out of the sanctuary."*

# 6

# A PULPIT PREACHER

Preacher's real message was taught from the pulpit of his own life through the expression of loving concern for his people. While his sermons were "born—not made" and were inspiring human messages, his real power came from the Almighty. He was a spokesman of God's Word as he found it in the authority of Scriptures. Knowing the ways of the world and the weaknesses of the wayward, he knew how the Bible spoke to those ways and filled the needs of all kinds of spiritually hungry people.

As teaching elder in the Presbyterian church, he took his role seriously; he taught by precept, exhortation, and example. The Presbyterian denomination is known as a "connectional church" because all individual churches are held together by a hierarchy of "ascending and descending" courts. Each congregation elects a court known as the Session which is made up of ruling elders and the teaching elder or preacher. The churches are bound together in a regional court known as a Presbytery and by a group of Presbyteries known as a Synod. A total representation of all Presbyteries constitutes a court called the General Assembly.

In the local church, the minister is the Moderator of the Session. Although they work cooperatively to oversee the life of the church, the minister has the primary role as spiritual leader and teacher of the Word of God.

When serving formally in that capacity at worship, Preacher wore his clerical robe, not for ritualistic purposes nor ecclesiastical piety, but to symbolize his function as one ordained to teach the Word of God. The ruling elders are ordained to help him do this through the work of the Session.

As Preacher describes it: "They and the minister assemble as a sort of cabinet, and all matters affecting the welfare of the church are decided at their meetings. In some churches there are also deacons who report on the temporalities, which means the finances and the upkeep of the church property. The deacons report to the elders, who are the governing and deciding voice in the church."

The Scripture is frequently read from the Bible placed on a separate lectern, but often it is read from the pulpit where the sermon is the focus of teaching the Word. The center of attention in the front of the Presbyterian sanctuary is always the Communion Table. Worship is the teaching and hearing of Scripture, praising God through hymns and prayer, and feeling the presence of the Holy Spirit as He is called upon in the Name of the Lord Jesus, whose Last Supper was eaten with His disciples gathered around him. Thus, a table for fellowship in communion with the Lord is prominent in the Presbyterian sanctuary in contrast to an altar which is the focal point in some churches.

Preacher emphasized this relationship by his own demeanor in conducting worship. Although every church includes praise, prayer, teaching of the Word, and the response of the people in its service of worship, every pastor has his own distinctive order of worship.

Preacher had a flare for the dramatic and natural flow of worship experience. While the Doxology is often sung at the Offertory, he liked to start the worship with it because the enthusiasm created by the singing of "Praise God from Whom all Blessings Flow!" is so exhilarating; he felt it was just natural and right to begin worshipping with this great hymn of praise.

56   BELOVED PASTOR

In the less formal, old sanctuary, the pulpit was located at the center of the rostrum. In those early days, Preacher did not wear clerical regalia, but, in a sense, the sexton did! Alex was a grey, nappy-headed, black man whom everyone knew and loved. Preacher had given him his old swallow-tailed coat as church attire because Alex was often called upon to pray and preach at the evening worship in his own church up the street just a few blocks away. But Alex also wore the coat to signify his self-appointed position as "door-opener" for Preacher.

Every Sunday morning at eleven o'clock sharp, when the steeple bell finished ringing, ole' Alex would appear in full dress, dramatically push open the door of the front corner of the sanctuary, make a courtly bow, and with great pomp and circumstance usher in his beloved friend. Under his

Preacher and Alex

breath, so only a few on the front row heard, he announced with dignity, "Dr. Gordon."

"Dr. Gordon" always timed his entrance so he arrived at the pulpit and started singing the first hymn before the organist had released the final chord of the introduction. This was a carry-over of his habit of "heisting" tunes when no musical accompaniment was available. His rousing voice, together with the excitement of the Doxology following Alex's magnificent entrance, always got things off to a flourishing start and provided some motivation for people to be on time for the start of worship.

After Alex saw Preacher through the door, he would retire to the ante-room to greet latecomers and help them find their way into the sanctuary. When the preaching began, he pulled up a chair by the open door into the choir loft and listened. He not only loved Preacher, but had a great respect for his book-learning and appreciation for his sermons.

One Sunday, when Preacher returned to his office, Ole Alex was waiting for him as usual to discuss some aspect of the sermon. Preacher greeted him warmly and asked, "Did you hear the sermon this morning, Alex?"

"Yas suh, I sure did."

"Did you understand it?"

"Yas suh; I heered it, and I understands every word of it, but I didn't quite get your meaning! Seems like you cut it short."

Preacher's concern for brevity in his sermons was not merely letting the Presbyterians out early so they could beat the Baptists to a favorite restaurant for Sunday dinner. His reasoning was more profound than logistical. He believed that not much more could be accomplished in a sermon after twelve o'clock. He said, "Ain't no use preachin' like everybody had come with a tub or a pail to carry the message home in. Some folks just have a little tin cup or a thimble or possibly only a sieve. You better make it simple, make it short, and make it the Word of God. Most folks can't hold too much at one time."

J. MacDowell Richards, President of Columbia Theological Seminary, recalls the first time Preacher asked him to be guest speaker. Just before the worship, Preacher led him into the sanctuary and, pointing to the big clock on the back wall which was clearly visible from the pulpit, told him kindly, but in no uncertain terms, "Now Mac, when that long hand stands at ten minutes before twelve, you slide for home!"

Preacher's very presence in the pulpit was part of worship. His sermons were always worth hearing, and they drew countless fringe Christians to morning worship. But, the charisma of the *man* in the pulpit, his appealing manner and down-to-earth translation of scholarly theology to simple explanations of faith and the Power of God were what packed them in. And when he offered this nourishment, he was wise enough to do so in bite-size pieces that could be fed to the young, the old, the weak, and the spiritually anemic.

A personal touch of admonition often added to the poignancy of his message. He reminded the congregation repeatedly that people should not be offended so easily or get angry at the slightest provocation. He would say that some folks have their feelings out on antennae, and he would make a gesture of pulling an antenna up out of his forehead. "They want to receive the slightest vibration that might get their feelings hurt. Why, even when they get mad at me or the Session, they will tell you, "I'm going to quit the church!"

"I visited a deacon of the church one day and found that he and his wife were having a party to which I had not been invited. I told them, 'You have deeply offended me. I don't see how you could do me that way. I have only one recourse; I'm going to quit the church.'" His point was understood, and a few listeners relaxed as if they had just lowered their antennae.

Asked whether he found it difficult to preach to college students, he answered with earnestness, "I don't preach to students; I preach to everyone. Can't see this business of being a man's preacher, or a woman's preacher, or an old folk's preacher. I try to throw the hay down where even the smallest goat can nibble, and that's not always easy to do."

"Everyone should love the church, magnify the church, and support it," he believed. "It doesn't make any difference which one you happen to belong to. Religion is a natural thing and the church is a fundamental institution of American society."

If religion was a natural thing, so was his preaching. People didn't find one man in the pulpit on Sunday and another in the street on Monday. No one was afraid to go to church nor hesitant to sit down in front because the whole experience with Preacher in the pulpit was so right, so easy, and so reverently worshipful.

One young matron who, as a child, had been a regular occupant of the front row, reminisced, "My young mind was usually not able to grasp and retain all the intellectual aspects of his sermon, but I learned the lesson of his text through the testimony of his life, which drew me to church in the first place. If my mind strayed to the stained glass windows or the maple wainscotting, I would abruptly be brought back to reality by Preacher's clearing his throat as if to say, 'Now, listen! This is important!' "

At the very outset of his ministry, Preacher had shown a native aptitude for holding an audience's attention. When he was still a student in Southwestern at Memphis, he held services during the summer at small churches in Panola County, Mississippi. On one occasion, he took one of his beloved aunts along with him to church. She lived to be over 100 years old but remembered to her dying day his sermon that morning. She told him after church as they were returning home, "Ulysses, you preached a good sermon this morning; but, son, the Bible doesn't say anything about any pickles in Jesus' feeding the 5,000."

The young preacher replied, "No, that's right, Aunt Sally, but whoever heard of a picnic without a few pickles?"

The paradox of this pastor's good preaching was that he *didn't* preach—not in the sense of laying down the law. His sermons began with a story, a moral tale, a parable of modern or Biblical days which kept everyone alert. He was not a reformer nor a lambaster, and felt he ought not to preach at people, but to be their pastor and teacher. He wanted to lead, not drive.

"When I get up to face the people, I look at them and realize they have had a hard time. Some have had broken hearts, sadness, financial trouble, and some are worried about their children. I felt I should try to offer leadership, guidance, kindness, and love." He believed that the way to reform society was to change the hearts of men and women. He used no force or coercion; but, he made it clear that one better take the Sermon on the Mount seriously, and Paul's twelfth chapter of Romans, and any of the many places in the Bible that tell us how we ought to live and to behave. "If you want to see the Kingdom of God, you better change your ways; you better quit being stingy, spiteful, and revengeful." Revenge is mine, saith the Lord.

Just as we can say that a television program is an emotional experience and not just a cerebral one, so it is that the hour of worship is a spiritual experience, not simply an intellectual exercise. The apostle Paul, said that wisdom alone was insufficient for us to understand the Power of God. In the same vein, the well constructed, well-reasoned sermon is not enough to transmit the love of our Lord. Preacher, himself, was a sermon!—because his way of life gave additional credibility to his interpretation of Scripture.

"My sermons are all based on the Bible," he explained. "I don't know too much about the economic situation, and I don't know too much about sociology—except what the Bible teaches us about being kind and thoughtful and generous to people who are in need."

As a spokesman of God, Preacher saturated his mind with what the Bible was trying to convey to us through its many inspired writers. This he would then transpose into practical lessons for our times. He read constantly, not only books and articles of Biblical import, but contemporary and historical works to understand the modern dilemma. He loved to read and re-read Bunyan's *Pilgrim's Progress* and all the classics which were beautiful expressions of life or considered to be the outstanding books in philosophy and the behavioral sciences. These, together with the Bible and his important laboratory of learning—the people—became the source and foundation for his preaching.

"I followed a more practical school of theology. Seminary study helps you greatly and is a wonderful training of the mind; but one must not live his life in a cloister because it is essential to be in touch with people and to experience life yourself."

He delivered his sermons with naturalness and ease. He spoke the language of the people with a baritone voice of tremendous carrying power. Those who were hard-of-hearing had only to sit near the front; there was no need for a public-address system.

He never used what some speech teachers would dub a ministerial tone—a singing of the vowels with artificial rising and falling inflections in measured cadence, half-chant, half-speech. When he said "Amen" at the end there was a downward thrust of his voice that had a finality about it. It never sounded like a question mark nor did it have any whispered mystery or hushed funereal suspense. When he said "Amen," it stayed put!

Also, he *said* "Amen," he didn't *sing* it. He always claimed that in singing one should open his mouth and sing ah-ah-ah-men; but in speaking, the vowel *a* should always be said like in the word, *pay,* and the word pronounced, ay-men.

He loved to hear chanting and to chant himself, but was amused by those whose delivery of sermons was half-song, half-speech—a sort of hybrid that has long since been much imitated in various degrees by those who have associated a sing-song, oratorical style with preaching.

"Do he intone his sermons?" Preacher would ask in fun about a newcomer preacher whose reputation as a stemwinder had preceded him.

Now, let it not be assumed that because he didn't use any communicative artificialities, Preacher's sermons were like conversational chats. Not in the pulpit on Sunday morning! He was forceful in his emphasis when force was needed. But emphasis by Bible thumping or bombastic, oratorical gesticulation was not his style. Sometimes he would make a 120 degree turn to face the choir at his left, or a 90 degree shift of his entire body to face the overflow crowd which filled the fellowship hall at his right. Leaning forward and taking off his glasses, he might quote a long passage from *Pilgrim's Progress,* or recite a Whittier poem or a Psalm, or just make a simple summary of what he had been saying, as if to encapsulate the point so one couldn't forget it.

But, there was one point in the sermon in which a gesture of emphasis could be expected. The huge, old, pulpit-Bible was always open and his sermon notes, boldly penned on cards with a black, felt-tip pen, were on a stack on the left side of the Bible. He carelessly, and usually without looking, lifted them one at a time from one side to the other as if following them meticulously. To the congregation, turning of the note-cards seemed more like a rhetorical pause than a mnemonic necessity for the speaker. But, as he came to his main point, he would gather both sets of notes in his left hand, shuffle them to his right, close the Bible with a flourish and put his mixed-up notes on top of it. Then, as he invariably took off his glasses, and held them in his hand like a pointer, one couldn't help but feel he was saying, "now, if you haven't paid any attention up to now, you better hear this!" Frequently, this major emphasis came when the long hand was approaching ten minutes to twelve and he was sliding for home.

Despite his concentration on his sermon, he was a perfect example of a speaker who could adapt himself to almost any kind of interruption and use it to his advantage. In fact, if things had not livened up sufficiently, he would create his own interruptions. For example, during the singing, if a late-comer hesitatingly tried to squeeze into the back row, no matter how the usher tried to prevent it, Preacher often waved to the person, and leaving his post, he would bring a hymnal to the worshipper while personally conducting him to the front. Between stanzas, he would call out to those piling up in the rear, "Come forward to the first pew!" Needless to say, the front pews were seldom empty after Preacher negotiated the latecomers. This procedure also encouraged the "regulars" to get to church early; it was the unsuspecting newcomers who got the treatment, or old friends who had dropped in from out of town.

One hot, summer morning in the old church on University Avenue, the stained-glass windows were open and the church was full, as usual. Preacher was approaching the main point in the sermon when the siren of an approaching police car was heard. The front of the church was only a sidewalk away from the street and all passing vehicles could easily be heard. So, when the police car came past, Preacher could not speak over the wailing siren, so he paused until it went on by. He had no sooner resumed his talk when, in the background, came the clang of a fire engine followed by the growl of its low-pitched siren and the grumbling of its overburdened engine picking up speed as it left the firehouse. Again Preacher fell silent and all heads turned to see whether it was the small fire-truck or the big tanker. Preacher had hardly begun to speak again when the two-toned, sing-song alarms of ambulances penetrated the stunned congregation. Finally, when this was followed by the screeching siren of the police chief's car, Preacher closed the Bible with a smile of surrender and said, "This church is on a busy corner; it ought to be on a busy corner of a major thoroughfare. Who wants to live in a community without a fire and police department?! A church belongs right in the middle of all the action; God help them to get the fire out and to save those who are hurt! Let us pray!" And that concluded the worship.

When Preacher said, "Let us pray," he meant it. He never asked "May we pray?" or, "Shall we bow our heads in a moment of prayer?" It was like he was echoing the words of Jesus who said in the Sermon on the Mount, "Let your *yes* be yes and your *no* be no." Preacher's *ay-men* had a finality about it, and his *let us pray* left no room for doubt that he was going to pray. "No need to ask them if they would be willing to indulge in a little prayer," he told the elders, "just *do* it." That was a lesson most everyone learned: one does not need to ask permission to pray, just begin—"Let us pray!"

His public prayers rarely omitted the firemen, the policemen, "and all others who wait upon the public good." He was greatly appreciative of their night watchfulness and felt they needed singling out as much as did the college professors, doctors, business men, farmers, factory workers, and housewives. Particularly when the church worship hour was broadcast, he would pray for all the people who "were working in the filling stations," or "fishing on Lake Wauberg." His was a natural and deep concern for his fellow man wherever he might be, and if Preacher were on-the-air, you could be sure there was a circle of firemen, policemen, and servicemen gathered around their station radios.

Preacher's prayers and sermons so captivated the hearers that even the deacons often forgot their responsibilities to look after the comfort of the worshippers. The sanctuary would heat up and the congregation flail away with the cardboard fans supplied by the funeral parlor, and the women would daintily wipe the perspiration from their upper lips and temples. When the deacons seemed not to notice, Preacher didn't send them an inconspicuous note about it, he called out from the pulpit, "For heaven's sake, why don't you deacons open some windows; it is hot as . . . torment in here."

Conversely, the transom over the pulpit was open wide on one Sunday morning when an unexpected wind and rainstorm descended. The water came through the window and splattered on Preacher's head without setting off any action from the deacons. "Do you suppose one of you deacons could pull yourself together to close this window so I don't get baptized while I'm preaching to you?"

Preacher entered into all parts of the worship with his whole being. He loved the choir and when it was singing a favorite anthem, he often sang bass along with it from his pulpit chair just in front of the choir loft.

Singing the hymns gave him special pleasure. He often sang the melody, particularly on the first stanza, to be sure they got started with gusto. Then he would shift to tenor or alto on the second stanza and, when his voice began to tire, he would sing a resonant and sonorous bass. He had a way of sustaining the last note of one stanza and letting it carry over to the first of the next as if to be sure the congregation didn't lose the tune. He was asked why he did this and his reply was, "It is because I am long-winded."

Even the collection was important to him — especially the collection. He made the offering a real joy-in-giving. His prayer of dedication was a sacred moment of presenting tithes and gifts of gratitude to the work of the Lord. When he referred to "the collection," it annoyed the sticklers who wanted the theologically accurate language — "offering." He often would hold the plates aloft when giving them to the deacons and mischievously say, "We will now take up the *collection.*"

During the depression, he was particularly sensitive to the fact that it was difficult for some to spare even a dime for the work of the church because of their own financial plights. In all sincerity and with no intent to jest, he sympathetically and tenderly added to his request for the offering this much-quoted assurance:

"If you can't put anything in, take a little bit out!"

While no one is known ever to have taken him up on that assertion, several "lodgebrothers" who had hunted with him took him at his word on "Shotgun Sunday." He had told his fraternity boys that if they couldn't afford to give cash, they could put a couple of shotgun shells in the collection. Several of them did!

He turned to a guest speaker one Sunday, when seeing a man slowly working his way down the aisle during the singing of the second hymn, and said, "If that ole' man doesn't hurry up, he'll miss the collection." He often said that where two or three people were gathered together in the Lord's Name, you should always take up a collection.

A church bulletin in 1948 paid tribute to Preacher on his 20th anniversary which concluded with this paragraph:

> Dr. Gordon's greatest love is the Church and its pulpit! His emphasis upon the stated services of the sanctuary has always been pointed and strong. In the sanctuary he unfolds the Word so that all may hear and understand. Words are not adequate to express the love and respect which we all hold for our pastor.

Yes, Preacher was a pulpit-preacher, a leader who loved the church and through its worship could bring people to know God, to become changed in heart, and to grow in Christian love for each other and for the Lord.

# 7

## MIKESVILLE'S CHURCH MOUSE

P<small>REACHER LOVED</small> a country church! While he was pastor of the large First Presbyterian Church in Gainesville, he loved to go to the surrounding country to help the people in the small churches. He knew practically everybody in the country, anyway, because he hunted and fished with most of them on their own property. He was just as at home with the farming Floridians as he was with the city's university clientele.

Often, these churches could not afford full-time pastors and they would get someone to fill the pulpit, or "supply" the church, on a given Sunday or even for weeks at a time. Preacher was one of the most sought-after pastors and if he couldn't go himself, he would get an elder or deacon, or Sunday school teacher to go as a mission effort of the Gainesville church.

One of the reasons Preacher was in such demand was his ability to meet all kinds of people at their own educational or cultural levels and make them feel completely comfortable in all circumstances and expectations. His natural ways in some cases were so uninhibited that occasionally they were downright unconventional. Those congregations who had never seen Preacher before sometimes did not understand his antics and were even shocked by them. Eventually, all were endeared to this natural, lovable man and each has his favorite story to tell about him.

One such congregation is located at Mikesville, about an hour's drive from Gainesville on modern roads. It is one of the historically significant churches of Suwannee Presbytery, a beautifully preserved sanctuary nestled under the southern live-oaks that make country churches in the South so picturesque. Along its side is a graveyard containing the bodies of three, four, and five generations of folk who worshipped there.

At Mikesville they still talk about the days when there was little money to pay the preacher, much less to keep the building in adequate repair. One might say they were poor as a church mouse. One Sunday night, Preacher was sitting in the pulpit chair during the taking up of the offering, a real church mouse ran across the platform underneath Preacher's chair and over to the other side and hid among a stack of hymnals stored in the corner. The eyes of everyone in the congregation turned to follow the mouse, each person showing a state of alarm in his own characteristic way. Some raised their eyebrows in dismay, others flinched in astonishment, and still others registered disbelief.

No one did anything about the mouse, however, except to move toward the center aisle in the pew, and a few women picked up their feet and sat on them. No one took particular note of the fact that Preacher had also seen the mouse. Casually he eased up to the pulpit and picked up a hymnal in his hand and took a firm grip on it. As he sat back down, he took aim at the corner where the mouse had disappeared. When the ushers assembled to come forward with the collection there was a sudden swish, and then a swash. Preacher had thrown the hymnal over to the corner catching the mouse between number 234 and 235. He had ambushed the mouse just as accurately as if he were flicking his fishing rod after a bass in the Oklawaha River.

"Will the ushers now come forward?" Preacher requested with an impish smile of saintly satisfaction. "Lord, we thank you for this offering of money for Thy Kingdom. We pray there is enough here to fix the cracks in the floor and stop the intrusion of unwanted guests during the worship hour." Preacher was noted for adapting his prayers to the needs of every occasion.

Since those days, the Mikesville church has been completely renovated, a new fellowship hall has been added, and it presents an appearance of care and devotion. Its bell rings every Sunday with the older boys all competing for the honor of pulling the rope. There is nothing as beautiful to behold as a country church with its antiquity preserved through care given by families of three and four generations. Especially is this important when the pride in the past is equalled by the excitement of plans for the future of these growing areas in God's country.

Preacher took advantage of every opportunity to worship in country churches as well as in large city sanctuaries. Some devoted followers went to church wherever he went because he led them into natural, worshipful, and inspiring moments of sacred reverence while simultaneously creating a joyful celebration—this is what people crave.

One of Preacher's closest and most affluent friends followed him out to Archer where he preached on a regular basis after his retirement. It was Easter and the Bethlehem Presbyterian Church was full to overflowing when the friend arrived late. The collection had already been taken, and there was only a single empty space in the center of the front pew. He waived the ushers to bring the lady down and, after some hesitation, she made her way to the front of the sanctuary.

At the next opportunity, Preacher acknowledged the out-of-town guests and with a bit of fan-fare he caressed a collection plate and took it to his good friend, saying as he approached her, "I noticed you came in late, sis-tah, and didn't have an opportunity to make an offering; I don't want you to feel neglected." She fumbled in her purse and put a piece of folding money in the plate. Its denomination might not have been Presbyterian, but the $100 bill found in the plate by the ushers had to be the contribution given by her.

One could never be sure what Preacher would be up to next. But when you saw his eyes start to dance and his mouth twist into a devilish contortion, you could bet your bottom dollar that he was about to turn an awkward or unnecessarily sombre situation into a mix of productive merriment.

It was at Archer that "ole Sam" worshipped regularly. Not long after Preacher started to preach at Archer on a regular basis, a doleful hound dog sauntered down the center aisle during the singing of the second hymn. An embarrased, but ineffectual, layman had tried to cut the dog off at the narthex-pass; having failed he hurried down the aisle after the poor critter. The faster the elder ran to stop him, the faster "Ole Sam" loped until he reached the third pew.

"Leave that ole dog alone!" Preacher called out in a commanding tone, "He ain't gonna hurt nothin'. If the dog goes, I go!" With that, the critter jumped up onto the rostrum and nibbled at Preacher's hand and then went and laid down under one of the pulpit chairs. Thereafter, in one pocket, Preacher kept dog biscuits for "ole Sam" – the other pocket held candy for the kids. From that day until the Sunday after Preacher died, "ole Sam" worshipped at the Bethlehem Presbyterian Church in Archer. When he thought it was time for Preacher to wind up his sermon, "ole Sam" would stumble to his feet and open his jaws and groan the dog-awfullest yawn you ever heard!

After the worship was over, he would follow Preacher to the front of the pulpit for the benediction, during which he would look up at Preacher with a look of utter devotion, waiting for Preacher to slip his hand into his side-pocket for a dog biscuit. He had learned to know that this was his reward for "not hurtin' nothin'." Far from disturbing the worship, he became an integral part of it – a blessing to all the hunters in the congregation and an eccentricity tolerated by those who didn't like dogs. He was a devotee of Preacher's sermons and few had ever seen such a spiritually sensitive dog as "ole Sam."

One might not know exactly what to expect of Preacher, but of one thing you could be sure—he would try to fit into all situations or bend them for suitable needs. His sermons were usually brief because he knew it was human nature not to listen too intently after the first ten minutes. One time he returned to a beloved country church unexpectedly as a worshipper. The young pastor of the church had talked for quite a while and passed up several good opportunities to end his sermon. Preacher got more and more fidgety and finally began clearing his throat, tapping his cane, and looking at his watch. When the service finally ended, he went to the young pastor, put a hand on his shoulder, and, affecting a Scottish brogue, told him how much he had enjoyed the sermon. "But you talked too long, me lad!" Preacher said. "You had enough points in that sermon to have lasted you all summer!"

But Preacher got hung-up on a long sermon himself one time. It was when he preached at a graveside worship out in the back country where mourners were disappointed if the sermon wasn't a long one. Preacher knew there hadn't been a clergyman in those parts for a long time. He also realized that this was an occasion for which people had gathered from all over—both to honor the deceased and to hear a good "fly swatting" sermon. So Preacher fortified himself with several psalms and three chapters from the New Testament. After reading a psalm or a chapter, he would preach without notes for as long as he could recount the significant meaning to be gleaned from it.

He had spoken for over two hours while everyone swatted gnats and stood in the sun with stoic attention. One of the chief mourners got so carried away, she didn't watch where she was standing and, as she shifted her weight in the sand, the wall of the grave gave way almost toppling her onto the casket. This did not seem to worry the crowd, however, and Preacher continued to speak. When his voice finally gave out and he had to quit, one good and true stalwart mourner came up to him and said, "That was mighty good preachin' you was doin', Preacher, but I saw those storm clouds gatherin' so I'm kinda glad you cut it short."

Preacher loved country people and a country church. He enjoyed the simple faith of the people and preached the simple theology they most wanted to hear:

"Jesus Christ is Lord of all; let Him be your Lord and Savior!"

# 8

## DON'T FORGET PRAYER MEETING

NEXT TO WORSHIP on Sunday mornings and evenings, Preacher loved the mid-week church meetings best. Sometimes these were big affairs of fellowship and food but often they were the simple, intimate worship through meditation and intercession commonly known as prayer meeting.

These were, of course, more frequently held in the chapel or any room smaller than the sanctuary, but during World War II when gasoline was rationed, neighborhood prayer sessions in homes were quite well attended. Everyone had an intense need to be engaged actively in prayer for loved ones in the military service. Togetherness in prayer provided families not only corporate petition but also comfort for the lonely.

One of these neighborhood prayer sessions was scheduled to be held in the home of a deacon who was also prominent in athletic affairs of the university. His wife was active in the women's church work, having hosted circle meetings frequently. This couple with their three boys constituted an exemplary Christian home where Preacher was often present for family meals or was guest of honor at parties. Their home, being in the center of one of the newest, most beautiful sections of university residences, was a natural place to hold prayer meeting and, of course, on this occasion Preacher was there.

The hostess was busily rushing about receiving the guests and neighbors but feeling a bit of pressure in the novel experience of having a prayer-gathering in her home. The baby was crying and the dogs were barking while the host was trying to make the men feel comfortable in the living room of the split-level house. A large crowd had arrived when Preacher announced that it was time to begin. After getting everyone's attention, Preacher called across the large living room to the lady-of-the-house, "Sis-tah, will you bring me a Bible so I can read the Scripture from your sacred, family Book?"

"Just a minute, Preacher, I'll get it," she replied, confident of finding it. She rushed to one book case and then to another and another; she called her husband who scurried to the same places, sure that she had overlooked it. They scrambled all over the upstairs and downstairs, and the boys looked in their own room, but nowhere was a Bible to be found. Mortification was mounting, and Preacher was enjoying it more with each passing gasp of the hostess who insisted, "It has to be here someplace; it just has to be. Oh, here it is!" She returned with a book, but it turned out to be a French dictionary.

Finally a neighbor slipped out the side door and ran home and sneaked his own Bible into the house, placing it on a table near Preacher. "Well, if you don't have one, I'll just use this one," Preacher winked at the amused neighbors who didn't know whether to enjoy the fun he was having or share the embarrassment for their Bibleless friends. No one ever forgot the incident, or the prayer meeting that followed in the wake of the confusion and chagrin shared by all in those fateful opening moments.

The sequel to the story was known only to the close friends who loved and laughed with this family through the years, including Preacher. The neighbor, who piously provided the Bible for the occasion, apparently had no further need of it, because he never asked for its return. It can still be found in the bookcase beside the "lost" Bible which had been there all along.

It was not that Preacher liked to embarrass people or see them embarrass themselves; rather, he enjoyed the humor in every kind of situation in any place. "There is enough to be sad about in life," he often mused, "and if you can't laugh at the things that are funny, you can be pretty miserable." This is a good adage for anyone of any age.

Prayer meetings at the church sometimes ended as humorously as the neighborhood meeting began. It was Preacher's custom to call on different persons to pray, and he rarely asked anyone whose willingness to pray in public was not already known to him. However, one night he called upon an old man who often sat in the back row of the chapel. He was hard-of-hearing and at the close of the meeting when Preacher called to him to dismiss the group with prayer, the old man apparently hadn't heard; he never spoke up. Preacher called to him again while all bowed their heads expectantly. After a third try for the man's participation, the perplexed worshippers heard him tell his wife in a loud voice, "I don't believe I'll mess with it!" Preacher closed the meeting with no further demands upon the poor man, but the story never finished going the rounds.

Reticence of the man who was hard-of-hearing was offset by enthusiasm of another beloved elder who normally prayed too long. Preacher always enjoyed watching the faces of the congregation when he asked the elder to pray because of their apprehension they might be in for a long seige. He allayed their fears on one occasion by adding to his request, "Make it a nice short one."

The poor fellow had kidney trouble and at times was found to be in a hurry. Preacher had asked him to lead the closing prayer before he noticed that the man had already stood to leave the room, presumably to go to the men's room. He responded quickly, though briefly, "Lord, make us ready to go when our time comes! Amen." He left the room after his shortest prayer on record.

The mid-week, pot luck, family suppers were always big fellowship affairs, but Preacher seemed to be partial to the dinners of the men of the church. He loved the women but instinctively realized that a strong church had to have a strong group of committed men if it were going to have significant impact on home and community. Admired and respected by men, Preacher always had a nucleus of sturdy followers to rely on. The men's dinners were not only fellowship, but they were educational, inspiring, and worshipful occasions as well. Good speakers with good ideas and personal testimony always drew a crowd.

A president of the Florida Bar Association, who was also an outstanding churchman, was asked to speak to the men on "The Christian in Politics." He did so in the presence of a banquet crowd of men who had filled the fellowship hall. At one point, the speaker spoke about our country being founded on belief in God and that we all ought never to forget that fact. He began jingling the money in his pocket as he built his speech to a climax. "Our forefathers were men of faith; they even saw fit to put 'In God we trust' on our coins!" He drew out a quarter and a half-dollar from his pocket and brandished them aloft to make his point still more emphatic. A businessman called out from the rear of the room, "Yes, but it's not on our folding money." Everyone started fumbling in his hip pocket for his billfold, including the speaker who stopped short to examine his own dollar bills.

Sure enough, "In God we trust" was not on the paper money. "Well," said the speaker, "It is *my* Christian responsibility to see my congressman about this; I'm going to do just that, I promise you!" After the applause had subsided, he went on with his speech, but he might just as well have quit because his point of a Christian in politics had already been made. He was as good as his word and, as a result, Congressman Charles Bennett from Florida introduced a bill in Congress that was eventually enacted that put this most significant motto on all our money.

Such can be the impact of a group of men gathered together under a banner of love and faith. Their hearts had been tuned by Preacher to Christian responsibility: they had listened to a speaker who inspired them; the speaker, in turn, received a mandate from the meeting that he acted upon through political channels. Such is the power of Christian concern and the capability of our political system! Preacher reflected Christ's constant message: Go forth and change the world by changing the hearts of the people.

Preacher was not opposed to women's rights, but he was very sensitive to the Scriptural admonitions declaring men to be spiritual leaders. Because of this conviction, he did not favor women holding ordained offices in the church. His concern was not so much keeping women *out* of ordained offices of the church as keeping men *in* ordained roles so they would not abdicate their Scriptural responsibilities as spiritual leaders of the church.

He loved the Women-of-the-Church and was loved by them. This was never more apparent than when he was given a hooked rug by the Women-of-the-Church on his 25th anniversary at First Church in Gainesville. The occasion was an Anniversary Prayer Meeting held in the sanctuary which was filled to capacity on Wednesday night for the celebration. He told the crowd, "It's worth 25 years of work to see this many people at prayer meeting."

He continued, "I have heard some folks talking about getting up this meeting, and one person referred to tonight as being my '25th wedding anniversary.' While there is not a word of truth in it, thank God for the rumor." During the evening, a ninety-year-old woman, who once had been Preacher's secretary, presented to him a hooked rug which she had made. She spoke eloquently that night despite the persistent arthritic pain in her body. The rug was only one of many presents given him, including a watch and a set of twelve plates with the church picture on them. But none could have meant as much to him as the rug put together by fingers that trembled and upon which tears of loving devotion had fallen.

And those women *did* love him and their hearts were lifted up and blessed because of his happy voice, devotion, and charm.

He admired and respected the tireless efforts of all the Women-of-the-Church. However, he was drawn most closely to the older generation whose lives he constantly punctuated with lively attention. He brought them to prayer-meeting, and took them to the hospital for visits, to the train or plane, and to any place they needed to be transported.

He carried one old sister to Ocala to the foot-doctor and almost got in trouble for doing it. She had, of course, taken off her stockings at the doctor's office to let him work on her feet. When she returned to the car, she carried them in her hand along with her pocket book. When she got home she found she only had one stocking and accused the foot-doctor of stealing the other one. Later, Preacher found it pushed way down in the front seat. He thought he would have some fun with her, so he took it to her one day. While she and her husband were sitting rocking on their front porch, he approached them holding the stocking out at full length, and sheepishly confessed, "You left your stocking in my car when we were out together the other day."

And visits? My conscience! He visited and talked to the shut-in old ladies continually. He always carried something under his arm for them from wine to Whitman's Samplers. After his death, when one elder tried to be a surrogate Preacher and visit one of his favorite ladies-in-waiting, she told him, "You are good about coming to see me and I thank you, but Preacher always brought me a bottle of wine." She got her wine on the elder's next trip!

On rainy days, when he couldn't get out, Preacher called them on the phone and carried on some kind of foolishness to brighten their day — and his. On his annual, family visits to Memphis, he couldn't wait to call the widow-ladies upon whom he had made an indelible impression as assistant pastor at Second Presbyterian Church in the mid-twenties. No sooner had he kissed his nieces "hello" than he made for the telephone and began calling.

He would begin by putting his handkerchief over his nose and mouth to help muffle his voice and then he would talk in a disguised high-pitched, nasal tone that was every bit credible. "Mary Green?" he would begin with tantalizing mystique. "This is the egg lady."

"The what?" she replied cautiously.

"The egg lady," he reiterated. "I heerd tell you was in need of a dozen eggs today. My chickens have near 'bout killed themselves laying, and I wants to know do you want some of them big eggs outn' my Carolina Blues?"

"Well, maybe I could use a few," came the innocent reply of the longtime friend. She had taken the bait, and Preacher was so tickled he could hardly continue.

"Well, with the change in the weather and you needin' to use most a dozen egg whites a day for them delicious angel food cakes, I figured you was ready."

"Who is this, anyway?"

"Well, it's the egg lady from Florida just passin' thu' and I. . . ."

"Preacher Gordon! You no-count rascal! Get yourself off this phone and quit foolishin' me. When are you coming over?"

He would die laughing and put his handkerchief half-back into his pocket and tell her he couldn't be there until in the morning because he had to telephone a few more good egg customers before the day was out. That was the first straight forward statement he had made, for indeed he had twenty more people to call before he would go to his room to unpack.

He was always the first to know when one of the ladies was sick, and he would be on hand at the hospital to receive her with a little handful of fresh pansies from his own patch. If someone's mother had come to town, he would find it out and immediately drive out to see her before she'd had a chance to settle in.

He loved a certain elderly "Southern belle," who visited from Louisiana. She was full of fun herself and had a "hot line" to her Maker. She was a benevolent matriarch of highest calibre who held nightly prayer meetings in her Christian home. Preacher visited there often, hunting, fishing, playing gin rummy, and swapping stories with her sons. He became an integral part of that distant family, too. His picture with Deacon and Elder hung in the sitting room near the massive canopy bed that dominated the family gathering place in this typical, post-war, Southern planter's three-story home. The plantation was called Fluker, a family name, and was just below the Mississippi border where Preacher passed often on his way to Baton Rouge to visit his niece, Helen.

"Miss Susie" never missed going to church wherever she was but she particularly liked to hear Preacher. She never understood, however, how he could be so saintly on Sunday and such a mischief on Monday. She arrived in Gainesville for a two-week visit, and Preacher drove out to greet her within an hour of her arrival.

He parked under a tree on the shady side of the street, shut his dogs up in the well-ventilated car, and started across the lawn with a box of Whitman Samplers under his arm. She came running out to intercept him; she was so glad to see him. But when she spied the candy, her own devilishness surfaced and she blurted out, "Here you come, you hypocrite, bringing me a box of sugar like you do all your sweethearts, and then you stand up so saintly in that pulpit on Sunday."

Her arms were outstretched to him, but he didn't see them for he had turned on his heel at the word "hypocrite" and headed back to the car with his box of sweets. He didn't like being called a hypocrite, and the rebuff had turned the candy bitter. But after putting the box back in the car, he returned empty handed to the "Queen of Fluker," temper cooled and quite composed.

That repartee had backfired, but the mutual bond between them was strong and easily spanned so slight a rift. After many more visits, the Queen of Fluker, as he always called her, suffered a stroke while visiting in Florida, and Preacher was a daily and hourly comfort to the families in both states.

Men, women, and children of the church came to Preacher at prayer meetings, celebrations and church suppers, and Preacher went to them in their homes where he honed the lives of hundreds into Christ-centered families. Many, whose habits, occupations, or life-styles kept them away from regular attendance at the eleven o'clock, Sunday morning worship, supported the church and its pastor, anyway. Some never missed a covered-dish supper; others never missed a prayer meeting. Many more included Preacher as a regular meal-time member of the family.

An elder and his wife regularly invited Preacher to dinner at their home on Wednesday nights, their preferred time to entertain university personnel. But, it was also Preacher's night for mid-week worship. "Preacher, why can't you ever accept our invitation for Wednesday night?" the elder asked.

"Well, you see," he replied in a high, squeaky voice but with double entendre, "my most main and principle elder, we have this little group of faithfuls who meet on Wednesday nights down at the church. I have asked the Session, as you well know, whether we should discontinue the practice during slack months, but the Session always says we should keep it going as long as two or more want to gather together in the Lord's Name. So, you see, my pal, we still have this little group; and, as for you, Doctor, don't *you* forget prayer meeting."

# 9

## CUTTING THROUGH RED TAPE

Love is blind, some folks insist. Maybe so! What is mistaken for blindness may be consideration and kindness. Inability to discern faults may more accurately be described as loving acceptance, and such acceptance is not just tolerance of flaws but willingness to regard them as part and parcel of the person loved. Only when the defective quality becomes detrimental to that person should a caring partner try to do anything about it.

Preacher loved the church and particularly the Presbyterian Church. He was not blind to its imperfections of polity but accepted administrative awkwardness of committee and court structure. He believed deeply in the "connectional church" and knew each church was stronger because of the interrelationship among all churches of the denomination. Only when the defective quality of incoordination and snail's pace movement of democratic processes became harmful and detrimental to the church did he become impatient and want to do something about it. When he came to this point, however, he was willing and able to cut through red tape and break the bottlenecks of bureaucracy.

Whether the tie-up was in church affairs or in local, state, or national government, or in the University of Florida, Preacher could get to the person or persons who could straighten things out. His communication with the university began with the members of its controlling board, the president and deans, the student government, fraternity officers, and student leaders at all levels and in every educational area.

When Preacher cut through the red tape of Presbyterian administration it was because he loved the church and the people who were serving in the name of the Lord. An outstanding example of his influence being exerted in this way had to do with policies governing the sending of missionaries into foreign lands.

One of Preacher's assistant pastors had tried to go into the foreign missions upon graduation from seminary. He wanted to go to Brazil where he had been born, but there existed a justifiable requirement that a new graduate spend at least one year in a church in this country before going abroad. The young minister had passed all the qualifying tests but in addition to his need for a year's experience, he needed also to find a wife. At that time, it was against Board of World Missions' policy to give a single man a foreign assignment for fear he would marry one of the nationals in the country where he was assigned.

Preacher Gordon was glad to take him on as an assistant pastor even though he knew it would probably be only for one year. After that year, the young man was asked to stay for two, which he was glad to do. He needed more experience and more time to find a wife.

Completing his two years of apprenticeship as assistant to Preacher was the best "on the job" learning he could have had, and it certainly helped him overcome any tunnel vision his zeal for foreign missions had given him. He was so strong on the message of missions that every time he gave a sermon, he talked about missions. Preacher finally took him aside and called his attention to the fact that there was work of the Lord to be done in Gainesville, too, and would he please talk occasionally on some other subject than missionary work. He also learned the art of pastoring from Preacher, whom he never failed to see in the halls of the hospital even on the Preacher's day off. You see, Preacher would sometimes get caught in his own red tape, and a schedule worked out with his assistant pastor was often broken.

After two years, this potential missionary felt he was ready for the mission opportunity, but had not *yet* found a wife. He wrote to the Board telling of his plight and requesting assignment to Brazil. He received a communication commending him for obtaining the required experience serving a church in this country, but advising that his single status would still mitigate against his chances of being sent abroad.

The young and very capable assistant showed Preacher the rejection letter and expressed his terrible disappointment. Preacher, having thus far remained a bachelor and realizing that being unmarried had not affected his successful tenure in the ministry, was incensed that the application had been refused because the young man was single. He picked up the phone and called an official at the top.

"You are the strangest people in the world," Preacher told him. "You send out tons and tons of literature begging people to go work outside this country, and here is a young fellow who wants to go to Brazil so bad that he can talk about nothing else. You say he can't go into the mission work because he doesn't have a wife! What do you expect him to do? — Get a wife like you get a heifer at the state fair?" The young assistant pastor was asked immediately to come to the next meeting of the Mission Board and was accepted and assigned as a missionary to Brazil.

But Preacher's having cut through the red tape to get this dedicated Christian servant on his way to spread the Gospel in another land was only the beginning of a story of how the Lord works in mysterious ways His wonders to perform. After completing a summer orientation program for young missionaries, the young pastor left for Brazil in the fall. Come Christmas, a God-incidence led him to meet a nurse from the States who had returned to Brazil to be with her parents who were missionaries working in a large evangelical hospital there. The bachelor missionary began dating the girl and they were married the following October, just one year and nine months after Preacher's famous phone call to the Mission Board. She was a citizen of the United States, born of parents who were citizens of the United States. However, his marriage did break a plank in the Board policy because his wife had been born in Brazil and hence was a national of that country. She was a citizen of both countries and so was he. Together, they went on to serve Christ's Church in Brazil for eight years before returning to the United States.

Preacher had not only cut through red tape, he had played a part in God's plan for the life of this young missionary who couldn't find a wife until he went to his field of service. How ironic that he had to go to Brazil to find the U.S. citizen who was propelled "home" to her parents because of the tragic death of her brother. One never knows when the disappointments of one circumstance will lead to the joys of another. One never knows how a phone call to cut red tape may lead to fulfillment of God's plan and purposes in an unexpected way.

For Preacher, the least said about some matters, the better. Words can become entanglements that act much like scotch tape — the more you try to straighten it out, the bigger mess you are in. He never used his own opinion when that of the Bible would do as well or better.

For example, the youth group was having a discussion at the church one night on the subject of the use of alcohol. Preacher happened to be passing by, and the leader asked for his opinion. Preacher quoted verbatim from one end of the Bible to the other, made no other comments, but walked out after fifteen minutes of reciting Scripture which they are still talking about. He had answered the question!

The greater hazard a situation posed for developing into

a lengthy, complicated, argumentative, overheated discussion, the more Preacher would use every opportunity at his disposal for cutting out some of the chatter. He always felt most problems were beat to death anyway, and that solutions, unfortunately, derived more from exhaustion than from persuasion.

He was very faithful and loyal to the Columbia Seminary and supported its work to the very best of his ability. He was asked to deliver the Invocation in Orlando at a Synod-wide meeting held to launch a financial campaign on behalf of the school. From several sources it has been reported that this was his opening prayer: "Oh, Lord, we pray Thee for Thy Presence and Thy Guidance in this meeting. Help us to get on with the business without any unnecessary palaver so that we can get on home."

With his local church Session, Preacher was especially effective. If there was any palaver at its meetings, it was done at the outset through his own story telling to get the elders in a good mood for the serious business to be transacted. As teaching elder, Preacher was the Moderator of the Session, and as soon as he called it to order with an opening prayer, matters were handled with dispatch. Here was the one place that the informal title of "Preacher" was dropped; friends of closest and longtime relationships respected the official responsibility that was theirs for properly conducting the business of the church. Preacher was addressed as "Mr. Moderator" and no one stepped out of place nor tried to take advantage of his friendship with Preacher. Elders with seniority on the Session made a special effort to cooperate with him. His agenda may not have been highly structured, but Preacher was "Mr. Moderator," the revered spiritual leader—the primary executive of the First Presbyterian Church of Gainesville.

He sought the advice and counsel of the Session in all matters of serious concern, but, knowing the clumsiness of committee competence, he often asked certain deacons or elders to take individual initiative in carrying out decisions of the Session or acting as fact-finders for future Session discussions. The Session had such esteem for the Moderator and for his churchmanship, foresight, and sense of Christian priorities that consensus was usually quite easily achieved in accordance with Preacher's recommendations. The men knew his only motivation was for the good of the church and for the on-going of the Lord's work; he had no desire for monetary gain nor ambition for personal aggrandizement.

There was mutual respect and love between teaching and ruling elders. Of the Session, Preacher said, "They were the finest group of people in the world to pass the buck to if you didn't want to make a decision about something. Always there was joint consideration given. We do not have an authoritarian organization in which the minister is an autocrat. It's a joint authority, and it's the most blessed system in the world. The highest type of men I have ever known have been elders of the Presbyterian Church."

Believing as he did in the hierarchy of courts of jurisdiction in Presbyterianism, Preacher served as a good presbyter—one who contributes to the business of the many levels of church administration. As Moderator of Suwanee Presbytery and the Synod of Florida, he played active roles in the endeavors at all levels of the governing process. He was well known in agencies of the General Assembly and served as a commissioner to this high court. He also was involved in the Division of Higher Education and trustee of several institutions. He knew church polity backwards and forwards and was on many commissions appointed to evaluate or judge alleged violations of the church constitution. In short, he was a great influence in every corner of the Presbyterian Church, U.S.

As he grew older, he became more outspoken and expressed the fear that governance had burgeoned at the expense of evangelical discipleship. The individual church, he felt, was losing some of its distinctive and simplistic means for "doing" personal evangelism and was weakened thereby in its own Christian growth. This, in turn, reduced the effectiveness of the church's outreach into the broader community.

Preacher believed strongly in the priesthood of all believers and in their role as personal emissaries or disciples of Christ. When church members actively give testimony of their faith and reach out to the needs of others, the church grows. The more each church gives unstintingly of itself for other struggling missions the more strength accrues to the mother church. As enriching programs are created and supported for its own membership and convenant children, greater becomes the response from non-Christians who want to be associated with such a lively, celebrating fellowship.

But Preacher held that as higher courts assumed more responsibility in these areas, the local churches tended to become more dependent upon the system and less upon their own initiative. Preacher's position was that preaching, pastoring, deaconing, worshipping, and personal witnessing must not take a back seat to the governing processes. As in all democratic institutions, danger lies in filling bureaucratic drawers to over-flowing with paperwork, surveys, deliberations of planning councils, recommendations on public issues, and reports of committees. Responsibility for self-government must not get out of the hands of the governed and into the offices of the bureaucracy. As followers of Christ, governorship should not be at the expense of discipleship!

During his forty-year pastorate, the First Presbyterian Church of Gainesville, itself the product of the mission work of a "mother" church in Kanapaha, developed missions in south, north, east, and west Gainesville. Three of these ultimately became churches, and First Church gave helping hands to its parent in Kanapaha and to all country churches in surrounding areas. Preacher thought it unwise for the university student-work to be taken out of the

# Cutting Through Red Tape 89

direct supervision of local churches and made a program of Synod because this would remove the supervising agency too far from the scene of the action.

Preacher believed that the higher levels of government in the "connectional church" should do the things that the local churches couldn't do alone, or that could be done better in aggregate rather than in separate congregations. This is a great advantage of the Presbyterian form of government. It is rooted in Scripture that churches are and should be inter-related and inter-governed. The strong should help the weak.

He became impatient with long, extended, or reconvened meetings necessary to accomplish the bureaucratic business of governing. Sometimes he omitted the argumentative floor debates and went only to the more inspirational sessions. In his mid-sixties, Preacher's assistant pastor for students had driven him to Synod which was meeting in Sarasota. He wrote that they had arrived in time for Preacher to attend Rotary Club where he was conspicuous by his hearty singing.

> Finally, we got to our suite of rooms. I set about unpacking. When I finished, Preacher was still in his room, and I assumed he was still getting ready to go to the opening session of Synod. I lay on the bed for a few minutes and smelled the pungent aroma of one of Preacher's cigars. Then I heard a low chuckle. This was followed by soft laughing. A few minutes passed and another chuckle. Finally, I went to the door of Preacher's room. He was sitting on the bed in his underwear, smoking a cigar and reading Aesop's *Fables*.

In later years, when his physical endurance had weakened, he often left Presbytery meetings early to get home to make his rounds at the hospital or to see an old man in the nursing home. It became more and more difficult to "cut through red tape" as the strands became tougher, more entangled, and wound interminably around the problems of governance.

Preacher loved the church and its people and felt there was nothing more important than being with the people and leading them in carrying out the mission of the church.

He was a Beloved Pastor, Spiritual Advisor, and a servant of the Shepherd of the Sheep.

# PART III

## SPIRITUAL ADVISOR

*". . . Because he had the divine gift to be our 'spiritual advisor.' "*

# 10

## COMFORT YE HIS PEOPLE

As spiritual advisor to people of every circumstance and degree of need, he lifted up the hearts of the sad and weary, the sick and dying, the bereaved and lonely, the troubled and broken-hearted. He comforted all who heard his voice, saw his smile, and felt his presence. His compassion was influenced by that of his Lord, who said, "Lo, I am with you always. Even unto the end of the world."

He was a human instrument for transmitting the Divine Love and encouragement bestowed so freely upon mankind by our Maker. By the Lord's Grace, an unmerited gift to us all, we can be healed of our anxieties, comforted in our grief, and lifted above our depressions. Preacher, a servant of mercy everywhere he went, gave spiritual consolation to anyone who could hear the joy in his voice and the melody in his laughter.

Those who knew him believed that the cap he wore stood for God's Grace. And in a sense it did! His green and white baseball-styled cap with broad bill was emblazoned on the front with the single word, *Grace*. The cap called Grace was his constant companion in his later years, and he seldom went anyplace without it and his "sympathy stick." Even when he was "dressed up" going to a dinner party, he often wore the cap for protection from the night's chill. After his

Preacher with Grace cap and "sympathy stick."

death, his close personal friend and surgeon, who had been with him at the end, was asked, "What of Preacher's belongings would you like to have as a gift from the family?" Without hesitation, the doctor said, "His cap!" Only a very few knew that Preacher had been given the cap by the Grace Fertilizer Company of Archer, Florida.

The truth was that God's Grace was sufficient for Preacher, and as a spiritual distributor in God's field that has no fences, he wanted to broadcast it as far and wide as he could.

In explaining the meaning of *Grace* in a sermon, Preacher concluded by telling this story: "A little boy had been disobedient at the dinner table, and his father sent him upstairs to bed without letting him finish his meal. Later, before his son fell asleep, the man climbed up the steps to the boy's bedside to tell him that he loved him, that God loved him, and that he was forgiven. He kissed the boy on the forehead, quietly left the room and closed the door." Preacher choked up as he then explained, "That was grace. The man was my father; I was the little boy!"

A woman volunteer, who went to the church office to help temporarily with the secretarial back-log and then stayed for thirteen years, was unintentionally privy to many private conversations with Preacher. At that time, his office was located over the secretarial room and was heated by an open grill that let the warm air from the coal fire on the first floor ascend to his "confidential quarters." When he came down from his office after hearing trials and troubles almost *ad infinitum*, he would think up an amusing story from the past, lift it out of his vast storehouse of memory and tell it to the secretary. By the time he had finished chuckling, his own mind and feelings were freed-up, and he was ready to take on another counselee.

Preacher's accomplishments as a pastor were not limited to keeping office hours for counselling. They derived also from going out into the field to find the lost sheep caught in a crag. His pastoring excelled more from his presence at the trouble spots than it did from advice given in an office setting, and he had a special instinct for being in the right place at the right time. An example of this occurred during World War II, when Preacher's assistant for student work was also chaplain to the Gainesville Naval reserve unit. One day the assistant received a long-distance call from the Navy Department requesting that he deliver a casualty message to a family. Believing that he was the first person in town to be notified, he immediately put on his uniform and went to the family's home. But when he arrived, he was both relieved and astonished to find that Preacher Gordon was already there and had spared this young clergyman a difficult task. "I do not know to this day," the chaplain said, "how Preacher got the news, but I do know that he had such an absolute sense of modesty and confidentiality about his work as a pastor that he would never reveal his source of information."

He seemed to sense where there were social gatherings or trouble spots like he smelled where the bream were bedding. Preacher was often heard to say, "I just lucked into it. I just hit it right. Caught three on one line." But if luck is equal to preparation plus opportunity, then Preacher had a lot of just such luck because he was always on the ready and never wanted for opportunities.

Of course, his timing was not simply luck. It was also his willingness to act on good impulses. If he thought, "You know, I ought to go see old man so and so," he would not just *think* it, he would *do* it. "If you have a good impulse, act on it before the moment passes," was his frequent admonition.

Some folks don't want too much help, though; he was wise enough to observe their wishes, too. A very close hunting companion, a professor at the University, was quite ill and not expected to live. His wife sent for Preacher; but, unlike her husband, she was not much on religion or, especially, praying. Preacher knew this; so when he arrived, instead of making a bee line for the sick bed, he sat and talked to the wife awhile. Finally, he asked her if she would like him to go in and have a prayer with her husband. She tersely replied, "Yes, but make it a short one." The length of the prayer must have been just right; the old man lived seven more years.

The reverse of this rebuff occurred one time at the hospital. A rather strong willed non-believer lay critically ill and near death. His believing wife requested Preacher to call on him, which he would have done anyway, because he liked the old man despite his gruff agnosticism. He went into the room to chat with his terminally sick friend and, when he had done all he could with light conversation, asked, "Would you object to my having a prayer with you?"

The expression on the dying man's face hardened, and he replied with resignation, "Go ahead and pray; I'm going to die anyway. If it will make you feel any better, help yourself." Needless to say, he made that prayer a short one too.

He didn't think it was necessary to pray every time one visited the sick, whether at home or in the hospital. He used to advise his elders and young preachers to sense the climate for prayer. "There are times when your very presence is a prayer and words are superfluous."

His purpose was to give what would best be heeded or needed. "Sometimes they don't need a prayer as much as a laugh," he advised. This certainly must have been true of the ladies in a four-bed ward who were out of danger but still out of sorts. He went every day to see them, and they were delighted. On occasion he would pray, but more often he would just sit and talk and give them something funny to think about. One day he noticed one of the ladies reading a murder mystery. With exaggerated astonishment he confronted her, saying, "Sis-tah, you have no business reading a book like this! Why, you ought to be reading the Bible!" With that he started out of the room, carrying the murder mystery with him. As he reached the door he turned, and with the devilish twinkle he knew how to turn on, said, "Besides, I haven't read this one yet." He stepped into the hall and left the ladies convulsed. He went immediately to a floor nurse with instructions to return the book promptly. But his mission was accomplished: the ladies had a much needed laugh, sometimes the best medicine for the day, and they had a story to tell their friends for weeks.

Preacher's smile and cheerful greeting was an anti-body for gloom. A favorite story of his that would liven up any sick room was about the veteran doctor who took his son on his rounds one day as he visited patients in their homes.

The son had just finished his internship and was coming back to go into practice with his father. "The best advice I can give you," counselled the experienced doctor, "is to cultivate your powers of observation. Diagnosis is simplified when you can detect the symptoms that are obvious before researching causes that are hidden and bizarre."

So, the father took his son to see three ladies confined to their beds at home. The first complained about her headaches. She was holding the novel she was reading within a foot of her eyes as he approached the bed. "Your headaches are coming from your eyesight; you need glasses," he told her and quickly left the house to go to the next patient.

The second lady was overweight and had poor color. As the doctor talked with her, he noticed on her bedside table a box of candy which was almost empty. "You ought to give up sweets," the doctor warned and then he left.

The third lady seemed very frightened, and he could tell that something indeed was wrong. Her face seemed flushed as if she might have quite a fever. He promptly got out his thermometer and began to shake it vigorously. As he was doing so, it slipped out of his hand and dropped onto the deep nap of the rug. He got down on his knees beside the bed to retrieve it. After taking her temperature, he shook his head with diagnostic decision, and pronounced the therapeutic verdict. "You will just have to give up your church work," he told her in no uncertain terms; without waiting to hear her protest, the doctor and his son left the house.

"Well, what have you learned today, son?" the doctor asked as they were returning home.

"Dad, I understand that the first woman was getting her headaches from poor eyesight and the overweight woman was eating too much candy. But, I can't understand why you told the woman with fever that she had to give up her church work."

"Son, you must take every clue into consideration. Did you notice when I dropped the thermometer?"

"Yes, Dad, I saw that," the son said uncertainly.

"Well," the doctor replied, "when I knelt down to pick it up, I saw her preacher under the bed."

Tales like this became Preacher's stock-in-trade. When he told that story in the right place at the right time, it was worth a whole pharmacy full of pills.

Preacher teased one good Baptist friend, who attended church infrequently, by telling him that being a Baptist beat being nothing at all. Then, years into their friendship, the man lost his wife. After the services which were conducted from the funeral parlor by their Baptist pastor, the bereaved husband went home alone. Early in the evening, who should ring the man's doorbell but Preacher Gordon. "First he prayed for me, then he prayed for all the living, then he prayed for my departed wife, and then we just sat awhile without either of us saying anything."

After some time elapsed Preacher called the man by name and asked him to make him a promise, to which he agreed. "Tomorrow is Sunday," said Preacher, "and I want you to get dressed up and go to the Baptist Church. This will be hard on you; but in time you will realize that what I am asking you to do will be for your good."

The friend did as he promised and has never missed a Sunday since. He wrote, "I thank him for the things he told me and taught me; O Lord, bless Preacher Gordon. I shall always heed his advice!"

Such a response expresses the kind of impact Preacher had on people. His spiritual medicine was sometimes hard to ingest, but if one could get it down, more than likely relief would follow. Preacher realized that truth was often hard to hear, but sometimes it was the only way. A contemporary Presbyterian minister of considerable reknown once asked Preacher how one should go about helping people when they asked for personal advice. His answer was, "Tell them the truth about themselves, as you see it; this might temporarily hurt their pride or ruffle their feathers, but in the long run it will help them."

He never forced himself into people's problems but always offered a considerate ear. "If I knew there was trouble of a marital or delicate nature in somebody's home, I would go to the friend and sit down and visit. Then, if they wanted to tell me about it, I would listen and try to help; but I never opened the subject. I didn't like to stick my nose into something that was none of my business." If it can be said one's very presence is a prayer that makes words superfluous, then good listening also can be a form of counselling that makes verbal advice unnecessary.

Preacher's trips to the hospital and visits throughout the community were so frequent that some folks complained he could never be found at home. His retort was kind but terse, "Well, if I stayed home you would complain because I wasn't out tending to my business." This dilemma is one that faces all good pastors, and it would do well for those who are impatient with their favorite minister to remember it.

Asked one time what he was going to do when he retired, Preacher mused, "Oh, I think I will just throw a shingle up in front of my house advertising COUNSELLING FOR WIDOWS AND SPINSTERS." But being a widow or spinster was certainly not a prerequisite for Preacher's concern and care. When he wasn't visiting face to face, he was doing it by letter. He wrote more letters to students in military service than anyone could imagine. He used a broad felt pen with a characteristic scrawl that was more appreciated than legible. When an envelope arrived from Preacher, it could be recognized by the handwriting alone; it was quickly opened for the words of assurance it invariably contained.

He could hardly answer the telephone without saying, "Hold on, there goes my doorbell." And he rarely answered the door but for the telephone's urgent request for his help. If it wasn't one, it was the other. People called or came by his house all day long; some of them just wanted to say "hello", or to sit with Preacher for a few minutes for no reason other than to tell or hear the newest joke or to start or finish their day on a better note. These daily encounters gave many people the energy they needed for the day. No energy crisis existed for those who drew strength from Preacher. Such life-sustaining fuel is accessible to all of us if we go to the same Source from which Preacher drew his—The Fountain Head, the Spring of Life from whence flows Living Water in everlasting abundance.

While Preacher engaged in a lot of foolishness and joviality, there was a more serious purpose behind it. "I think people need to laugh and be happy," Preacher told the historian. "Everybody ought to have some joy in life and that is what my religion has meant to me. It's made me happy and joyful. I believe God has put us here in this world for some wise and benevolent purpose. All things will work together for good if we try to do His will—try to serve Him. We are all imperfect; but there are ideals and goals we strive to approximate, and we can always give someone else a bit of happiness along the way." Such was the intent of his jocular nature.

His was not a sickly smile, his words not pious platitudes, and neither was his laughter void of merriment nor his eyes dry of tears. He was a square shooter in all respects and never engaged in frivolous arguments. If an intellectual, not of Christian persuasion, approached Preacher for debate just for the fun of it, to test him or his faith, he would gracefully fade into the woodwork or otherwise refuse to pick up the challenger's gauntlet. Jesus told his disciples to "shake the dust from your feet" and go on to the next place or person where there was a receiving heart.

Even when amidst trouble or unhappiness, he exemplified how to rejoice in tribulation. He was grateful for all things, knowing that increased strength comes from overcoming the rough places of life, and that the very act of being joyful can free us to think more clearly and to thread our way through our emotional labyrinths.

While Preacher was a fairly optimistic man, he became terribly depressed on occasion but never dispirited. He thought of depression as a state of mind that came from being too shut up within one's self. "Thinking about yourself all the time is enough to make anybody depressed. It's a good idea to go out and try to do something for somebody else and forget yourself. Our own physical make-up casts a shadow on the spirit," he said. So, Preacher's anguish in the midst of his own melancholy or despondency was overcome by giving joy to someone else, laughing with them and enjoying them, comforting them, and thereby being, himself, comforted.

After a sad funeral, he was often known to visit a home where he knew he would find a happy outlook to which he could contribute his own laughter and work his way out of his own distress. Preacher knew full well there were some people with whom he could have fun and others who didn't seem to know how to be happy; they enjoyed poor health or pessimistic outlooks on life. Then, there were those who just seemed to be pestered by things that kept them miserable.

One such person was a good old soul whom Preacher loved and called Aunt Ruby. She lived nearby the manse and explained her troubles daily to Preacher whether they were real, feigned, or just imagined.

"I loved Aunt Ruby devotedly; she used to speak to me as her son, and she came nearly every day. She was lonesome. Her husband was a little bowlegged man who lived to be almost a hundred. Aunt Ruby came over one day to ask me to come pray for him, because he was upstairs drinking himself to death. I asked her how old he was, and she said he was 96 years old. I told her, 'Well, why don't you just go and be sweet and good to him; he's not going to quit, and it probably doesn't hurt him any at his age.' "

She kept on, "You get my mind off what I came for. I know where he keeps his liquor, and I wish you would come get it."

Preacher told her, "I don't want it; I don't have any need for it. But I'll tell you what to do. Get the bottle, say your prayers, drink it all, and hop in the bed with him."

She still wasn't satisfied, and argued, "But when he gets drunk he gets to swearing; I can stand anything but profanity."

"I agree with you," Preacher concurred quietingly. "It is an inexcusable fault. The devil catches people with every kind of bait in the book, but he catches the profane swearer with a naked hook."

Aunt Ruby was Preacher's beloved friend, but he knew how to humor her and keep her from thinking about herself too much of the time. Back in the old sanctuary in the days when he didn't wear his preaching robe, he used to tell her that he was ashamed to stand up in the pulpit in front of the choir because his pants were so thin in the seat that the sopranos could see through them. As expected, she replied that she would buy him a new suit of clothes. He didn't particularly need a suit of clothes, but he did want to give Aunt Ruby a diversion to occupy her mind.

* * * * * *

His influence as a comforter was felt so strongly that upon his death a movement was begun to build an interfaith chapel in a local hospital and to name it the Preacher Gordon Memorial Chapel. He had become an integral part of the hospital and was loved by patients and staff alike for his warmth, humor and compassion. Because he had been of comfort there to all people, the chapel was designed for people of all faiths. Incorporated into the plan are four symbols of universal significance: rock, water, fire, and earth. (See Appendix C)

Rare was the day when Preacher was not in one or all the hospitals of the city. He was a great supporter of quality medical care. He frequently referred people to a physician when they had sought him for counsel. In his latter days, he, himself, was beset by all manner of physical ills: arthritis, failing eye sight, cancer. But his mind and spirit did not deteriorate with his body. His flesh grew frail and weakened, but his mind remained alert and his spirit embraced the world.

He walked the hospital halls and lighted a candle in the hearts of patients in every room. He gave encouragement and appreciation to every employee. The corridors echoed with his certain but slowing steps and, although the years hampered him physically, they never dimmed the twinkle in his eye. Little wonder that the stained glass window at the left of the entrance to the Chapel contains both a replica of Preacher and the inscription which he had taken so to heart: "Comfort Ye My People." (See picture p. xvi)

# 11

## THE CANDY MAN

ONE MIGHT ASSUME that after a half-century of service as a pastor, an eighty year old man would need a young assistant to keep children and youth work in focus. Not so with Preacher Gordon! While he could no longer stand the physical exertion it took to keep up with the younger generations, he was way ahead of them in thought and spirit. Upon his retirement the city newspaper ran a picture of him holding a young boy in his arms and whispering a secret in his ear. The inscription read, "Preacher Gordon is loved by young and old, a warm tribute to a man's forty years of priesthood in one church."

The reason he was loved by children was because he loved them. He noticed them and gave them recognition in every possible way. Children are quick to respond to someone who is attentive to them. The old adage to the effect that children should be seen and not heard, did not fit Preacher's idea of how to get along with kids. He lived by a different philosophy: "Children should be seen, heard, noticed, disciplined, and taught."

A new arrival in town would be surprised, not just by the early visit from the preacher, but by his greeting the children and calling them by name. He did his homework beforehand and learned the name, age and sex of all the children in a family. He had a stick of gum for each one as well as the legendary buckeye for every older member of the family. The gum wasn't important—the attention was.

From the outset he was a friend of the entire family: youngsters, parents and any oldsters that lived or visited in that home.

Each Sunday morning he filled his clerical robe or suit pockets with sticks of gum or individually wrapped candies; after the worship, families would hover around until the "candy man" had distributed his love-token to each child. This way the whole family was kept together, and the pastor was able to identify with the children while simultaneously greeting the parents. All loved the ritual, and it was enjoyed by onlookers as well as by the group being recognized. The candy was neither a reward nor bribe; it was a silent giving and receiving of a mutual bond of friendship.

As soon as a child was born into a church family, Preacher was right there with a pair of blue or pink booties. He also kept on hand ready-wrapped presents for the fathers of new-borns; he loved to hand these out before the "It's a boy!" cigar was given to him. He occasionally knew the baby had arrived before the father did!

The guidance given by him to children was simple and to the point: "You are fast becoming what you are going to be." That takes in a lot of psychological territory and can be translated into variegated circumstances and patterns of growth. Nonetheless, it was good advice for Preacher knew that "the child is father to the man."

Some parents hold that a child should not be forced to go to church while he is young but be allowed to make that decision when he grows older. The trouble with that reasoning is that growing up just doesn't work that way. A child whose spirit is not awakened as a toddler cannot be expected to become a church-going believer as a teenager. Development of good religious habits is as important to spiritual maturation as exercise is to physical growth. Also, giving good moral and religious instruction to a child is as vital as preparing a pupil's mind in mathematics. Body, soul, and mind—these three—are the triune measures of human growth and development. Children, parents, and grandparents are *all* "fast becoming what they are going to be."

But Preacher did not expect his children to be "goody-goody." He knew there was mischief in a child as there was mischief in himself. He wanted the boys to give him a good strong hand-shake and the girls to give him "a little peck on the cheek." He would often lean over and whisper in their ears, "Have you been a good boy? Be good, but not *too good.*"

What he wanted most was for them to become children of God. On Palm Sunday, following completion of a six week's Communicants Class, Preacher would have twenty-five to fifty young twelve year old boys and girls whom he confirmed into the full fellowship of believers. As they knelt in a line from one side of the rostrum to the other, he would put his hands on their heads as he passed down the line praying God's blessing on them. "Be God's boy; God's girl," was his loving supplication.

Frequently, if a teenager was playing the carillonic bells, he would make a special trip up to the control tower above the balcony to request the carillonneur to play "Children of the Heavenly King." His favorite bell rendition for Easter was "Jesu, Joy of Man's Desiring." It was hard for him to take the time and exert the energy to climb the stairs, but the youth of the church were foremost on his mind and, in consequence, the girls playing the bells always felt they were playing especially for Preacher. He recognized young people as an important part of the church service. Their future and that of the church itself was dependent in large measure on the emphasis placed on their spiritual lives and education during their formative years. He didn't want the children to run the church, but he wanted the church to be reminded constantly of its responsibility for nurturing them and including them in all forms and manner of worship.

# The Candy Man    107

One time, two ladies responsible for the upkeep of the lawn of the church complained to the Preacher that the preschoolers who played in the central courtyard were making it impossible to grow grass. "They keep it roughed-out about as fast as we can plant it," they deplored. "Well, sis-tahs," the candy man quickly countered, "You will just have to decide what we are trying to do here—raise children or grass."

He never grew too old to be intrigued by small babies. They were all "Cho tsweet, cho pretty and cho tsmart." He held them tenderly when baptizing them and was never ruffled by their crying or wiggling or even wetting him while he was sprinkling them.

He did seem to get rattled when his niece, who was living with him at the time, was getting ready to bring her premature baby home from the hospital. The brand-new mother's sister—a career woman who never married—was the only family woman well enough at the time to help him in this emergency which had arisen five weeks ahead of

schedule. She had never travelled by air, but despite her fear of planes, she flew to her sister's aid for this critical occasion.

An antique wooden crib on a rocker base had been sent on ahead by the grandparents. It had arrived by express in ample time and in good condition; moreover, the mattress was in excellent shape because it had been wrapped in straw and wood shavings held by gunny sacks sewn together with hemp twine to make a complete burlap covering around the bulging mattress. The problem was that the baby's early arrival gave Preacher and his unmarried niece only a day to put it together and make the crib-bed before the homecoming of the mother and tiny infant.

Neither Preacher nor his niece were experienced in matters pertaining to babies; yet they had to lock arms and undertake to make the baby's bed. Not knowing that the straw and burlap were only shipping excelsior, they began by leaving the wrapping on the mattress. They knew they needed to provide a waterproof foundation as well as a padding that would make the bed more comfortable. How to overcome the bumpy knots of twine, the rough burlap folds and the protruding sticks of straw became a major problem.

They accomplished their purpose only after layer upon layer had been applied to smooth out the little one's nest to perfection. First, there was a cellophane sheet to protect the burlap, followed by a cotton pad with a sheet to hold it in place. Then, a blanket was added to cover the rough spots and a sheet to cover the hot, prickly blanket. This still did not satisfy them so another soft pad was added which was covered with yet another sheet of silk with a sheet of cotton on top of it to let the silk breathe. Finally, the little rocker crib was clean as glass, as firm as a board and as smooth as a hammock. No bed-making has ever been taken more seriously nor done with more intense, tender-loving care. The only trouble was that after the first wetting, the laminated cradle had to be stripped and done over, a process that took an equally long four hours.

When this little fellow grew to be a toddler, his great Unkie taught him to be tolerant in all things, including bumpy bunks and rumpled layers of discomfort. Preacher reminded him that he must not expect everything to be smooth and easy and he must learn "to accept adversity with a meek and uncomplaining spirit." How that spiritual counseling was repeated by a little boy just beginning to talk can be better imagined than spelled.

If bed-making was not his forte, Preacher's story telling was. In addition to his two nieces, he had a nephew. In the early thirties Preacher's nephew came to live with him in Gainesville to be a companion for Preacher's mother, who was living with him at the time. A man and his wife lived in a house next door to Preacher, and their bedroom was just three feet from Preacher's study. The nights were warm, and everyone kept windows open. The neighbor, who later became an elder in Preacher's church, recalled:

"Nightly we would hear Preacher's clear voice as he taught his nephew the great truths of the Bible. That summer of waiting for our own baby's arrival was one of the best in our lives for we were filled with Biblical truths as only Preacher could give them to a small child, his nephew. In our room we became as small children sitting at the feet of Preacher, as he taught the Gospel that he preached and lived throughout his life. Would that we had more and more great preachers in our world to guide our children's footsteps aright."

As he exited one house, and before he entered the next, children would run to greet him, watching his hands closely as he approached. His patterned movements always yielded one or two surprises. Having reached into his pocket he would withdraw something concealed in his closed fist to be deposited in the outstretched palms of their hands. Anxiously, they waited to discover whether it would be a stick of chewing gum or a peppermint lifesaver.

One lady, who is now a mother herself, will never forget the comfort Preacher was to her when as a youngster, she had the traumatic experience of discovering her father dead.

> On that Easter Sunday morning, I had wakened early, not especially to find my Easter basket and eggs, but to retrieve the comic book my father brought me each Saturday night. Not finding it in the usual place I rushed to the living room and to the horror that awaited me.
>
> As our family huddled together a short time later with the friends who began arriving, Preacher came to us between the sunrise and morning worship, dispelling with a comforting and calming reassurance some of the fear that had gripped me. His words and prayers gave me hope that stability would return to my life and our wounds would be healed. After this loss, Preacher continued to serve as a paternal influence for me and always kept track of me in a way that showed how much he cared.

Yes, Preacher was the "candy man" to many a growing child, but more important than his sweet handouts was his sweet love, understanding, guidance and spiritual leadership of youth. He made them feel important to him, which indeed they were. It was also important that the church see and hear these young worshippers—the future deacons and elders of the next generation.

Sunday nights, prayer meetings, and often at the main worship on Sunday morning, Preacher had one or more of the young men "help" him with the service. They would announce the hymns, read the Scripture, lead a prayer, or just sing and be there with him. Sometimes a little tot would come crawl up on his lap or sit quietly in the extra pulpit chair just to be near Preacher. There was a magnetism about the man that drew children to him; he was a spiritual Pied Piper!

# 12

## "SHE'S STOLEN MY TEETH"

D<small>R</small>. U. S. G<small>ORDON</small>, S.A. known by the sobriquet, *Preacher,* was not only a spiritual Pied Piper for the young, but a mischievous saint for the old. It can be said that a person's inner qualities are most clearly seen in the manner in which he treats the young and the old. So it was appropriately said that Preacher's elaborate courtesy and loving concern for the older members of his following was beautiful to behold.

He treated the aged with kindness, forbearance and compassion. Sometimes if an older person became apprehensive or suspicious, Preacher could enter the privacy of their thoughts with a good will and humor that lifted them out of their fretting frustrations and left them with smiles of satisfaction and trust.

There was no nursing home, convalescent clinic, or retirement facility in the area that didn't await Preacher's visits. In many of them he was regarded as the chaplain, and Preacher was needed not only for spiritual comfort but as arbiter of quarrels among the residents. If the food was not good one day, one of the old ladies would call Preacher to complain. If an old man's daughter didn't visit at the usual time, Preacher got the call, not the daughter. When somebody's birthday was coming up, it was Preacher who was asked to arrange a party.

Not infrequently he was called by the manager or house-nurse to settle disputes between the patients. Or, the disputants, themselves, would slip to the phone and whisper their problems to Preacher. Early one evening one of them caught him by telephone just as he was leaving to go visiting.

"Dr. Gordon?" the ninety year old respectfully inquired.

"Yes'm. Ain't that Miz Johnson?" he echoed with a soft, aspirated imitation. "Where are you, in a closet?"

"No! I'm right here at the desk, but I don't dare let anybody hear me."

"What's the matter? Can I help?"

"I don't know whether you can or not; a terrible thing has happened and I can't tell anybody about it but you."

"I'll be right out," he assured her and departed immediately for the nursing home where she lived. When he arrived, he went straight to her room and found her pacing the floor with a veil draped cautiously over her mouth. As soon as he entered, she closed the door behind him and looked around the room suspiciously.

"She's stolen my teeth!" she wheezed and sputtered.

"Who's done what?"

"You know that old woman down the hall that is always wandering around making believe she doesn't know where she is? Well, she came in my room while I was in the bathroom; and when I came out, I looked in the glass by my bed, and my teeth were gone—uppers and lowers! I just know she has them because she hasn't let me see her face since she took them."

Preacher had difficulty to keep from laughing at the poor soul because he could hardly understand her with her teeth missing and her face half covered with a veil which kept puffing in and out with every word she spoke.

"When did this happen?" he asked.

"Right before breakfast. I haven't been able to eat a thing but orange juice, coffee, and soup all day."

"May I use your bathroom a minute?" Preacher asked rather abruptly. He reassured her that everything would be all right and for her not to worry. Leaving the bathroom door ajar, he looked on the back of the wash basin and all around the room before bending over to pick up the waste basket. He carefully lifted out a solid object wrapped in several layers of tissue. He did not unwrap his find until taking it to the toothless, miserable woman.

"Could your teeth be in here?" He slowly lifted the corner of the thin gossamer, and then another and another, until the beautiful dentures were exposed right there in his hand. She grabbed them up, and demanded, "How did you know where she had hid them?"

"Well, now, sistah, you have to remember that when we get older we get a bit forgetful; and I expect you wrapped them this morning while you were thinking about ole man Jenson down the hall. When that woman surprised you by wandering into your room, you mistakenly brushed them off into the basket when you were cleaning up your counter. You know, Miz Johnson, you are one of the best housekeepers I ever knew. You have always kept such a clean home you can't help tidying up the place behind yourself. Don't you fret about it anymore. Just put in your teeth and walk down the hall and find that old woman and look her straight in the eye and smile—so she can see your teeth!" As if to emphasize the point to make the lady less self conscious about her false teeth, he then parted his lips and pushed his tongue against his partial plate until his own front dentures dropped into view.

He had an uncanny way of turning a crisis into a joyful happening. The old sistah who had accused another of stealing her teeth—uppers and lowers—made a new friend of the woman with wanderlust and smiled at her every day. What fools we mortals be, and how little it takes to make us laugh. Makes one want to go right out to the nearest special-care institution and smile at someone and, by doing so, bring a wave of pleasure to a whole wing of lonely hearts.

To be sure, there will be times when all that can be done is to whisper a prayer over the bed of a patient who is comatose. But there are other times when the mentally keen and alert are crippled only of body and not of communication. What release it is for them to get a laughing-pill.

Preacher visited one such man who did nothing but complain about his terrible predicament. He deplored not only his own condition but the general tragedy of growing old and useless. Preacher listened for awhile and let the man get it off his chest, and then began to smile. Seeing the twinkle coming into his eyes, the man said, "I know what you are thinking. You are thinking I have gotten too old for sinning."

"You're right," said Preacher laughingly, "but you have many a fond memory you are enjoying, haven't you?" The amusement that ensued not only cheered the doleful man but brought queries and resulting guffaws from all to whom the story was repeated.

One of his earliest student assistants went on to become the pastor of one of the largest Presbyterian Churches in the mid-south. He claimed Preacher had taught him more than once how to accept embarrassing situations and take them in stride. All of his life the assistant had remembered the funeral he conducted one time in Preacher's absence. At the cemetery, several elderly ladies walked by the open grave and each dropped a rose upon the half-lowered casket. Astonishingly, one of the ladies tripped and fell right onto the casket. A husky pallbearer had helped her out of the grave; but the assistant had been in a state of nerves ever since the incident until he could talk it over with his mentor. "I nearly panicked," the assistant told Preacher later. "What could I have done that I didn't do to prevent this catastrophe? What would you have done, Preacher?"

"Well," Preacher mused as he patted the assistant comfortingly on the shoulder. "I always knew that poor old sistah had one foot in the grave, anyway." Preacher could say and do almost anything.

The reason he enjoyed such freedom was because he purposely exercised it to please others and to give them some fun. "The older they are, the more they need to laugh," he used to say. In fact, the older Preacher got the more *he* had to laugh. He never laughed *at* people; he laughed *with* them. This was probably never more true than it was in the prayer for which he became famous. It is believed to have first been prayed at mealtime in a small and intimate home for the aged where he was known by everyone. It has also been attributed to an Invocation he gave at a gathering of World War I Veterans of which he was numbered.

It doesn't matter where he said it first because it was appropriate to so many situations that he was often asked to repeat it:

> O, Lord,
> Bless these old folks,
> They don't want much;
> They don't need much;
> They ain't gonna be here long anyway.
> Amen.

Let the reader understand once again that here was a spiritual advisor who lifted up the hearts of all with whom he came in contact. His prayer for the old folks included himself. It was not irreligious but humanly realistic. We are where we are, and the best we can do is to be cheerful and willing to have God's plan unfold about us.

# 13

## "BE YE STEADFAST"

A MARK OF a good advisor, or leader, is his ability to watch a counselee improve without himself trying to take the credit for it! The really great man or woman gets true fulfillment from the joy of knowing that he or she has been helpful and contributory to another's well-being. A good teacher, for example, may often be out-performed by his pupils and receive less public recognition or praise. But for the teacher, it is often enough to know that someone else has benefitted from his precept and example.

Some persons in positions of authority try to prevent their subordinates from rising above them in reputation; this is counterproductive. Wise leaders glory in having assisted some understudy in acquisition of fame or fortune; this often reflects the leader's own stature. A selfless counsellor who enjoys seeing his protegé succeed is, in the long run, recognized in his own right. Such an outstanding person's influence is compounded, like monetary interest, without loss of principal, until the aggregate is of such magnitude as to touch the lives of followers down through generations.

A case in point is the influence of Preacher Gordon whose steadfastness, and modesty in all his spiritual advisory relationships and associations has been a hallmark of his greatness.

Seminary students who spent summers assisting him in his pastoral duties came to know his greatness and goodness, albeit their complete understanding did not come until they reached their own maturity.

One great churchman, who had been fortunate enough to serve under Preacher's guidance for several summers, recalled how much responsibility he had been given in the work assigned him and how willing Preacher was to suffer the consequences without complaint, if the student flopped. "His kindness and lack of carping criticism, his he-man and down to earth Christianity, his leadership and tutelage by example, all went into the molding of my ministry. I shall ever be grateful to him."

The last assistant serving under Preacher before his retirement was especially appreciative. He came to town directly from Seminary and felt confident and self-assured. "I was cocky and smart and thought I could teach Preacher a thing or two. I took myself too seriously and thought I knew something about everything. I was short on height and long on answers. But, he had a way of knocking me down to size that somehow didn't offend me. In fact, the more I knew Preacher the more I knew about myself. After breaking up my conceit, he began rebuilding my confidence until I was no longer only *self*-assured; I was *Preacher*-assured. I owe him so much for what he did for me—I can only hope I can pass on to others some of what I learned from Preacher."

Preacher's eminence derived, in part, from his simple acts of pastoral care—going anywhere he was needed to look after any of God's children. One cold, biting, winter day he took a Presbyterian preacher from a neighboring town with him out to a village in Florida's panhandle where a university student had asked Preacher to hold the graveside funeral service for his mother. In the 1940's a trip that far was not an easy one to make, and he had asked the friend to accompany him. Additionally, riding together would give Preacher a better chance to know his companion. To be asked to go somewhere with Preacher was an honor; but Preacher saw his invitation as an opportunity for killing two birds with one stone: he could get closer to his colleague while giving pastoral care to the university student.

The two nearly froze before getting a third of the way because Preacher's black Ford didn't have a "stove" in it, as he used to say. They went into a service station and warmed themselves around a pot-bellied heater burning lighter'd knots. After they started out again, in order to keep warm, Preacher sang all the way to the funeral and back, and that was a lot of singing. It was the last car he ever owned without a stove.

His favorite style of extending friendships was through unexpected, pop-in social visits. He had certain places he liked to frequent because he could kill a half-dozen birds at one time. Business establishments, fire stations, courthouse, post office—these were where he could always find six or eight people to talk to and pass the time of day. His "quickies" were short and snappy high-spots in otherwise routine days for those favored by a visit. He always had a joke to tell or a piece of business to transact or an interest of some kind that made each person realize how Preacher cared for him. And they knew they could count on him if they should ever need him.

At one of the savings and loan offices downtown, he was a regular visitor. "Preacher came at least twice a month and took great delight in talking with the younger members of our staff," said the chairman of the institution's board. "In fact, he always made a point of speaking to one employee whom he had baptized as a baby and of seeing my son-in-law, whom he had recently married to my daughter." It was as if one of his missions after retirement was to keep up all these acquaintances without slack or stint.

There is little doubt but what his bachelorhood made this persistent tour of camaraderie possible. Whether marriage would ever change his style remained to be seen. He was able to be a part of every family in the church and to be, as well, a part of the bank, the police and fire-force, and the business life of the community. There was something special about the mutuality of these relationships; he needed the friends almost as much as they needed him.

As long as he could do so, he took the long walk to the post office to get his mail from his box. He could have had the mail delivered, but he then would have missed seeing the many old timers he met along the way or who waited for him in the lobby. Getting-the-mail became a ritual of friendship appreciated all the more by the recipients because of the physical effort Preacher exerted to keep up the practice.

Until his later years, Preacher regularly smoked cigars or a pipe. He was conscious, however, that these might be offensive to some even if tantalizing to others. He certainly did not want his habit to become a stumbling block to anyone or to get in the way of effective relationships. A non-smoking assistant pastor, immediately upon his arrival, was initiated into this addiction by Preacher, who invited him into his office specifically for that purpose. Closing the office doors, pulling down the window shades, Preacher motioned the young fellow up to the desk and pulled out the bottom left drawer. "Man, let me introduce you to sin." The drawer was full of cigars and smoking tobacco. They both laughed together for the first time as official colleagues while Preacher continued, "Now, I don't want you to take up smoking; if my cigars will be a stumbling block in your Christian career, I will refrain from smoking them—in your presence."

They never were a detriment to anyone's Christian journey; but, instead, the aroma that wafted through the building from Preacher's office was always a comforting sign that he was near by. As offensive or tantalizing as the smoke may have been, Preacher was identified with it; any objections one had were over-ruled by willing tolerance.

For example, Preacher had been the long-time guest for dinner of one devout lady member of the church who despised smoking. On each occasion he would push back his chair after the dessert, take out one of his favorite cigars and say, "Sistah, will smoking this cigar hurt or cause you in any way to err in your spiritual life?" She always assured him that it would not. Later, she acknowledged to others that it didn't really matter to her because he was such a good friend, good conversationalist, and good company that his presence invariably insured a dinner party's success.

Willing tolerance and understanding also existed for his hesitancy to give someone a loan. Preacher would give you his eye teeth or the shirt off his back, but he wouldn't lend you a dime! A young minister associate went to him one time to ask him to endorse a note for him at the bank so he could get a loan to buy a new car. Preacher proceeded to tell him that he couldn't sign the note because he didn't want anything to mar their friendship. He said that on previous occasions when he had lent money to people who later couldn't or wouldn't repay, he would see them downtown crossing to the other side of the street to avoid meeting him. "Perfectly good friendships can be broken up over money." Some years later, when the young minister and his wife and children were struggling to get re-situated in a new call, Preacher sent him a gift of $500 towards the purchase of another much needed new car.

Preacher's steadfast friendship led this clergyman in later years to write:

> I am so glad and grateful that the Lord saw fit to bring into this world the person we know as Preacher Gordon and for his willingness to ask me to participate with him in ministering to those in spiritual and physi-

cal need in Gainesville. I will be forever indebted to him for his kindness. It can truly be said that the Lord made only one Preacher; and when He finished, He broke the mold; there will never be another person like him.

Preacher was so committed to his work and so engrossed in every aspect of his pastoral responsibilities that he took little account of his own needs. It was difficult to find anything to give him that he would not immediately give away. He lived very simply and attached little importance to his own creature-comforts. He was glad for others to have the luxuries of life, but he was happy just being what and where he was.

Every year he fought off the budget committee's recommendation that he be given a raise. His annual retort was, "I will not accept a raise in salary! If you pay me more, I won't do any more; if you pay me less, I won't do any less, so you might just as well leave it like it is."

Preacher never deprecated the importance of money. He really appreciated its value and went to great lengths to be sure the church received enough contributions and tithes to carry out the programs it undertook. He did not believe that *money* is the root of all evils. "That," he would say, "is an incorrect quoting of the Bible which says that the *love* of money is the root of all evil."

Preacher also believed that all of us should strive to look our best for the Lord. On Easter, the overflow congregation was apprehensive for fear it would be scolded for sporadic attendance during the year while breaking out new bonnets, hats, dresses and suits for Easter. Instead, he preached, "You ought to put on your best bib and tucker for the Resurrected Lord, including your best smile. No need for a hang-dog look or a sense of embarrassment because Easter is the only time you go to Church. We are glad you are here today and hope you will be so spiritually nourished that it will last you a whole year. But, if you need more, try coming back next Sunday, and the next, and the next."

Sacriligious? Nonsense! More money was offered that day for the Lord's work than on many previous occasions. The constant and unchanging loyalty and the unconventional naturalness of the man made people want to be a part of a Christian fellowship so warmed by his personality.

One of the pastors of the adjacent First Baptist Church loved to tell about a community Thanksgiving service held by Preacher when the new sanctuary of the Presbyterians was being dedicated. All the participating ministers, as well as Preacher, were decked out in their clerical robes; the entire worship had been appropriately dignified and impressive. The time came for the offering, and Preacher went to the front of the communion table, folded his arms behind him and said, "We are now going to take up the offering for the needy of our community. I've looked over this crowd, and we ought to be able to give at least $500 tonight. These offering plates are gold-plated, gifts from the Baptist church next door; I have counted them, and I want to see them all back up here after this offering—full! Choir, I don't want you to start the Doxology until I look over these plates and estimate that we have given at least that much. Let us pray!"

Then he prayed, and the offering was received and placed reverently, plate by plate, from one end of the communion table to the other. Plates in place, the congregation, organist and the choir waited patiently while Preacher walked down in front of the table, estimating the amount in each glistening plate. At the end of the table, satisfied, he turned to the congregation, threw his head back and in his inimitable style started the congregation singing, "Praise God from Whom all blessings flow!"

There was always a close, cooperative relationship between the Presbyterians and the Baptists. One hot, summer day several years earlier the Presbyterians stopped service at 11:50 so everyone could hear a ten minute concert on their new carillonic bells. The old churches were not yet air-conditioned and the windows were all open at the Baptist church because of the heat. The Baptist worship included the Sacrament of Holy Communion, and all was silence as the elements were being passed. Only the soft tones of the organ were playing when, up the street, the Presbyterian bells pealed forth in their first daytime concert. The Baptist organist, a great improvizationist, simply played accompanying chords; the Baptists took Communion to the tune of "Rock of Ages" played on Presbyterian bells, with organ accompaniment in the Baptist's own sanctuary.

Preacher was a contributor to the work of many other churches and did not ask others to do anything he was unwilling to do. He often led a fund-raising drive by pledging the first one thousand dollars. He also donated freely to civic causes and to special funds. He gave a sizable sum to the Catholic Church when it was conducting a drive for a new building and then apologized because he could not do more. "But," he explained, "I am a little short on rations myself these days."

He kept a separate charity checking account into which he put his personal funds for give-away purposes. This amount was in addition to his tithe to the church. If anyone had any legitimate need for funds, Preacher was always ready to help out. The scoutmaster, for example, had only to tell Preacher when the scout troop's money was exhausted, and Preacher would write his personal check to cover what was needed. He also wrote meal-tickets for wanderers who came by the office claiming they were hungry. He seldom gave cash for fear the money would be misused by the beggar; but, if he were indeed hungry, a personal note from Preacher would be honored at a number of downtown restaurants. "We didn't have any United Fund in those early days, but sometimes you miss something by not doing something personally for people. You miss the satisfaction of sharing yourself along with what you have. The gift without the giver is bare. 'Who gives himself with his alms feeds three, himself, his hungry brother and Me.' "

Preacher gave generously and advocated that one should receive graciously. He always said that if someone wanted to give you something you should always accept gratefully even if you didn't want or need it. In doing so, you could make three people happy: the person who gave you the gift, the person to whom you, in turn, could give it, and yourself as recipient and giver. He meant this seriously, for he felt keenly that the joy of giving should be encouraged by one's thankful receiving. "Take tarts while they're passing," was an expression he had learned from a wise and wonderful lady friend.

The women of the church had always given Preacher a warm winter coat when they saw him wearing a worn-out ragged one. They finally quit the practice because they noted that within two weeks he always gave the new coat to someone in need and then broke out his old one again.

He lived his life for others — giving a kind and reassuring word when one was needed, always present in times of adversity, and maintaining extensive correspondence with the lonely and troubled. His salary was given away as fast as he received it — for baby shoes and silver drinking cups for the newborn, flowers and cards for the sick and infirmed, gifts for newlyweds, telegrams and Bibles for high school graduates, candy and gum for children, bountiful food for fellowship and cash for those with meager incomes. All young men who attended his church, whether Presbyterian or not, received from Preacher a New Testament with a personal message of inspiration in it.

His house and church office were filled with gifts from grateful friends who cherished the opportunity for expressing gratitude to their "pal and lodge-brother." Some of these were merely "dust catchers" as he called them, and were of no practical value, but he wouldn't part with them and kept many on display. His dining room table, refrigerator and kitchen counter were heaped with pies, cakes, hams, roasts, jellies, preserves and cookies from the many women cooks who wanted to do something to help. Other practical gifts ranged from cigars to furniture and from coal to cars. One group of men maintained his car for him, replacing it when he needed a new one. Others kept a private trust account for his emergency needs; and women were constantly giving him clothes, hooked rugs, and hand sewn patchwork quilts.

One of the most novel gifts he received in his later years was a supply of bagged coal that lasted him the rest of his life. He loved his fireplace and had commented that wood burned too rapidly, and coal was too hard to find. A close friend through the years sent his own company truck to a neighboring city, had it loaded with fifty pound bags of coal and delivered to Preacher's garage. Some of it was still there upon his death. He never failed to gather everyone around when the "coal-man" was with him to tell about how his life-long friend had warmed his heart by keeping him warm in body.

He was constantly giving and receiving gifts from widows and unattached maidens. This exchange of interest and attention kept alive the notion that Preacher would, indeed, someday find a wife. A beautiful lady of grace and beauty who was full of fun and good Christian spirit would always arouse and keep Preacher's interest. One, in particular, he visited often, although she was not Presbyterian. He took flowers to her and was always included on her invitation party-list. He frequently was paired with her at other people's dinner functions. When she went to Tennessee to visit her family he wrote, "Gainesville is *pale* because you are not here."

Through his advice, charm and personal steadfastness, Preacher enabled men and women to achieve their highest purposes in life. Because he remained such a genuine, constant, and faithful friend, his influence had indeed been compounded and handed down to all generations. He has well-earned the title: "Spiritual Advisor."

# PART IV

## BOUNDLESS FRIENDSHIPS

*". . . Because he was good, but not too good, and people could identify with him: rich men, poor men, beggar men, thieves, doctors, lawyers, merchants, chiefs."*

*". . . Because he met you where you were and walked with you to help carry the load."*

*". . . Because he could walk with kings and not lose the common touch; his influence reached from the low places of life to the leadership of state and nation."*

*". . . Because his friendship knew no bounds of church, denomination, status, race or creed."*

# 14

## THE MUSCLE DEACONS

ANYONE CONNECTED with the University soon became aware that Preacher Gordon was the unofficial pastor to the entire educational community. He lived only two blocks from the University and was always present to welcome students with open arms. Preacher was a familiar sight on campus: tramping through the dorms, into fraternities, and onto the many athletic fields and adjacent grounds. He was unexcelled in his ability to get students more conscious of their spiritual needs and Christian calling and to become involved with the church.

While he was well known to almost all students, he was particularly friendly with the fraternity boys. As he drove past a fraternity house with his car windows open, he would call out across the street, "Fray-ter-ni-ty!" The boys called back, "Hi, Preacher, come on in," and they waved back wildly for him to stop. It is said that he knew the secret grips of 15 or 20 fraternities and the songs and rituals of half of them.

Ultimately, his work with all the students resulted in the creation of a Presbyterian Student Center and the organization of student religious work led by his "student elders." However, the best known of his university groups was a tightly knit, burly bunch of fellows he called "muscle deacons." These admirers constituted his earliest and most famous, or infamous, followers. He often took one along in the car as "tire changer" when he went on a pastoral errand. The grown men of this coterie still call themselves "Preacher's Muscle Deacons."

"Come forward to the first pew," Preacher would call out to the back of the sanctuary when he saw a couple of his boys brush up behind the ushers. But the first pew usually was already occupied as was the second and the third. Chairs often were placed in a ring around the pulpit, and when they were filled, more were added on the rostrum where they sat *with* Preacher.

During the 1930's and 40's the muscle deacons were his strongmen from the all-male student body at the University. They were varsity football players, track and basketball stars, handball partners, athletes and border athletes. Their carriage and physical prowess identified them as strongmen but their response to Preacher's, "Come forward to the first pew," identified them as strong followers of their pal, Preacher Gordon.

Where was Preacher leading these fellows? First, he met them where they were: on the handball court, tennis court, on the practice fields, in the dorms and fraternity houses, on the streets of the campus. Wherever there were students, Preacher could be found mixing it up with them. He led them to his house, the manse, for a meal or a chat in his smoke-filled, dog-haired den. They were invited for breakfast at Preacher's which was better known to those boys than "Breakfast at Brennans" in New Orleans. The point was to get these big, overgrown boys out of bed on Sunday morning and propelled into a Christian orbit.

The affection that existed between Preacher and those rough and tumble he-men was beyond belief or description. Some came for the food, for in the early thirties such a breakfast might have been their only muscle building meal of the week. A few managed to get to the early morning breakfast as a way of putting a night-cap on their Saturday nocturnal adventures. Most of them came, however, just to be with their "podnah," Preacher. As time went on, they all counted themselves proud and most blessed to have been associated with Preacher as one of his muscle deacons. They realized, as they grew out of college and graduated into the realities of life's "jungle," that they had been exposed to a great Christian; they wanted, not only to follow his footsteps, but to follow the Lord towards whom Preacher had been leading them, step by step, in personal fellowship.

Many men of this early and good vintage ripened into great church laymen and preachers, state and national politicians, military generals, and outstanding leaders in all walks of life. One deacon, who was baptized by Preacher during those years, continues to boast a bit about it; and well that he should, for he became one of Florida's most respected governors. Another, who later became a U. S. Senator, told Preacher that he certainly had enjoyed sleeping through his sermons when he was in college. Preacher was quick to return the compliment. "Well, you didn't sleep all the time because I have recognized excerpts from my old sermons in your political speeches." There is no way of counting or recounting the influence these muscle deacons have had through the years on local, state, national and international affairs; they have left their own footprints for yet another generation.

The muscle deacons arranged a special celebration for him on the occasion of the 25th anniversary of his University of Florida ministry. A program was planned in his honor following the football game with Tennessee, and gifts and speeches marked the afternoon. The day was marred, however, by a great tragedy. Dr. J. Hillis Miller, then President of the University and a good Baptist, was to have made one of the tributes, but he had had a heart attack only a few days prior to this fateful Saturday. The following announcement was made at the stadium over the public address system:

President Miller, who is still confined to the hospital, has expressed deep regret at not being present at today's game. At his request, the honors of the University are being given to the Reverend U. S. Preacher Gordon, Pastor of the First Presbyterian Church of Gainesville, who is seated in the President's box. In celebration of his 25th year of pastoral service in Florida, alumni and friends of the University have arranged to honor Preacher Gordon at a reception in the Presbyterian Student Center adjacent to the campus.

Later in the afternoon, about two-thirds of the way through the program for Preacher, word was brought to him of the death of Dr. Miller. With a characteristic sense of urgency and priority, Preacher interrupted the speaker, and stood up to announce, "Dr. Miller is dead. Let us pray!" Whereupon in the middle of joyous reminiscences and laughter, Preacher moderated the mood and prayed a prayer of assurance and comfort, the impact of which none present will ever forget. Then Preacher left immediately to go to the President's widow.

Birth and death wait for no man — neither doctor nor

preacher. When it comes, all need to stand ready to rejoice or to give comfort and assurance when the first pangs of pleasure or pain appear.

During the muscle deacon era, a devout Roman Catholic athlete was co-opted by Preacher as an associate muscle deacon. Because this good Christian wanted to attend his own 7 A.M. Mass, he couldn't come to Preacher's house on Sunday morning. He wanted to be of help, though, so he offered to become Preacher's "bed-shaker" and get all the Protestant athletes up for breakfast at Preacher's.

Thirty years later, this student stepped down from his important post as Chief Justice of the Florida Supreme Court to accept the presidency of the University of Florida in Gainesville. In his inaugural address, he said, "There is no greater burden for a man to bear than a debt of gratitude he feels he cannot adequately repay." He had received his higher education at the University of Florida; he was now in a position to repay his indebtedness by skillfully leading his Alma Mater through the years of confrontation, riots and insurgence in the late 60's and early 70's. President Stephen C. O'Connell's experience as "bed-shaker" must have contributed to his well-rounded college career.

The informally organized muscle deacons may well have been one of the first really successful and exciting forms of pastoral work on campuses of state universities and colleges. Preacher's charisma mesmerized the men and instilled in them an interest in soul-building as well as body-building. He used to tell them, "One pull on the bar-bell does not make an athlete, and one prayer on Sunday does not make a Christian."

There was no facility then in existence providing religious focus and fellowship for college students. Preacher played handball with them, shot the breeze in fraternity living rooms, rooted for them on the gridiron. He had the reputation of being the best handball player on campus and was acclaimed the champion in 1939.

Preacher, himself, was the focus; and his home was the place where muscle met spirit. He weekly held prayer sessions in his study at the manse. A good crowd of students assembled. A lot of foolishness was carried on, but sometime during the evening they sat down to a sincere, but simple, session of prayer. If anyone refused to pray aloud, Preacher claimed he would "put the sacred paddle" on them. Their program was play, prayer, and performance.

At breakfast on Sunday, Preacher asked a muscle deacon, a wide-end on the varsity football team, to give the blessing. It caught the athlete off balance, but he managed to raise his arms and stammer, "O Lord, put Your Name on this table. Amen." What a great prayer! What a great play. That athlete reflexively reached up and grabbed the ball in mid-flight and held onto it for a completed pass. Preacher was amused by the embarrassed, unexpected reception for the Lord, but he slapped the athlete on the back and said, "That was a fine prayer, my pal; the Coach would be proud of you."

Most of the muscle deacons finished off Sunday morning by coming down to the first pew, and became not only an integral part of worship but an inspiration to the younger kids who knew these fellows by their reputation on the athletic squads. It was impressive to see them with heads bowed in the front rows, singing lustily off-key on the hymns, and listening intently to the sermon.

But being the spiritual leader for this motley crew of collegiate heroes was not always easy for Preacher. It was sometimes downright embarrassing. On one occasion Preacher lent his car to one of the boys so he could take his girl to a picture show on Saturday night. During the course of the evening they drove out of the county to buy some whiskey because Alachua County was dry. They got back all right, but the fifth turned upside down and saturated the front seat of the car. They tried every way imaginable to camouflage the odor, but to no avail. They opened the car windows and drove around town frantically all night. When they thought they had eliminated the telltale evidence, they pulled into Preacher's driveway, closed the windows, and put the keys under his doormat as he had instructed them.

The next morning when Preacher went to get in his car to pick up two widow-women for church, he was almost choked by the fumes that filled the car. He couldn't go to church smelling like a brewery, so he arranged for someone else to pick up the ladies and Preacher walked. During the sermon he pulled out his handkerchief from his hip pocket to blow his nose, and the bourbon-bouquet nearly knocked him over. The handkerchief had picked up the smell while Preacher had been sitting on the seat where the bottle was spilled. Later, he admonished the couple with such kindly concern that their relationship with him was intensified rather than destroyed.

Another evening, during summer school, an undergraduate took his date and another couple to a local restaurant where they were "prepping" themselves with some suds before getting to a dance. Preacher and his dogs, Deacon and Elder, came into the student hang-out to buy a cigar and, naturally, joined them for a nice visit and some limeade. As he got up to leave, he said, "Be sure to make it to church tomorrow morning!" They did get there on time, and Preacher's greeting to them after the worship was, "Good morning, my beer deacon."

A law student, who later became an outstanding Florida figure, recalled the days when he was rooming off campus with three other boys. After making the rounds of the house parties one Saturday night, the four students returned to their apartment to fix some bacon and eggs to top-off the evening. Subsequently, they fell asleep on the living room floor. When Preacher Gordon came over about 6:30 Sunday morning to be sure they attended church, he found them in this predicament. Finding the situation was completely harmless, Preacher left them to sleep it off, but he never let them forget that embarrassing moment. The attorney later reminisced, "When I became Chairman of the Board of Regents for the University, he telephoned me to state that he never in all his fondest dreams had expected me to turn out so well, and that he wanted now to claim me as one of his own."

"No finer men were ever developed than the muscle deacons and student elders of those early days," Preacher acknowledged as he reflected on his early Gainesville ministry. "We had a lot of those fine fellows. I received a good many of them into the church. One of the warmest sensations one could possibly ever feel is to have these successful men come back to see you. They are grown men now, some with grandchildren, but one looks back with a deep sense of appreciation and gratitude for what they have meant to church, state, and society."

In addition to the specific emphasis upon the muscle deacons, Preacher had wide influence on all students. He was national chaplain of the Pi Kappa Alpha fraternity for about twenty years and attended their bi-annual national conventions. He claimed that he was not involved in the activities of the local chapter, but one would have to infer that he meant only that he was not officially connected. "By being a national officer, I would go over there occasionally and eat a good meal. They had good housemothers—very worthy women who resided there. I used to tell the housemother, 'Keep them from going native.'"

One social fraternity sponsored an annual Mother's Day tea to which not only the mothers of members were invited but other women connected with the university and community as well. Each year Preacher also attended as an honored guest. One year, however, he failed to show up; he sent no regrets nor did he drop by the house for his customary chat. It appeared that the fraternity was considering the employment of a woman of questionable discretion as a housemother, and Preacher knew of no better way to express his disapproval than to boycott the affair. Needless to say, Preacher attended the first Mother's Day tea *after* her release. Such was the public admiration of his personal judgment and wisdom.

After the University became co-educational and sororities came to the campus, one sorority whose chapter house was located near the manse enjoyed referring to Preacher as their "house-father." He was asked to give the Invocation at all their public functions and at the dinners when there were to be invited guests. His chief concern, however, had always been for fraternities and he was frequently involved in settling disputes among them.

The Pike house was directly across University Avenue from the Sigma Alpha Epsilon fraternity. Located on an intersection, both houses also faced on a U. S. highway. It was a critical corner and the scene of many so-called friendly victory celebrations in the 40's and 50's. Unfortunately, it also became the rallying spot for riots in the 60's that became anything but friendly. However, in Preacher's hey-day, the corner was the focal point of fraternity pranks that zeroed in on Leo, the SAE lion. This stood proudly on the fraternity's front lawn, and one of the responsibilities of the pledge class was to keep the statue guarded and properly protected. All of the meticulous attention was simply an open invitation to other fraternities to attempt painting the lion without being apprehended. If he was caught, the offender was wrestled into the house and held until the whole chapter could be assembled. Then, one of them cut the villain's hair off and shaved him bald-headed. Such was the penalty for desecrating the lion of Sigma Alpha Epsilon Fraternity.

As champion of the PIKES, Preacher tried to ameliorate these attacks and counter-attacks particularly when they involved any of his muscle deacons in either "fray-ter-nity." On one occasion he successfully presided over a truce, and on another he became the only go-between in a really serious encounter between the two chapters.

One alumnus vividly recalls the circumstances that led to a meeting on neutral ground to exchange documents of a cease-fire. Leo had been re-freshly painted by the SAE pledges in a beautiful coat of antique gold. This was like waving a red flag at a bull. The "bull PIKES" wasted no time in destroying Leo's rich coat. Late one night a group of PIKE pledges, moving on orders from the active chapter, sneaked across University Avenue armed with automobile tires and cans of gasoline. They put the tires under Leo's belly, on his back, hung one from his tail, and put one like a wreath around his neck. After pouring oil and gasoline on the tires until they were soaked, they backed away, threw a firebrand into poor Leo's pyre and took off down the highway.

Retaliation was not long in coming. The PIKE's were electing their chapter sweetheart at a dinner to which all of the girl friends were invited. Since the PIKES had no lion to desecrate, their next most vulnerable symbol was their sweethearts' dinner. There seemed to be no prankery developing in connection with this affair; little did anyone suspect that the entire PIKE chapter and all of their lovely guests would, the next day, come down with Montezuma's revenge.

At first, no one was in any condition to do any detective work, but as time went on, a careful questioning was undertaken of the SAE's pledges and members; but the inquiry was less than satisfactory. Finally, the PIKE brothers began asking their own cook whether there could have been anything wrong with the food. Had she left the potato salad out of the cooler too long? She stopped to think what had been different from other meals she had prepared. Puzzling over it, she said, "Could it have been them biscuits the SAE cook sent over for the party?"

"That's it!" the investigators reacted in chorus. "Those blankety, blank SAE's; we'll get them yet." Finally, they forced an SAE pledge to confess. He glowed with satisfaction as he told how he had devised a way to get the SAE cook to prepare some southern style, home-made biscuits to give to the PIKE's cook; but this pledge had slipped a laxative into the dough while the cook's back was turned. His motivation for this act of revenge was that he had been the pledge who had had to clean up Leo's carcass after the previous cremation.

Well, things had gotten to such a fever pitch that Preacher was asked to intercede. He made it clear that fun was fun, but things had gone too far, and they better call off this feud before someone got hurt. So one Sunday afternoon a table was set up in the middle of the street separating the two fraternities, and representatives of both chapters were seated at it, all dressed in formal attire. Preacher Gordon, also in his tux, presided over the ceremonies. He made a speech which "almost made Christians out of them," and it was so full of humor and wit that his serious admonitions were well accepted on all sides. Truce documents of good will were exchanged, and the era of traditional rivalry as it pertained to pernicious prankery seemed to have come to an end.

Things went well for several months until one morning it was discovered that Leo had disappeared. He had been pulled up by his concrete roots and carted off. No one was able to uncover the slightest shred of evidence as to who was involved and how this horrendous task was accomplished. PIKE athletes were strongly suspected because they were the only ones with a sufficient motive to attempt the act of lion-napping. Months passed and still no clue to Leo's disappearance was uncovered. Finally, a couple of Preacher's closest and best muscle deacons swore him to secrecy and then showed him where Leo could be found. They took Preacher to a distant and secluded spot near a vast prairie where they pointed to a bog and said, "He's down there." They never did tell him how Leo got there or who did it.

The mystery had outworn itself, and the SAE's were about to buy a new lion; so the culprits told Preacher he could reveal the secret if he would not expose them. Having been asked to be the emissary to the SAE's, Preacher took them out in his car one day and pointed to the bog and said, "Why don't you try digging down there?" This they did; and in due time Leo was resurrected from the watery grave and returned to his spot where he was then planted in a four foot slab of concrete.

Preacher once again prevailed over the forces of evil and his devilish muscle deacons had come forward to the front pew.

Fraternity boys were not always so cooperative and congenial; and he occasionally had run-ins with them. This was particularly true of the fraternity house immediately adjacent to Preacher's residence. The boys were nice enough, and he had a lot of fun with the individual members. But, as a fraternity, it was little different from any others in the conduct of their Saturday night parties. The house was not really large enough to hold a dance inside so the outside patio was included as part of the affair. Naturally, the music had to be heard at full volume outside as well as inside, whether anyone was dancing to it or not. Large outside speakers were installed in the patio and operated at full throttle.

Preacher politely told the chapter that he couldn't sleep with all that racket going on until the wee hours of the morning, and he needed to be ready for his busy day on Sunday. It was agreed that they would tone it down after midnight, but no one ever seemed to notice when the witching hour arrived. After several weeks of non-compliance with his courtesy compromise, Preacher thought of a way to reinforce his request. He took the speakers of his own stereo system and put them in the windows facing the fraternity house. After the fraternity party finally closed down and the boys had wobbled off to bed, Preacher let them get about three hours sleep. Then, at six o'clock on Sunday morning he put some records of good, rousing hymns of praise on his player and piped the glorious

142   BOUNDLESS FRIENDSHIPS

church music into the open bedroom windows of the boys next door. Two or three weeks of this, and a truce was reached.

* * * * * *

As a result of Preacher's ministry and fund-raising, the Presbyterian Student Center was built about 1940. It provided a gathering place for all students wanting religiously oriented fellowship. It gave a great boost to the work with students, enabling Preacher's pastoral assistants to develop activities of special value to young men and women who were away from their home church. Some years later, the Student Center became a responsibility of the Synod, and the local church was relieved of its direct administration.

The program thus being supervised by a distant court of the church produced some problems, but it never curtailed Preacher's efforts in behalf of the Center nor of his work with students. After his death, a fund of $50,000 was discovered in the assets of Synod for student work called the "Gainesville Campus Crusade Fund." No one seemed to understand where it had originated. A special committee was appointed to investigate and clear up the mystery for the Synod. It was found that Preacher Gordon had wanted to see the Presbyterian Student Center able to expand its facilities. The price for adjacent land was considered too high so a purchase was not made, and the money that had been raised was held in trust for future capital improvements. The minutes of that special investigating committee for Synod said, in part:

> It was concluded that the funds were raised primarily through the efforts of Preacher Gordon, in a campaign in which $300,000 was raised for Columbia Seminary, $50,000 was raised for student work at the University of Florida, and another $50,000 for the work at Florida State University in Tallahassee. The FSU funds were largely spent in operations rather than capital outlay.

Preacher with Charles J. and Edna Williams of Jacksonville, Fla.

144   BOUNDLESS FRIENDSHIPS

The students who rose to leadership roles at the Presbyterian Student Center were called "student elders." They comprised an unofficial Session for the Center which developed its own by-laws, rules, and programs. Preacher always believed, however, that the students should go to Sunday worship at one of the local churches. Study groups and prayer meetings were encouraged at the Center, along with the activities and fellowship programs; but he was convinced the Center should not become a church nor a clique of young people that were more interested in self-preservation than in self control. They could feed themselves but they should not feed *on* themselves. The Center should be a satellite for all the churches, serving to aid in collecting students and communicating directly with

them, but it should ultimately point them to worship in the established churches of the area. The issue was debated, but it was Preacher's point-of-view that prevailed.

Throughout his ministry, he remained vitally concerned about the students and their welfare. His student elders and deacons were important to him as he extended the arms of the Lord to them through his pastorate. They were always a significant part of his parish, and he knew all of them personally and had nicknames for most of them. In turn, many of them named their boy-babies after Preacher, but, so far as is known, no one accepted Preacher's request for someone to name a girl-baby after him. He always said he wanted to have one girl named "Preacherina."

One student remembers all too well why Preacher called him his "lamp lighter deacon." One night after a football game, the student found himself trying to get out of the stadium after he had too many drinks during the evening. Not knowing who Preacher was, he weaved up to him with a cigarette hanging out of his mouth and asked Preacher for a light. He got a light off Preacher's cigar, and Preacher offered to walk him home. This he did, and thus began a friendship that resulted in the young man becoming his "lamp-lighter deacon."

Another became known as "Deacon Rattlesnake." The student had seen a huge snake in a farm yard by the road as he drove into town. He borrowed a shotgun from the farmer's wife and gave the snake both barrels in the head. He was well over six feet and had thirteen rattles and a button. "We brought the snake back to Gainesville," he said, "and decided to clean it for the hide. We were on the sidewalk between my fraternity house, Alpha Tau Omega, and my friend's, Phi Delta Theta, as we cut the snake open. Preacher Gordon came up with his dogs, Noah and Nicodemus, just as we exposed the snake's heart and found it was still beating." Preacher supervised the skinning of the snake as he related some of his own snake stories.

From that time on the boy was called "Deacon Rattlesnake." When he went off to war, Preacher gave him a New Testament as he gave all his young men. The inscription was "To Deacon Rattlesnake from his podnah, Preacher." He carried the Testament all through the war, and put with it the many letters he received from Preacher during his days in service. After the war, that New Testament was used for reading the Scripture when Preacher officiated at Deacon Rattlesnake's marriage.

Thirty years after one student elder's graduation from the University, Preacher was worshipping in a West Florida city where the student had lived. Preacher looked all over the sanctuary for him and didn't spot him until the deacons and elders were taking up the collection. As his podnah handed him the plate, Preacher leaned over and loudly proclaimed, "I might have known you would be *on the job.*"

Throughout all of his active ministry, including years of retirement, Preacher seemed to be able to remain contemporary with youth. While he was worried and exceedingly unhappy with much of what he saw happening in their subculture, he was able, in many ways, to defend and support the latent potentialities of the now-generation.

"I don't like the drug traffic," he said, "nor the promiscuity. After all, homes are the foundations of our country, of our church, and of our synagogues. We cannot live promiscuously and not reap the consequences of it in our society. But, I know a lot of individuals who are just as fine as can be. We must remember that young people live in a different world from the one I grew up in. Whether they have become wiser, I will not say; but they have access to more knowledge at twelve and fourteen than I had at eighteen and twenty. Life isn't simple like it was. My earlier life was in an agrarian civilization. We got our pleasure in the woods and the fields and in sports. I think we forget that our youth are born into far more complex situations. My main complaint is not with youth but with parents. Some of them are falling down on the job. They don't give any

Student deacons and elders

discipline nor any instruction, and children cannot live without both. It may be self-righteous to say this, but my parents gave us all the love and freedom we needed; but, by George, we towed the line when it came to being disciplined; we didn't have everything our own way."

So, the muscle deacons and the student elders were among the many groups Preacher fostered because his friendship to others knew no bounds. He met them where they were and walked with them helping to carry the load until they grew into men and women of influence in high places in Christ's Kingdom. He was good, but not too good, and students loved him. For years yet to come, his deacons and elders of all ages will remain *on the job*.

# 15

## A FISHER OF MEN

A WOMEN'S GROUP was having a study meeting in the parlors of the church; Preacher was there for one reason, and one reason only: he had been asked to make a few remarks to introduce the Bible lesson. He sat in the back row looking out the window when the chairwoman requested they all bow their heads for a few moments of concentrated meditation, focusing on the outreach of women's work in the church. Preacher continued looking out of the window as if already in a deep trance. After the silence, she directed her first question to Preacher. "What were you thinking, Dr. Gordon? Please share your thoughts with us."

Without a moment's hesitation he said, "Madam Chairman, I was thinking what a great day it would be to go fishing!" Hilarity reigned.

Preacher did love to fish! He especially liked fresh water fishing, but would fish salt water if they weren't biting in the lakes and streams. As he grew older, the strenuousness of fishing in the Gulf or Atlantic kept him inland where the whole outing—boat ride, picnic lunch, lazy drift—was more relaxing and soothing to his mind and body. He had any number of casting rods, but his favorite was a cane pole. In his prime years, he fished so frequently at a coastal city,

Cedar Keys, that his favorite fishing spot is still called "Preacher's Hole."

One time when he was visiting in Mississippi, a kinsman took him fishing at the Sardis Dam. Preacher did not have a license valid in those parts but they decided to risk it anyway. They were well into their fishing when they saw a game warden heading toward them. The relative whispered, "Preacher, what can we do? There's the warden." Preacher quickly answered, "Man, you do the talking, and I'll do the praying."

Fishing can be one of the most sedentary of sports. Perhaps this is why so many ministers of the Gospel like to go fishing. More men-of-the-cloth can be found in boats and on banks of streams on Monday than perhaps any other recreational place. Ministers like to take Monday to recuperate after the strenuous week-end. It gives them a chance to relax, reflect, and rejuvenate — the three "R's" of successful vacationing.

But, for Preacher, fishing was not just a sport, it was an obsession! When he rode with anyone to new country, he would ask the driver to stop at every bridge, lake-side, pond, or culvert. He always had to ask himself, "are any fish in there?" He would get out and stand with his hands on his hips and stare at the water and sniff the air. Finally, he would pass judgment. "I believe there are bream in that pond," or, "I know there are catfish under that culvert."

Fishing was an equalizer for him. People went fishing — all kinds of people — and Preacher loved to be wherever there were people. He could ply his trade at a fishing camp as well as in the pulpit. He was a fisher of men! A gregarious person, he enjoyed the associations as much as catching the fish.

People also are look-alikes when they are in fishing clothes. Hunters are not as well camouflaged from each other as fishermen. One's affluence is often revealed by the style and condition of one's hunting wardrobe, but not so with fishing garb. Any old rag will do; and the more commonplace the rag, the better. With wide-brimmed sun hats pulled sloppily over the face, and shirt buttoned up around the neck to stunt the rays of the sun, with a can of worms in one hand and crickets in the other, with a paddle and a pole under arm, a banker looks like a preacher and a painter looks like a teacher. In fact, the look-alikes actually act alike. The banker will tell you the percentage of chance there is to catch fish that day; the preacher will persuade the banker that the odds are better than he has figured. The painter will teach the professor what bait to use; the teacher will explain the merits and demerits of reel vs. spinner. Everyone is equal in the eyes of the fish, and all are a good catch for Preacher.

Rare was the excursion from which Preacher came away empty handed; for his catch was not fish, it was men. The more he could engage in repartee with new acquaintances the better he liked it, and often he caught two or three on one hook. When Preacher cast, waves of charisma went out in ever expanding circles as he made friends at every fishcamp, landing, pier, flat bottom boat, or sleek canoe. More than likely, new-found friends who were having poor luck were given a buckeye which they later swore had turned the tide for them and fish started jumping into the boat.

Not only had a fishing spot been named Preacher's Hole, but many other places and gear were named for him. There was Preacher's landing, Preacher's bait, Preacher's boat, Preacher's pond, and Preacher's joke. Every fish story Preacher ever told has been repeated so often that the recent versions bear little resemblance to the original. Phrases from one tale find their way into another, and jokes he retold became attributed to him as if he had initiated the tall tale.

For example, there was the time when Preacher was going down the Wacasassa River in a row-boat with a friend; and as they slipped under an overhanging cypress bough, a big moccasin dropped into the boat. Now this *did* happen! Preacher was deathly afraid of snakes of all kinds including non-poisonous ones, but he especially abhorred moccasins and rattlers. It is also true that he carried a gun and shot many a snake coiled up on a log or slithering through the reeds. But, there is no verification of the report that Preacher killed the snake that had dropped into the boat by shooting him, causing the boat to sink from the gaping hole in the bottom.

It *was* true that one of his favorite references to almost any other denomination than Presbyterian grew out of his fishing repertoire. "So, you're a Methodist," he would chide a new friend. "Well, you *can* get to Heaven being a Methodist, but you're in a mighty leaky boat, and you're going to have to row hard and bail fast or you'll never make it."

Yes, fishing was a great social event for Preacher, and he was at his best when he met people where they were, talked their language, and shared their rations. "We are cut off the same cloth," he liked to tell someone he had just met. There was immediate comaraderie, whether rich man, poor man, beggar man, thief, doctor, lawyer, merchant, chief. Fishermen were people before they learned to fish, but Preacher used his mania for fishing to learn the people. He knew them and was known of them. He walked with them to help carry the load. That is, he helped with the load unless it was a motor or the heavy end of the boat. He usually took a strong companion with him when he went fishing—"to tote the kicker" or "to paddle the boat."

One companion was a ministerial colleague who tells this story of his fishing adventure with Preacher.

> After suitable apprenticeship, I was promoted to paddler first class. One March day, when the bream were bedding, we went to Bivin's Arm to catch us some fish. Preacher was in the front of the boat; I was paddling. He would sniff in the air and motion me over to a stand of lily pads. In a confident undertone he disclosed, 'There will be one right under that bonnet.' And sure

enough, as he dropped his bait carefully into that specified spot, the bobber sank and the pole bent almost double. Preacher was pulling them in right and left.

As we approached the other side of the small lake, we came upon a brother-of-color sitting on a limb which extended out over the water. He, too, was fishing but seemed not too busy at it. Preacher struck up a conversation.

"Brother, are you doing any good?"

"Naw suh; but y'all seem to be doing right well."

Preacher smiled pleasantly and teased, "Any man ain't catching fish today must be doin' something wrong. Are you living an upright, Godly life?"

"Oh, yas suh."

"But, are you a churchman, and do you go regularly to the Lord's house for worship?"

"Yas suh. I'se a deacon in de Baptist church."

This did it for Preacher. He knew what would tickle the man's humor so he went on.

"That's it! That's it! You ain't paying your Preacher enough!"

"Naw suh, dat ain't it. I puts in de collection every Sunday."

This gave Preacher cause to stop and think, and he finally came up with, "Well, you must just be a hard luck Jonah not to be catching fish today. You got to do something to change your luck. See this fella paddling for me? He's a preacher. Preachers ain't no count for fishing; but if you can get one to paddle for you, it'll absolutely change your luck. Getting a preacher to paddle for you will do more to change your luck than carrying a rabbit's foot or even a buckeye."

"Ain't you Preacher Gordon?"

Preacher threw back his head, had a big laugh with the brother, pulled in his line, gave me a signal to start paddling, and called back, "Brother, if I was you, the next time I came out here I'd see if I couldn't get my preacher to come paddle for me. Paddle on, Reverend; you're doin' real good."

As Florida became more populated both the hunting and fishing were affected. This happens in any part of the country, but Preacher had a most unique explanation of why the fishing wasn't as good in the 70's as it had been in the 20's when he came to live in the state. "There have been so many Baptists immersed in these streams that their sins have been washed into the water polluting it and killing all the fish."

A local physician, a member of Preacher's congregation, was an ardent fisherman who liked to fish the Gulf. Preacher saw him one Saturday and asked him whether he could be in church on Sunday. The doctor looked so ashamed and guilty that Preacher quickly added, "Never mind, I suspect you are going fishing. Well, you ought not to do that on Sunday morning but if you go, you can bring me an eight or ten pound grouper."

The doctor took his chances and went fishing that Sunday morning. During the day, in the open water, a storm came up; and he made for the mouth of the river. The rain and darkness that accompanied the storm caused him to take a wrong fork in the network of channels through the coastal marshes; and when he finally tied up at a safe place with some high ground, he had no idea where he was. Nightfall came, and there was no way he could wend his way through the maze of navigable water, so he slept in the boat. Wet, cold and scared, he rested the best way he could and set out again at day break. After following a countless number of hopeful looking routes only to be led into impassable waters, he finally ran out of gas. He had left his high ground mooring and was far into a finger of salt water completely surrounded by tall rushes that kept his boat hidden from view.

Meanwhile, the alarm had been out since Sunday night that the doctor had not returned to the landing slip, and boats had gone down the river to see if he had had motor trouble. He could not be found; the hunt was called off until daylight and the seas had calmed. All day Monday the fishing craft searched for him but could not find him. Several times the doctor heard their motors but he could not be seen even waving his paddle high in the air. Nor were his shouts heard above the roar of motors, and no one ventured up his little pass. Monday's daylight came and went with no sign of the doctor. Back in Gainesville, people were in panic by Monday night, and many rushed to the ramp with search boats on the ready for Tuesday daybreak, including Preacher.

Sleep finally overtook the doctor, and he rested during the wee hours of the pre-dawn Tuesday just as the tide was turning. As the full swell gave way to receding waters, his boat was pulled away from its improvised mooring to the reeds and began to carry him with the drift towards the open bay. Shortly after daybreak, one of his rescuers noticed a boat drifting into the Gulf and investigated. There in the bottom of the boat was the doctor—fast asleep, sunburned, hungry, exhausted, and embarrassed. His embarrassment was not alleviated when Preacher, who was waiting at the ramp, asked him, "Where is my grouper?" A laugh, a prayer, and a good breakfast sent everyone back with a story worth writing home about.

A sports columnist for the local Gainesville paper had come to Florida at the same time Preacher did "when game was most abundant and fishing was at its best." He wrote, "I remember one moonlight night we were fly fishing from a canoe when Preacher suddenly said, 'Take me toward the middle of the lake. I've got a nine-pounder on!' Many a laugh we had later when that bass turned out to be only a two-pounder."

Preacher was the first president of the Alachua County Sportsman's Association and the first to receive the "Book of Golden Deeds" award of the Exchange Club. He was honored by many organizations in various ways. On one occasion, when his prowess as a fisherman was being praised in fervent and exaggerated detail, he interrupted the speaker to inject, "*You* know all of that is not true, and *I* know it's not true, and *God* knows it's not true, but say it again!"

Preacher's hunting and fishing reputation caught many a "follower" which he persistently played with his Christian charisma until he had him in God's boat. Three of his student elders and deacons were on their way to church one Sunday morning when they saw sitting on the curb, all by himself, a big blond-headed guy who looked real lonesome. They stopped in front of him and asked if he wanted a lift. He said "no" just as one of the muscle deacons recognized the boy as one of the freshman football prospects. "Come on and go to church with us and meet Preacher Gordon. He is a real, all-around, regular guy; hunts and fishes, but more importantly, makes going to church worthwhile!" The athlete didn't want to go to church, but he did accept a ride uptown with them. By the time they arrived, they had convinced the big fellow to take an hour off and go to church. After listening to one of Preacher Gordon's down to earth, personalized sermons, the visitor said he would like to meet the Preacher. The inspiration that Preacher passed on to the big football player initiated in him the desire to become a preacher, himself. He subsequently did so and became a most successful and popular minister. (See Appendix C.)

Jesus said, "Follow me, and I will make you fishers of men." Fishing may have been Preacher's obsession; but attracting people to the Lord, Jesus Christ, was his real cast in life. Like the disciples, he did not ask, "What's in it for me?" He just followed! He didn't ask how much time it would take; he just followed! Having become a disciple of Christ, Preacher spent his lifetime bringing others to Him.

It was a toss-up as to which Preacher liked best—hunting or fishing. He seldom went deer hunting because he

could not bring himself to shoot "those beautiful animals once they looked you in the eye." But quail and doves were another matter. Everyone who hunted with him reported that his cocker spaniels were the best retrievers in the field. And there was good reason for giving the dogs such superlative credit. A county commissioner, recalling early hunting days, put it this way: "Preacher would find a nice shady tree to sit under with his two faithful dogs, Deacon and Elder. As others in the party, or I, would shoot down doves, Deacon or Elder would run out and pick them up and bring them back to Preacher. He would take the dead bird, pat his faithful dog on the head and say, 'Now,

Deacon, you know that bird does not belong to me,' and then would calmly put the bird in his hunting-coat pocket. By the end of the day, Preacher would have a fine mess of doves and not have wasted any shells."

That Preacher came home with *all* the birds didn't matter to the cronies, for they knew he would give them all away anyway or invite them all over to his house to help eat them. The fun was in companionship, not in counting who shot the doves.

There was more than one field replete with covies of quail which were posted against all trespassers except Preacher. Many a hunting party was ousted by the owner with the explanation, "These birds are all saved just for Preacher Gordon."

For a number of years Preacher had an early morning devotional over the radio. Hundreds of people all through the county heard him and became familiar with his tone of voice and individual accent. One winter, during hunting season, he was out dove shooting on a field belonging to one of his friends. Unintentionally, he crossed over into a stranger's field and was immediately hailed, "Hey there! What are you doing shooting doves in my field?"

Preacher breached his gun and walked toward the speaker and apologized. "I'm sorry, brother; I did not know this was your property. I thought I was still within the lines of my friend's land."

The offended farmer heard the familiar voice and immediately recognized it. "Ain't that Preacher Gordon?" Preacher readily admitted his identity, and the irate farmer turned with friendlier tones and said, "Then, Preacher, you can go on and hunt as much as you please!"

Preacher did not always get out of scrapes that easy. He and a crony were hunting together when one of Preacher's dogs, probably Nicodemus, caught and killed a guinea chick about one week old. A tough farmer came out and threatened to have them arrested when Preacher pooled his resources with his hunting companion and bought the guinea for $17.50. That was a lot of money in those days. It certainly taught Preacher a lesson, but whether it had any effect on Nicodemus will never be known.

Both hunting and fishing put a lot of pressure on Preacher to hold his tongue and not let go with expletives in a crisis. One comrade was not so restrained, however, and when he fired and missed, he let loose with "damn-it-to-hell!" A little later, Preacher, too fired and missed. He looked helplessly at his friend and finally said, "Say it for me, pal, say it!"

Another hunter, who went on to become the Chief Justice of a United States District Court, also can attest to the fact that Preacher's dogs could be depended upon to pick up all the dead or wounded quail in a field no matter who had shot them. He tells about the time he and his cousin were hunting quail in the woods and met up with Preacher. They had some cold drinks in their vehicles so they sat down and had a visit. Preacher got off on one of his dogs that had been misbehaving, and he ended up by telling the attorney, "You know, that damn dog hasn't acted right all morning." The judge couldn't help but grin. Preacher quickly tried to right his wronged tongue and said, "Now, counsellor, you have to understand; I was not cursing. It's just that that dog has been a damn dog all morning!"

"Preacher was a wonderful man," recounted the judge, and in doing so wrote an opinion shared by all. "I have heard it said that the highest tribute that can be paid any man is that it can be said of him the world is a little better place in which to live because he had lived in it. There would be, I am confident, complete unanimity among all of us who knew him in paying him that tribute. Certainly, none of us will ever forget what he did for us and what he has meant to us. We will be thankful all our lives that his life touched ours."

Such was Preacher's friendship that knew no bounds. He was following the instructions of his Lord and was truly a fisher of men.

# 16

## PLAY A GOOD GAME

As the best handball player on the University campus, Preacher was an honorary member of the F Club, the organization of athletes who had earned their letters for participation in collegiate sports. Preacher earned his letter not only through his companionship play at handball, but because he also served as unofficial chaplain of squads in every sport. Like Vince Lombardi, he played to win, and he encouraged everyone with whom he played to do the same. "But above all," he would say, "play a good game."

In handball, he was always known as "The Cloth." There was no question about where he stood on fairness, honesty, good sportsmanship and swearing. Expletives he had, but never blasphemy. A student, who was a frequent competitor in the sport, claimed that Preacher got more mileage out of "bagnabit" than the students got out of the more colorful words. They all loved to hear him call them by name and by "my pal" or "my podnah".

There was one student whose game gave Preacher a lot of trouble and who occasionally even beat him. He was nicknamed "Coppersmith" because in II Timothy, 4:14, Paul wrote, "A coppersmith did me much evil, the Lord rewards him according to his works." The student was proud to explain his play against Preacher had earned him that special title. He never knew Preacher dubbed him with the name because he didn't always play fair.

For Preacher, the time finally came when this strenuous sport had to give way to one less demanding. To continue with a competitive sport, he joined the "Sunset Shufflers," a group of ten older men who met on Tuesday and Friday afternoons to play shuffleboard. Preacher seldom lost a game because his long arms gave him a greater reach than most of his opponents and he "played a good game."

His chief indoor recreation, however, was gin rummy. He was an inveterate and astute player and never refused a game. Since many variations in the rules of the game were preferred by different players, he made clear on the front end the rules by which he would play and then followed them explicitly. He always used cards with the large size figures on the face so his waning eyesight would not play tricks on him. Many a contemporary crony remembers with happy nostalgia the frequent evenings of gin rummy with Preacher. It was a relaxation for Preacher as well as his opponent because it took concentration, was fun, and it kept their minds off other matters. A well known practicing attorney was upheld during his college days by Preacher and gin rummy. He recognized the value this association was to him.

> I was running for President of the University Student Government and discovered that I received a great emotional uplift by sitting with Preacher in his dimly lit study, playing gin rummy. Preacher would expound on his adventures and previous students that he had known while I absorbed all of his "country" knowledge and did my best to beat him. Our gin rummy games continued thereafter throughout my student years, and we continued to insult one another about our respective gin rummy abilities for the rest of his life. He was a great man! I treasure the moments I spent with him.

His great nephew, who as a baby had been bedded down in the ten-ply cradle, in his late 'teens became an accomplished tennis player. Once when he was on the varsity tennis team of Louisiana State University, he was playing in a championship tournament with the University of Florida in Gainesville. He stayed with Preacher, and they spent the eve of the finals match playing a rousing game of rummy. In fact, it turned out to be a better game for Preacher than anyone expected. The tennis champ served Preacher a hand that he had been waiting for all his life — he dealt Preacher a perfect gin rummy hand! After their surprise and laughter subsided, Preacher told him, "Well, son, I hope this game is not a harbinger of your tennis match tomorrow." All through the years, Preacher never failed to introduce his great nephew by chiding him about the incident. "I want you to meet the tennis player that served a perfect gin rummy hand. I've never been dealt one before nor since."

\* \* \* \* \* \*

Preacher not only believed in playing a good game, but he tried to help those who had been thrown out of the game of life for misconduct. For a ten year period from 1950 to 1960, he held an early morning Sunday chapel service twice a month at a local road camp of the Florida State Prison System. It was a short service of worship consisting of prayers, hymns, the reading of Scripture, and a brief sermon. It always conveyed the idea to the prisoners that God loved them, and that they were not forgotten during their period of confinement.

One text is particularly appropriate to this ministry. It is from Acts, Chapter 26, beginning with the 25th verse.

> About midnight Paul and Silas were praying and singing hymns to God, and the other prisoners were listening to them. Suddenly there was such a violent earthquake that the foundations of the prison were

shaken. At once all the prison doors flew open, and everyone's chains came loose. The jailer woke up, and when he saw the prison doors open, he drew his sword and was about to kill himself because he thought the prisoners had escaped. But Paul shouted, "Don't harm yourself! We are all here!" The jailer called for lights, rushed in and fell trembling before Paul and Silas. He then brought them out and asked, "Men, what must I do to be saved?" They replied, "Believe in the Lord Jesus, and you will be saved—you and your household."

Preacher, in a sense, re-enacted this drama by his worship within the gates of the prison. He took a group of high school and college students with him who could play musical instruments and sing. After gathering at Preacher's home for a 7:30 A.M. breakfast, they went to the prison camp where they sang and played hymns, joined in the prayers, and gave testimony by their presence.

There was another way in which Preacher assisted these men who had broken the rules of life's game. As the prisoners worked along the roads and highways of the State of Florida during the week, they killed snakes that came out of the ditches and brush. In their spare time, the prisoners converted the snake hides into billfolds. Sunday after Sunday, Preacher could be seen buying four or five wallets in order to give those prisoners a little spending money. In a year's time, his purchases amounted to around $500, which over a ten year period was equal to his annual salary.

In those days, almost every Presbyterian in Gainesville, and a few Baptists, Methodists, and Episcopalians, carried a snake-hide billfold given to him by Preacher.

During this decade, Preacher often brought a carload of inmates to the monthly men-of-the-church dinner meeting. On one occasion, an older prisoner among Preacher's guests exhibited some less-than-acceptable table manners;

he poured his coffee into his saucer, blew on it to cool it, and then drank it. Preacher was quick to see the shocked look on the faces of church brethren around him and the hurt expression in the eyes of the offender. To relieve the situation and show complete kindness, understanding and compassion, Preacher quickly poured his own coffee into the saucer, blew on it, and drank it. The important thing was to encourage these men and not to hold them up to unnecessary ridicule and contempt. None are so perfect that there are not times when a face-saving gesture to get one off the spot would not be appreciated.

By and large, the prisoners who attended the services were grateful and appreciative; many of them stopped by to see Preacher following their release in order to express thanks for the prison ministry. Often, they received a suit of clothes and a small financial gift to help them back into the competition.

The prison ministry was as significant to the students Preacher took with him as it was for those to whom the ministry was directed. It was an earthshaking experience for those who were occasional helpers. To those who went regularly with him, it was fulfilling and humbling. Along the way, each participant got the distinct message that "there but for the Grace of God, go I." The whole worship and fellowship was not 100 percent successful, but more were saved than lost.

His constant coaching and befriending of those who were inclined not to play a good game reached into the jails of the city and county as well as the state prison where sentences were being served. Again, he lost some and he won some, but an outstanding example of helping to get a young fellow straightened out had to do with a recalcitrant who couldn't seem to stay out of trouble.

A Baptist friend of Preacher had hired a university student to pick up laundry and dry cleaning at fraternity houses and bring it to the plant. The student was given an auto for this purpose, but one week he got too much to drink and, while inebriated, took the car to make a trip to his home in Georgia. While there, he ran the car across a lawn, breaking a water hydrant and smashing up against a tree. He returned to Gainesville without the car and never reported the accident or returned to work. The boss had both the car and the student picked up, placed charges against the boy, and had him jailed by the sheriff.

The boy's mother had been friends with Preacher for a long time; and, of course, she called him immediately to try to get her son out of the clinker. But, when Preacher went to the sheriff, he found out that this was not the first encounter the sheriff had had with the boy; and he wasn't a bit in the mood to release him on bail, much less to the custody of Preacher. Apparently, the student had not only been in trouble before but had been in jail several times. When Preacher telephoned his Baptist friend to withdraw the charges, he found that the sheriff had beat him to the draw and had already called to advise against any such procedure.

Not to be thwarted, Preacher took his Baptist friend and went to see the sheriff, who was a member of the Presbyterian church. Preacher arranged to see the boy in his cell in order to use his predicament to talk some sense into him. Finally, all worked out a compromise to which everyone agreed: the young man was to stay at Preacher's house, run errands as necessary, and for six months he was to go to church every time Preacher went. After a few weeks, the fellow went to the dry cleaning boss who had pressed the charges and pleaded with him to put him back in jail because he just couldn't go to church that much. However, a bargain was a bargain; it was adhered to by all concerned. The repeater never got in trouble again but grew into a fine man and friend of both his boss and Preacher.

This was not the only case where Preacher assumed custody of a young rascal and turned him into a decent, law-abiding citizen! He taught many a person how to play the game of life fairly and squarely. Most of all, he played a good game himself, made friends with the opposition and enjoyed the challenge of competition. He won some, and he lost some; but even when he lost, he won!

# 17

## WALK HUMBLY

As pastor of First Presbyterian Church of Gainesville, Florida, for forty years Preacher's ministry spanned the administrations of four presidents of the University of Florida, several acting presidents, and innumerable vice-presidents, deans, and department heads. Of the presidents, one was Methodist, another a Baptist, the third was Presbyterian and an elder in Preacher's church, and the fourth was Roman Catholic. Preacher was a close friend to all of them as well as to the students.

Just as the University was a training and proving ground for many state and national leaders, so Preacher's association with them was a contribution to their leadership development. In the earlier days, when the student body was under 5,000 male souls, there wasn't a student, faculty or staff member who had not heard of Preacher Gordon. He was such a distinguished affiliate that when alumni thought of their Alma Mater they also thought of Preacher.

It was said that Dr. Tigert, the president who arrived in Gainesville the same day as Preacher, became almost envious of the esteem that friends of the University held for Preacher. President Tigert and Preacher were very close friends and admired each other greatly, but Dr. Tigert became a little peeved at returning alumni who seemed more concerned about Preacher's welfare than they were about the University. When a distinguished senator came to the campus for an official visit and walked into the President's office, the question never was, "How is the University?" or "How is your family?" or "How is the budget?" No! The ex-student turned statesman would inquire, "How's Preacher Gordon?"

This didn't really annoy Dr. Tigert, but he did think he needed a ready answer for this question since it was asked so frequently. Thereafter, as alumni came into the office of the President of the University and asked their inevitable question, he gave them this reply: "He's just fine! He's out walking on Newnan's Lake." Dr. Tigert had his own kind of wit!

It was during these early years that Preacher was elected an honorary member of Florida Blue Key, a leadership fraternity of active students and alumni whose purpose was service to the University. Its major responsibility was conducting the affairs of Homecoming. The most important event, of course, was the football game; but almost equal in importance was the Blue Key Banquet attended by active and alumni members and their guests—who were often political figures in the state, the Florida Congressional delegation and court judges. Several featured speakers later went on to become presidents of the United States, such as John F. Kennedy and Richard M. Nixon. The significance of this dinner and the smoker which preceded it cannot be over-emphasized. One of the most popular figures present was Preacher. His tales about the student capers of the distinguished alumni were a highlight of the evening.

With his left hand on the shoulder of a state senator he would be shaking hands with a federal judge and saying, "Shall I tell him about the time you . . . No, I better not tell that; it might get you in trouble." It was believed that if Preacher told all he knew about people, he would have to leave the state and go into hiding. He thoroughly enjoyed these reunions, however, and got a big thrill out of seeing his young friends become men of prominence and stature. He was humble about any recognition he received for his role in the making of these leaders. To the oral history recorder, he observed,

> Yes, I was an honorary member of Florida Blue Key and received an honorary degree from the University. I deeply appreciate those things, but one must not let it make you think more highly of yourself than you ought. The New Testament says, "I say through the grace that is given unto me that everyone that is among you not think of themselves more highly than they ought to think, but think soberly according that God has given to every man a measure of faith."

From an old Dutchman who had taught him church history he had learned that one better be humble. His teacher had said, "Young man, don't try to climb too high. If you climb high, they'll see your naked little 'hindness'." Not bad advice for starters.

Dr. J. Wayne Reitz, an elder in the First Presbyterian Church, was President of the University of Florida for more than a decade. Preacher loved and respected Dr. Reitz, hunted with him, and counselled with him as a friend and pastor. Dr. Reitz, in return, was devoted to Preacher and willingly gave of his wisdom and good judgment as an active ruling elder on the Session. In bestowing upon Preacher an honorary Doctor of Humane Letters degree, President Reitz called him a distinguished pastor, teacher, public servant and friend.

> You have endeared yourself to thousands of University of Florida students and faculty members . . . and have recognized and exemplified how scholarly achievement best serves the public good when embodied with a spirit of compassion, forgiveness and forbearance. (See Appendix C.)

Preacher said of each of the four University Presidents with whom he was closely associated—Dr. Tigert, Dr. Miller, Dr. Reitz and Dr. O'Connell—"As we say about Queen Esther, she came for such time as she did come." And it was true that each assumed the presidency at a time in which their particular knowledge, expertise and administrative talent was needed for the successful growth and educational achievement of that great institution of higher education.

But in the midst of the austerity of intellectual pursuits, Preacher always retained his comely commitment to being his own natural self. He could quickly modulate from the intricate melodies of English poets or Greek philosophers to cracker barrel tunes of great people of the soil. One day, as he was taking his usual "constitutional walk" on the campus, a hard-shelled Baptist friend approached him to request that Preacher accompany him to conduct a funeral service in the country. The man persuaded him by saying, "These people love you and need you. After all you are only an educated Primitive Baptist preacher who has come to town."

Most of the folks at the graveside worship only had a fourth or fifth grade education. One of the dyed-in-the-wool countrymen walked up to Preacher after the funeral and paid him what Preacher regarded as one of the highest compliments he had ever received. "Well, I shore am glad to meet you. You know, I heered every word you said. Some folks say that a city preacher is so high educated a country man cain't understand him, but I heern every word just as plain."

Preacher told him that he was a good man and that God, too, was a country man. The good fellow replied, "Sure 'nuff? I bet he was as good as them city fellows were crooked."

Anyway, as Preacher and his Baptist companion drove back to town, the friend reflected on how privileged he was to live his life during the years Preacher was around helping people. Later, in a tribute, he paraphrased Preacher's language when he said of him, "He was not so critical, but critical enough; he was not so straight-laced, but straight-laced enough; he was not stuck up, and his piety showed in his deeds but not in his mannerisms."

\* \* \* \* \*

During World War II, a commissioned officer and a non-com both arrived at Preacher's the same day on leave from nearby Camp Blanding. They were invited to spend the night if they didn't mind sleeping together in the double bed. They gladly accepted the chance to spend their precious leave-time with Preacher. In the middle of the night, Preacher could hear from his own room as the sergeant pleaded with the officer, "Will you please move over, SIR?"

Students from Columbia Seminary were often guests of the church, and many of them ate or spent the night, or both, at Preacher's. A choir from Columbia Seminary sang a concert at the church, and a group of them were eating breakfast with him when he discovered that one student had brought some flash cards with him to work on his Greek vocabulary while on tour. Immediately Preacher stopped the frivolity and, congratulating the boy on his studious tenacity, asked to see the cards. The boy flipped one card after another onto the dining room table as Preacher correctly gave the English equivalent of each Greek word flashed before him. The neophytes were impressed with the freshness of his command of the language after so many years out of Seminary. It was good for these students to see an alert, scholarly mind honing its metal against their own academic knowledge when, only a moment before, he was strictly a plain pastor and hail-fellow well met.

As the years went by, new students arriving at the University or visiting from Seminary considered Preacher Gordon to be a timeless legend. When they heard some of the memories he had of their fathers and mothers, they were witnessing flashbacks into the early 30's. "At the same time," an elected state official said of his first meeting with Preacher when he had come to school as a freshman, "Preacher had an intense interest in us and made us feel at home with his friendliness and his capacity to be in tune with our generation of college students."

The College of Business Administration of the University of Florida took the occasion of its fiftieth anniversary in 1977 to publish a booklet giving the history of the College and its founding faculty. It gave account of some of its most notable students and accomplishments of the college throughout its distinguished academic curriculum and service to the State of Florida. It is of more than passing interest to note that the booklet gave space to recognize the interweaving of Preacher's ministry with the warp and woof of academia. It reported: "Scores of students and faculty members were parishioners of Preacher Gordon, and it was not uncommon to find him walking through the halls of the college seeking one or more of his lost sheep."

Preacher was never one to boast of his wide spectrum of close friends nor of any part he might have played in their successes. He appreciated being singled out, however, and received all compliments gratefully and graciously. He liked whenever possible, however, to turn plaudits away with a shield of wit that eased everyone's tensions including his own deep down emotion.

As he was approaching his seventieth birthday, he was unexpectedly feted after a regular monthly church supper. Preacher could not understand why there had been such a crowd at the dinner. There were accolades and gifts galore, all climaxed by the presentation of keys to a new car. Preacher was beside himself with tears and laughter. When it came time for his response, a sudden "hush" fell over the assembled flock which was fearful the emotion-packed program might have been too much for the beloved pastor. But Preacher, who may have been beside himself, was not undone. He stood up promptly, ripped off his glasses,

wiped away a persistent tear from the corner of one eye, brushed the opposite cheek and broke into a paroxysm of laughter until he finally was able to talk. "I have just two regrets about this gathering: that I can't take up a collection for the church, and that I will not be able to stay to help with the dishes." That put a cap on the climax!

Then with his inimitable Presbyterian spunk, he continued. "I know you think that just because I will soon be seventy years old you better say all these nice things while you can. I want you to know that I am like my grandfather who broke his leg playing polo at 97 — I plan to be around for a long time yet. But if there is anything the Lord will get me for on Judgment Day, it will be to make me eat all my idle words . . . I feel very close to all of you . . . I thank you for all you have been to me! I hope to be with you for many more happy years during which I will try to preach to beat Hell every Sunday!"

# 18

## BREAKING BREAD TOGETHER

ONE OF THE subtle and destructive changes gradually creeping into the style of modern home life is the deterioration of family fellowship at mealtime. Table-clothed dining has all but been eliminated in today's home. Parlors have given way to living rooms; and, in turn, living rooms have been replaced by family rooms, leisure rooms, and television parlors. The activity of eating has migrated from dining rooms to breakfast nooks and T.V. trays. Busy schedules allow little time for seated, corporate eating. Instead, it is done in shifts at kitchen bars with bulletin boards to describe what can be warmed in the microwave. Very little intra-family communication can take place because it has to compete with the stereo, television, and telephone.

The generation growing up during this period of erosion of the family mealtime may need to be reconditioned to the institution of breaking bread together as an integral part of home life. The familiar adage needs to be amended to read, "Those families that eat together usually pray together." Short-order kitchens and fast-food restaurants are convenient, but they are not conducive to family solidarity and nourishment of the soul.

Preacher was a great believer in the fellowship that accompanied the consumption of food. There is no better time to create good will, to exercise laughter, and to give encouragement than through sitting down to a good meal. Just as Jesus was "known of them in the breaking of bread," so was Preacher famous for his breakfasts and dinners that provided not only generous portions of food but ample measure of compatibility. His home presented a twentieth century version of the fellowship of Jesus' disciples as they met and ministered to the people after the Holy Spirit came to them at Pentecost.

Everyday they continued to meet together in the temple courts. They broke bread in their homes and ate together with glad and sincere hearts, praising God and enjoying the favor of all the people. And the Lord added to their number daily those who were being saved. (Acts 2:46-47)

Breakfast was Preacher's main meal of the day; he loved a big breakfast and believed everyone should have a substantial one to start the day off right. Formal invitation

Perry Foote, Jr. and Maxie Dell drop by for breakfast

was not necessary; the welcome mat was always out, there was plenty to eat, and breakfast was always a special and unforgettable occasion.

If one was hungry and merely showed up at the appropriate hour, usually between seven and seven thirty, he would find the white-clothed table piled high with grits, eggs, ham, bacon, sausage, preserves, cakes, biscuits, toast, plenty of milk and hot coffee, and steak or chops. Preacher took great pleasure in presiding at the head of the table and filling everyone's plate with food. He always insisted that everything be eaten, constantly admonishing the partakers that they weren't doing his fare justice. "I don't want you to leave here undernourished and say you didn't get enough to eat at my house."

A festive mood always prevailed around the table. The atmosphere was one of lightheartedness, warm humor, and conviviality. Before, during, and after the meal, jokes were told, hymns were sung, and prayers were offered. Without any previous warning, a guest might be called upon to recite a verse or to read from the Scipture. There was never a dull moment!

During his years in Gainesville, thousands of souls were guests at Preacher's table. Many were university students or other young men who were lonely and away from home for the first time. At Preacher's table, they always found a spirit of Christian love, concern, and friendship.

One student remembered his three years in law school when he lived off campus and contrived to walk a route to school so that he always passed Preacher's house. Often Preacher would yell over to him and give the welcome invitation, "Tow-bye, come over and get some breakfast!" Toby would always oblige and was never reluctant to take advantage of this occasion this way!

> Breakfast! Feast would be more descriptive: turkey, hash, cornbread, toasted pound cake! We would fellowship and share the goodness of God together with the

ever present cigar and Joe, his loyal weimaraner dog. Following breakfast, Preacher, his cigar, Joe and I would walk a block or two along the way to the law school. These experiences always nourished and fortified me physically and spiritually for the rigors of my work as a law student. They also gave me an unforgettable taste for good "ceegars"!

In trying to give Preacher something as an expression of appreciation he asked him what kind of "ceegars" he might like best. The priceless reply was, "Just any *given* brand."

One Sunday during hunting season, Preacher announced in church that he wanted to see John, Jack, and Phil in his study after the worship. He was somber as he made this request. The three college boys were all shaken up as they thought he had discovered something for which they would be remonstrated. When they met Preacher in his study, he immediately directed them to sit down. After a period of nervous silence, he smiled and asked, "How would you three 'brothers-in-the-bond' like to come over to my house tonight for a quail dinner?" Without a wife, he was free to issue this kind of impromptu invitation.

The hope never waned, however, for Preacher's house to be enhanced and himself made more happy by acquisition of a wife. Widows and spinsters continued to pursue him, and some made rather bold efforts indeed. While his mother was living with him, she served as the "lady of the house"; but when she died, he became exceedingly vulnerable. Early one morning, a taxi drove up in front of his house and a widow-lady got out. She came up to Preacher's front door with a suitcase in each hand and proclaimed that she had come to take care of him. Without pausing a moment, Preacher firmly but courteously turned her around, pointed her towards the cab, and said firmly, "You would not be happy here because my three dogs sleep on top of the bed in the guest room, and I already have a 'woman of color' who cooks my meals and makes my bed."

He thanked the dear lady profusely but managed to get her back in the taxi before it left. Like previous attempts, this foot-in-the-door technique had been foiled by Preacher's adept dissuasion.

The "woman of color", about whom Preacher had spoken, was his cook and housekeeper; she waited on him with faithful devotion. He called her the "African Queen." She was a person of limited formal education but possessed a great deal of common sense. Over the years, Preacher developed a special relationship with her, and each knew just how far the other one could be pushed.

The African Queen was an extraordinary cook and was especially good at preparing game birds such as quail and dove. She also excelled in frying speckled perch and bream. Cleaning the house was not her long suit; but she reluctantly attempted vacuuming, dusting, and keeping up with Preacher's clothes. When a telephone call came in Preacher's absence, she was known to give out advice and Christian consolation to the bereaved. When she answered the phone, "Doc-tor Gard-en's res-aye-dance," her dutiful presence was a welcome sound and second only to Preacher's, "Hel-law."

Her great failing was her unquenchable thirst for beverages with spirits. Her weakness caused her to be absent from her domestic duties from time to time, but she would always return after a few days. She knew when her time was up because she would get several threatening calls from Preacher. He understood and tolerated her leaves of absence, but for only just so long. The degree of his tolerance was determined by when he tired of making his own breakfast.

Often his concern for her health, as well as his need for his own breakfast, led him to make frequent visits to her house to see for himself what her condition was. One time he discovered that she had been arrested for a minor matter and was on her way to a court hearing. He immediately went to the courthouse to appear as a friend of the accused.

When the judgment was handed down that she was to pay a fine of $25 or spend a week in jail, he asked her, "Well which will it be?"

She said, "If I go to jail, you don't eat." Without hesitation, Preacher forked over the fine and carried the Queen back to work.

One summer, she had fallen from grace so many times that Preacher had to go to her house on numerous occasions to try to get her back on her feet. He finally became so frustrated that he told her she better shape up or the devil would get her. Straightway, he went on vacation to see his family in Tennessee and Mississippi. While there, he wrote a letter back to the Queen which recited all her weaknesses and exasperating escapades with the bottle, and how she was not treating the man she worked for with proper diligence and dependability. The letter was quite explicit and firm and concluded by saying, "You better have his house straightened up and vittles laid by in time for his return next Friday." The letter was signed, "THE DEVIL."

Good friends frequently gave Preacher a bottle of wine for him to take as a tonic for appetite and good sleep. He sometimes referred to it as "sacramental wine." Not infrequently, he would find a bottle missing, and the African Queen was always the sole suspect. He would call to the kitchen from his bedroom suite, "I believe I see where there have been *hain'ts* in here." She was deathly afraid of ghosts and was haunted by the very thought of them. That Preacher suspected some had been there and made off with a bottle of wine was enough to keep her out of his "tonic cabinet" for a month.

On one occasion, Preacher called from the church to tell the Queen to pack his suitcase. He told her he had been summoned to another city to settle a church fight. He came home, picked up his packed grip, got in his car and drove to the city where the trouble was. When he reached the location of his appointed task and checked into a motel, he proceeded to unpack. When he opened the suitcase, on top of the clothes, where she had thoughtfully and protectively placed it, he found his favorite pistol. Whether the Queen meant this as a joke or thought Preacher might need a gun to settle the fight is not known.

She did her utmost to take care of the "Doctor." She adjusted to his moods and idiosyncrasies with devotion. She cooked the best meals, fed all the dogs and became a part of the mystique of the manse. Cleanliness, however, was just not her cup of tea. In earlier years, Preacher's niece, who was temporarily living with her Unkie, tried to help Preacher by teaching the "Queen" some basic rules of cleaning and keeping a house. This help was not only ineffective, it was totally rejected. The situation became so tense one day that the niece fired the housekeeper. After the "woman of color" had gone home and the house-dust had settled, the niece was filled with remorse at having taken things into her own hands and quickly went to the church to tell Preacher what had happened. "You won't believe it, but I have just had the audacity to fire your cook!" He relieved her anxiety by saying, "I back you in any way you handle the domestic scene." But the niece, realizing her error, insisted that the recalcitrant *cook* be reinstated, and Preacher arranged the details. After all, it wasn't the *cook* who had been fired as much as it was the *housekeeper*. All's well that ends well. The African Queen not only survived this firing but many more that Preacher himself administered when the spirits had captured her, or she had captured the spirits, whichever the case may have been.

One time, among many, Preacher brought home a car full of ordained ministers, commissioned officers and elected politicians. A meeting had been going on in town, and so Preacher had told the African Queen to prepare a complete and comprehensive meal with all the trimmings. When everyone had washed up for dinner, he waited until all of them were in the dining room when he called out in a commanding order, "Fannie, come on in here!" The cook came running, accompanied by at least the two spaniels, Deacon and Elder, and maybe the hunting dog, Mrs. Smith. Amidst the hubbub, Preacher intoned, "We have been honored to have many of the Lord's servants at this board; but they have all been foot soldiers, muleskinners and cup bearers. Today, we are feasting with the Lord's heavy artillery. The very sound of their names strikes fear into the heart of the devil and all his legions."

"Praise de Lawd! Hallelujah!" cried the Queen. Elder and Deacon took up the "Amen."

She loved to join in the repartee with Preacher. Sometimes she knew he was funning with her, but at other times she wasn't sure. His language was sometimes placed so far over her head that she wasn't at all clear about what he had said, but she usually tried to adjust to his mood.

Her tolerance, though, sometimes was tried beyond testing. Ole Joe, the weimaraner, always came to the table with Preacher. He was a big dog and liked to lay his snout on the table cloth and sniff all the enticing foods he coveted. Although he never doubted that he would be given morsels of each before the meal was over, he took great delight in circling the table, sniffing and begging. One Sunday morning at breakfast Joe got carried away. His snout had come to rest right by the butter plate. He snapped at it, took a huge gulp, and with one swallow a quarter pound stick of butter suddenly disappeared. Preacher thought this was the most humorous trick he had ever seen his comic-dog pull, and he laughed long and loud. The Queen, however, took a dim view of this performance and threatened to slit the dog's throat. This only added to the humor of the situation, for Preacher knew she loved Ole Joe as much as he did — well, almost as much.

The days of fetching and taking her home came to an end when Preacher's health began to fail. She then acquired a bicycle which she rode to and from work well into her eighties.

One time, Preacher designed a dinner that was planned to worry his guests as well as give them a good time. The

Synod of Florida was meeting at the First Presbyterian Church of Gainesville in order to honor Preacher because he was retiring. A special ceremony for this purpose was being planned for the second evening during which the Moderator of the General Assembly was to speak. Preacher, ignoring what he knew would transpire at that evening session, invited some close friends who were attending the Synod meeting to his house for dinner. By very insistent, preplanned, and careful calculation he had included such people as the President of Columbia Seminary, the President of Eckerd University in St. Petersburg, and two ministers formerly associated with him in Gainesville.

They had a most delightful meal together and did much reminiscing and prognosticating. They even speculated on what words of wisdom would be spoken by the Moderator in this climax session of Synod. All knew the speech was going to be a testimony about Preacher's contribution to the work of the Synod and especially his pioneering mission with students. Preacher, however, suppressed knowledge of the purpose of this final evening. As the time was approaching when they should leave Preacher's table to go back to the church, one of the presidents tried to terminate the animated conversation by saying, "Don't you think it is time for us to be getting back to the church?"

"No," demurred the host. "Let's not go back tonight; we are having so much fun, let's just stay here and relax; they can get along without us."

The other president joined in. "Surely, we must go back; you know the Moderator of the General Assembly is to speak at your church tonight. As host pastor, you must be there." The dinner socializing was finally terminated abruptly by the guests, as they carried the much amused Preacher off to the program being given in his honor. All had had a great time at dinner, and Preacher had secretly planned and enjoyed everyone's nervousness. He was the only calm participant in the crowd.

Preacher never missed an opportunity to accept invitations to break bread at other people's houses. In fact, if a homemaker was having a particularly good dinner some night, she would invariably call Preacher to ask him to come eat with the family. It was not unusual for Preacher to have a conflict, but he did not let that deter him from accepting. He would say, "Sure, I'll be glad to come eat with you, but I can't come tonight; I can come tomorrow night, though." Of course, he would be asked for the next night even if it resulted in much change of plans or preparation of an entirely new meal. Just to have Preacher's presence made any inconvenience only a small matter.

Occasionally, Preacher used a novel means for getting an invitation to a meal when none was in the offing. Once, he approached a dear friend and asked, "Why don't you and your husband come over to my house and have supper with me tonight. I'm having some cold, fried okra left over from breakfast."

"Preacher!" she replied, "If that's all you've got to eat, why don't you come over to eat with us; we are having steak and French-fried potatoes?"

"What time?" he replied instantly to the surprised housewife.

No account of breaking bread with Preacher Gordon would be complete without giving at least a couple of the cook-out recipes for which he was famous. These appeared as Culinary Crinkles in the Junior Welfare League Cook Book of 1941. They are worth trying.

### Fried Fish (camp style)

Take a 2 pound bass, draw and clean. Put 2 strips of white bacon inside the fish; then, wrap fish in wet newspaper. You can wrap it in mud if there is no newspaper handy—in that case omit the bacon stuffing.

Dig a shallow hole under your fire and place the fish

in it. Cover lightly with ashes and dirt and cook under slow fire until done. Smaller fish, squirrels or chickens may be cooked the same way.

### Tallahatchie Camp Stew

One iron pot or large skillet, two cans tomatoes, one can corn, three squirrels, two pounds onions, and two pounds fried potatoes diced fine, one-half pound raw bacon.

Add okra, pepper and salt to taste. Let simmer slowly over wood fire until meat and vegetables are thoroughly cooked. A dash of ashes does not impair the flavor.

Take one pound of bacon or side meat and fry to a crisp. Pour this into the larger pot and stir thoroughly. Serve in the pans with bread. A dozen eggs broken in the stew if there are no squirrels or chickens handy to give a good thickening to the stew.

Preacher Gordon

Fish-fry or camp-out stew, church supper or breakfast at Preacher's, fellowship went with food like ham goes with eggs. Meal time was mission time for this delightful pastor who knew that the way to a man's soul was often through his stomach.

# PART V

## A MISCHIEVOUS SAINT

*"... Because he understood people's weaknesses and forgave them, found some good in everyone, revealed the mischief in himself, was empathic with those in trouble and could become emotionally involved without losing his composure."*

*"... Because he could break tensions and 'cut the fool' with wit tempered by good will and a profound human kindness."*

# 19

## TEMPERED WIT

"It is a good thing he is a preacher; there is no telling what would have become of him if he hadn't been." These were the words of one faithful and devoted sis-tah. She loved him from the day he arrived in Gainesville and until the end of her days. As with many other widows, Preacher gave her much attention and she maintained an active participation in the church throughout all her life. Like others, she recognized Preacher's mischievousness and loved him for it.

Preacher's good humor employed both *tempered* wit and *wit* tempered with profound human kindness. He frequently turned tense situations around by engaging humor rather than temper. This use of wit to control embarrassing temper can be thought of as *tempered* wit.

Wit that is tempered is quite a different thing; it is the control of one's joking so that it is never hurtful to somebody because of barbs or cutting sarcasm. Preacher never intentionally joked at someone else's expense, and he didn't appreciate that style when he heard it used by other people. Laughter, he felt, should always serve a constructive function and never have a demeaning or harmful effect.

Even on very sensitive issues he could be honest in his

differences without taking aim to shoot someone down. Shortly after his retirement from First Church, the Session voted to make women eligible for holding church office. Subsequently, one of his favorite and long time widow-friends, whom he dubbed the Duchess of Suwannee, was elected a ruling elder; she had been ordained and was active on the Session. From that time forward, despite his own opposition to women serving as ordained ruling or teaching elders, he good naturedly called this widow-lady, Elderina. The first occasion he had to tease her was at the post office. He called out to her, "Here comes my Elderina."

She replied, "Preacher, I didn't know whether you would speak to me after you found I had been elected and ordained."

"Now, you know I love you just the same." But he came up to her just as close as he could get and chuckled in her ear, "Now you know if there should *ever* have been an Elderina, it would have been you."

There was an elderly man, however, who used to badger Preacher every time he saw him by saying how sure he was that Preacher didn't like him. Preacher always turned the affront with a laugh but it never deterred the grouchy complainer from repeating his claim. Finally, after this had continued for some time and Preacher had grown tired of hearing this ridiculous accusation, Preacher yielded, hoping it would give the old man some satisfaction. He said, "Yes, it is true that I don't like you, but my heart is filled with Christian compassion for you."

This was not the only time he was confronted with a personal attack. One time when he was visiting in a nursing home, an old sister asked him, "And who are you, my good man?"

Preacher was unabashed and replied with assurance, "Why, I'm Preacher Gordon, the Presbyterian pastor."

To this, the old lady rejoined, "Yes, and I'm sure that you are not all you are supposed to be, either!"

It was with gaiety at the joke on himself that he would

tell others that he replied to the sis-tah, "Too true, too true." When Preacher could relieve a situation by a joke on himself, he was in tall cotton.

He was never left without a response. One Sunday he had preached on "All have sinned and fallen short of the Glory of God." On Monday, as he was making his rounds of the various stores and establishments to visit the members of his flock, one sister was waiting for him to tell him in no uncertain terms that she had never sinned! Preacher paused for a minute of reflection and then conceded, "Well, sis-tah, I've just got a whole lot better congregation than I dreamed I had."

Despite the efforts of the congregation to find Preacher a mate, they never considered one attractive widow to be a candidate because she was so much older than Preacher. He made pastoral visits to her often, however, beginning with his early days in Gainesville. In later years, when she had become quite old and feeble, she would tease Preacher by telling him how, as a young man, he was always so prim and proper whenever he came to see her. She reminded him of how he always sat in the uncomfortable, antique chair next to the front door. Preacher hastened to claim, "I used to sit there so I could get out fast in case you tried to seduce me."

Preacher was very much aware of the match-making designs concocted on his behalf. He continued successfully to avoid entanglement. However, he was caught in one happenstance that stumped him. He went to a doctor for treatment of what is commonly called tennis elbow. He was told by the physician that he should have his arm placed in a splint for several weeks to rest his elbow. Preacher promptly told the physician he didn't have time for that. The doctor told him it would only take a few minutes to prepare the splint.

"You don't understand," Preacher told him, "I don't have time to explain to every good lady in Gainesville why my arm is in a sling."

There were times when Preacher's jocular moods and uninhibited personality got him into some unusual situations. He usually managed to scramble out of them, but sometimes it was a tight squeeze. Once, when a student pastor was driving Preacher to a Presbytery meeting in West Florida, they passed through a small town with only one traffic light. Although the light was green, they had to brake the car to a screeching halt because a tough gang of boys was sauntering across the street against the traffic. Preacher stuck his head out of the car window and hollered, "You boys better watch out, someone's going to get hurt." The tallest boy in the gang was a hot tempered red-head.

"You go to hell!" he yelled back at the car.

Preacher told his driver to stop the car. He got out and started walking back toward the gang while the student pastor joined him as his second. When they approached the rowdies, Preacher challenged the big, red-headed boy with, "What did you say?"

The teenager clenched his fists and reddened with rage as he spit back, "I said, you go to hell!"

Preacher looked him square in the eye and said with a finality to the exchange, "Well, I just came back here to tell you, I ain't going!" The raucous toughy relaxed his fists and face and then broke out in a big smile.

Clothes were often the subject of chiding. While Preacher loved to be dressed up in a new suit to go to a proper affair, he gave but incidental attention to the freshness of his everyday apparel. One of his deacons owned a haberdashery across from the church in the early days and was always trying to get Preacher to buy new clothes from his store. He claimed he had the best line of clothing in town. Preacher told him, "Well, it's a poor frog that don't croak in his own pond."

"But Preacher, your old suits make you look like a traveling salesman," the deacon insisted.

"I *am* a traveling salesman, Brother! I carry the Greatest Line of Goods in the world and it would behoove you to come into my shop on Sunday as regularly as you try to get me into yours on Monday."

Another time, in the days of greater modesty and conformity in habits of dress, Preacher was attending a Women of the Church meeting when a full-skirted maiden aunt indignantly searched him out to reveal a most alarming indiscretion. "Preacher," she whispered starchily, "I am the only one here wearing a petticoat!"

Without a second thought he disposed of the problem by stating a very obvious, if inaccurate, fact. "Well, sis-tah, what difference does that make? I'm the only one here wearing pants."

Such retorts gave credence to his oft-admitted sin of not curbing his chattering tongue. One of Preacher's noncommissioned buddies (that is, a non-member of his church with whom he enjoyed repartee as a crony and friend), was walking home with him from the Legion Hall in the 1940's. He was a successful criminal lawyer, and Preacher recognized his professional, legal skill. Preacher complimented him by this endorsement: "I went up and heard you trying a case the other day and I want you to know that if I ever go to jail, I'm going to send for you."

The attorney took advantage of the opening to enter his own rejoinder. "I will make an agreement with you Preacher. I will keep you out of jail if you will keep me out of hell."

"Now, counsellor, you know that is an unequal agreement!" Preacher was not going to enter into any plea bargaining even for a Legionnaire buddy.

A medical doctor who had been Preacher's radiologist all through the years likes to reflect on the many beautiful associations he had with Preacher. He remembered the time in the years immediately after Preacher came to Gainesville when an elderly man collapsed in church. The deacons stretched him out on the hard, curved pew while one of the physicians in the congregation came and listened to his heart. The doctor pronounced the man dead and then left. In a little while, the man began to stir and sat up. Presently, he stood up, walked out of the church, unhitched his horse-and-buggy and galloped away. Preacher remarked, "That's what I call stamina."

Another time, the radiologist recalled, one of the dear ladies of the church had jumped on Preacher for never being at home. Preacher asked her how she knew. She said she went by his house the day before and he wasn't there.

"How did you know I wasn't home? The bell was out of order," claimed Preacher. She said she had gone in looking for him and went all over the house, and he wasn't there. This was too good a chance to let pass, so Preacher thoughtfully and mischievously reflected, "Now I know who ate my fresh apple pie I had left on the dining room table."

When thinking of these incidents, the elderly doctor reflected, "I have never enjoyed anyone's company as much as I did Preacher's; there was nothing put on about him and he was so natural and unaffected. I loved Preacher and miss him every time I walk past his house."

He remembered also the woman in the congregation who was somewhat of a hypochondriac. She took pleasure in describing her ailments and telling everyone how sick she was. Every time she was admitted to the hospital she would tell Preacher that this time she was going to die. After he had heard this three or four times, Preacher allayed her fears by telling her, "Yes, you might, but think how much happier you will be where you are going."

There were occasions in which Preacher's temper showed more than his wit. He was exceedingly sensitive to the fact that some well-meaning people thought that, since he had not yet acquired a wife and was so much a part of so many families, he did not consider the manse to be his own home. It was, indeed, his home and he never left any doubt about that if someone seemed to question it.

He and his assistant pastor were invited to a church family's home for dinner in September during the hurricane season. Preacher was deathly afraid of storms especially when there was lightning. A hurricane was passing up the east coast of Florida and doing no damage inland except for an occasional gust of wind. One of these gusts snapped a limb in Preacher's front yard and it fell on the corner of his porch. After surveying the damage, he and his assistant proceeded to go to dinner. Following the meal Preacher said, "I'd better be getting home to see whether everything is still O.K. after the storm."

"Home?" thoughtlessly queried the assistant. "You don't have a home." The young man had meant only that the storm had damaged his house. But the damage to Preacher's feelings had already been done, and there was no retrieving the remark.

"You're mighty right I have a home. I have a home just as much as anybody. Just because I'm not married—yet—doesn't mean I don't have a home. And don't you forget it!" Preacher had bristled at this unintentional goof of the assistant pastor. But the point had been made and the young assistant never forgot it.

Just as Preacher's temper occasionally out-witted him, his humor sometimes was at the expense of discretion. He was not a man to swear by his temper, but he would use a swear word in jest when the situation called for it. *Never* was he known to blaspheme! But one Sunday morning, as he greeted the departing worshippers, a man who had apparently been drinking came up to Preacher.

The stranger said, "That was a hell of a sermon you preached today."

Preacher answered him politely, "Brother, I am glad you enjoyed the sermon but I wish you wouldn't use words like that here on the steps of God's House."

The drunk continued, "Preacher-man, that was such a damn good sermon I put a hundred dollar bill in the collection plate."

"The hell you did," was Preacher's startled reply.

The man went on off just as startled as Preacher was,

but he kept shaking his head as if he were saying to himself, "Ain't he something? I'll be back next week, for sure."

There were other circumstances in which righteous prevarication was employed as the better part of persuasion. A Presbyterian evangelist, a good friend of Preacher's, always stopped to see him to bring him news of all his relatives back in Mississippi. The evangelist was going blind and had been advised by his friends not to drive his car any more. His response to this advice always was, "I ask the Lord to take care of me when I start out on a trip and He always does." That is a rather hard position with which to take issue.

It was left to Preacher to come up with a plan that might influence this devoted servant of God. The next time the good fellow came to see him, Preacher reported, "Brother, last night the Lord gave me a message to relay to you. He told me to tell you when you came today that He wasn't going to take care of you any longer, so you better quit driving!"

Until his later years, Preacher would not publicly drink any beverage that had alcoholic content. As he got older, however, he occasionally accepted a glass of wine, giving this explanation, "I think I have tramped long enough in God's vineyard to enjoy a little of the fruit of the vine."

Once, at a wedding party, no one had offered him a glass of champagne. He was sitting next to one of the young bridesmaids who was about to sip on hers.

He reached over and took the stem from her as he scolded. "You are too young to drink this." Whereupon he put the glass to his own lips and drank every drop of her champagne.

He may have had a double purpose in taking the girl's drink, but there were some things he did, or jokes he told, that were done just for fun. He loved to laugh about the seminary student who was admonished by one of his teachers because he and his wife had had three children during the three years at school. The old professor scolded him saying that they should exercise family planning until they could better afford to provide financially for children.

The student explained. "Well, I just can't help it. It's that six a.m. train that goes by every morning and wakes me up. It is too early to get up and too late to go back to sleep."

Another slightly risque joke he used to employ concerned two churches across the street from each other with similar names. The situation almost always prompted someone to ask Preacher what difference in belief kept these two churches separated. "Well," he would stroke his chin and explain somewhat secretively, "the church on this side believes Pharoah's daughter found Moses in the bulrushes, but the church on the other side believes that is just what *she* say."

A trick Preacher played on more than one unsuspecting acquaintance was revealed on a rainy day, when a Gainesville lady's car stalled on one of the downtown streets. She tells that she had several appointments to keep and was pressed for time so she hailed the taxi that was coming towards her. Having waved it down, she got into the back seat and gave instructions to the driver. As she looked at the man wearing the driver's cap she thought he was either Preacher Gordon or his twin. Realizing his identity had been discovered, Preacher turned to her with a prankish grin, tipped his cap, and asked, "Can I give you a lift, sis-tah?"

It seems he had just put his car in the garage for repairs and the cab company had loaned him this off-duty taxi to use for the afternoon to make his calls. The driver's cap was in the seat so Preacher had played the role to the hilt. This was not the first time Preacher had played cab-driver and fortunate indeed were those lucky enough to be chauffeured by this mischievous cabby.

# 20

## "BLEST BE THE TIE"

THE CHOIR soprano was in the middle of her solo one Sunday worship when the electricity was interrupted and the organ whined a dying chord. The beautiful soloist froze with mouth agape not knowing what to do. After a seemingly eternity, Preacher jumped to his feet and took control.

"Well, we can't help that; let's all stand and sing one stanza of Blest Be the Tie." He proceeded to heist the tune and the congregation sang with gusto and glee.

The familiar hymn, of course, continues, "Blest be the tie that binds our hearts in Christian love." Love transcends life and is the hope in death. It is the most important ingredient of marriage and funerals. Without the rudiments of spiritual bonds, the legal and physical union of couples oft comes unfastened.

> Love is patient, love is kind. It does not envy, it does not boast, it is not proud. It is not rude, it is not self-seeking, it is not easily angered, it keeps no record of wrongs. Love does not delight in evil but rejoices in truth. It always protects, always trusts, always hopes, always perseveres. Love never fails.
> (I Cor. 13: 4-8)

The *Gainesville Sun* (May 12, 1968) said of Preacher Gordon that he had probably married more couples than any other minister in the city. "He recalls marrying three generations of some families, and, of course, he has married many young people whom he had baptised as infants."

Preacher believed that religion is especially important in marriage and that couples should go to church together, pray together, and raise their children in one church regardless of which one it was. "I often send couples together to other churches to keep the family together," he said. Other advice he gave couples seeking his premarital counselling was not to marry with the idea of reforming the partner. "I've seen many girls who tried it only to come to much grief."

Although Preacher believed marriages should not be undertaken on the spur of the moment, he was the first to admit that he, himself, might have waited too long. "When I was young, I was too particular and as I grow older, I am less desirable." While this was his quip for turning away inquiries, he always left the question of his own intentions for marriage unanswered. Kiddingly, he told one good church sis-tah that he wanted her to arrange his wedding reception and he was going to ask the church soloist to sing "The Fight is On."

He often told about the two university students who came to him about ten o'clock one night and asked that he marry them. He told them to come back the next morning at ten and he would consider it then. The young man came the next day but not the girl. "Now," said Preacher, "they are both married — to different people and are happy that I made them wait until daylight."

There was a period of time when the assistant pastor, the director of Christian education, and Preacher were all three unmarried. The question often was asked about how much real marriage counseling could take place when none of the staff knew any of the basics from first hand experience. Only a novice would ask that question, however, for there was something about Preacher's perception of love and life that made him eminently qualified to inspire a couple to consider their relationship from a spiritual perspective.

The truth about Preacher, that some folks never stopped to consider, was that he knew when words and advice were not as persuasive as friendship and warmth of relationships. He never gave long-faced instruction when jocular fellowship was more helpful. Several young women whom he had baptised and known all their lives remember that his marriage counseling had consisted of one leisurely half-hour chat, during which he offered the groom-to-be a cigar, and then commented that he never did much in those sessions except to advise the bride to cook some good meals for her husband. In those instances, that may have been the very best thing he could have said or done.

If he knew before the conference that they were well aware of the spiritual as well as physical and legal union that was about to take place, he might make the counselling session perfunctory. If he was unsure, he laid the matter squarely on the line and went over every particular of the Christian ceremony in great detail and with emphatic clarity. One thing is for sure, no one ever forgot Preacher's marriage counselling session. He always assured himself that the bride and groom fully understood the religious vows they would be exchanging. He wanted them to appreciate the significance of what they were about to do and that it was in accordance with the ordinances of God.

He never read the ritual at the wedding but gave all the sanctified words from memory, speaking them from his heart and impressing them upon theirs. He often told the groom during the ceremony, "Don't look at me, son; look at her. Make your promises to her, not me."

As a pastor and as a friend, Preacher was more interested in the spiritual attitude of the bride and groom towards each other than he was the superficial particulars of the ceremony or the psychological, physiological or economic details of pre-marital counseling. As he commented to a financier whose kids he married, "When I marry a couple, I want them to stay married."

While Preacher always made a wedding a most sacred experience, this did not keep him from having a lot of fun at wedding rehearsals. In fact, the contrast between his jocular mood before a ceremony and his sanctified reverence during the wedding was so well defined that it served to amplify both.

Rehearsals, in particular, brought out the mischief in this saintly man. During the war, a muscle deacon had asked Preacher to please come to a distant city to participate in his wedding, for which, the soldier said, he would be in his officer's uniform. He agreed to go, of course, but he was late getting to the rehearsal. The Methodist minister, who was the girl's pastor, had quite properly started the rehearsal without him and it was proceeding with dignified solemnity when in came Preacher panting for breath. In his usual loud voice, he called out as he got about two-thirds of the way down the center aisle, "Where is the couple that told me they *had* to get married?" The cream of society in that town were shook up for a while but soon Preacher had charmed everyone, as he always did. He just had to tease the muscle deacon about his "military wedding."

When a bride gave birth to a full term baby just six months after her marriage, he gave reassurance to her by saying, "Well, that quite frequently happens with a couple's first child but seldom with the second."

His associate pastor for the student ministry once asked him how he should counsel a coed with an unwanted pregnancy. Preacher jested, "Why don't you ask the Methodist student pastor? He has more knowledge and experience with that kind of counseling than Presbyterians."

In the 40's, a man Preacher knew from a neighboring farm community came to the church offices with a woman he wished to marry. The man was wearing a white tee-shirt with the sleeves rolled up displaying huge muscular arms. His girl friend looked every bit as powerful. Preacher asked the fellow whether he had obtained a license.

"What did you say?" the man asked. He was apparently hard-of-hearing, for he wore a hearing aid in one ear.

"I said, do you have a valid marriage license?" repeated Preacher.

"I sure do," he responded, finally, as he tugged the proper legal document from his hip pocket. He was then asked whether he had brought any witnesses with him. When Preacher found there were none, he asked the church secretary and the receptionist to serve in that capacity. Preacher was not reluctant to perform the ceremony in these particular hasty circumstances because he knew the man was trying to make public, legal, and holy the estate which they had been enjoying for a long time.

At last the time came and Preacher propounded the vital question: "Do you take this woman to be your loving and faithful wife?"

The groom stared at Preacher hesitatingly and asked, "What did you say?" The question was repeated a little louder until the big fellow kind of grinned and winced as he exclaimed, "I sure do!" The receptionist and the secretary each picked out a knot in the floor at which to fix their glances to avoid looking at Preacher or they all would have broken out in unceremonious laughter.

Afterwards, the groom asked how much he owed and Preacher told him, "Not a thing." The man went on to say that he repaired tractors for a living and that business had not been too good this year. Preacher repeated that he wasn't owed a thing.

The muscular mechanic turned to his buxom bride and said, "Give the man a dollar."

At a rehearsal of an affluent girl who was going to have six bridesmaids and a sophisticated wedding with all the trimmings, Preacher carefully stepped around the stands of ferns and palms staggered at each side of the fully decorated wedding arch, which was heavily braided with ivy and orange blossoms. After wending his way to the center, he complained, "You know, I'm afraid of snakes! If you keep all this greenery in here, we are liable to attract a couple of them. Tomorrow, I'm going to come in my rubber, hip-boots." Needless to say, the decorations were toned down a bit for the wedding day.

There was a time, however, when Preacher could not avoid wearing boots. He had been hunting and had car trouble on the way home. He arrived in town just before the ceremonies were to begin, so he had his hunting companion drop him off at the church. He put his robe on over his blood stained pants and his leather boots as he solemnly joined the processional. Aside from thinking his shoes needed polishing, no one seemed to take any notice of his boots!

Going from the sublime to the ridiculous was never more in evidence than during the picture taking between the ceremony and the reception. Preacher was always very good about making himself available for these, but he was not always good about standing still in one place until the photographer was ready for him. He usually was out in the sanctuary talking to some of the bride's relatives or the groom's cronies. When a wedding director and professional photographer were present, things usually ran more smoothly because everything was planned out ahead of time.

When Preacher married his great niece, there were relatives on all sides and of several denominations, all of whom received his individual attention and most of them received at least one practical joke in the bargain. As the director got everyone arranged for a picture, she then had to get Preacher's attention away from his own galavanting to join the group. When he stepped into the grouping, he then fixed his eyes on the lady giving instructions as if he were entranced with her. She was a good looking person with a bubbling personality, and Preacher just had to have some fun with her. As soon as she finally got everyone in position looking toward the bride and groom, she glanced over at Preacher and found he was staring at her rather than smiling at the bride.

"Dr. Gordon, please don't look at me; look at the bride!" Then she instructed the photographer to wait until she could get Preacher's cooperation. Finally, after she had requested him two or three times to please look over at the bride and not at her, he broadcast to everyone present:

"But, I just can't keep *my* eyes off of *you!*" If any more ice needed to be broken, this did it. Everyone fell into a pool of merriment that didn't quit rippling until time for the reception.

Funerals were another matter. Death of a loved one is a dreadful experience, and Preacher never tried to be pollyanna-ish about it. To be sure, Christians have hope and faith in the everlasting life of the spirit. Much comfort can be derived from the Scripture concerning the love of God which is in Christ Jesus our Lord: "For if we believe that Jesus died and rose again, even so them also which sleep in Jesus will God bring with Him. Wherefore comfort one another with these words." (Thessalonians, Ch. 4)

Preacher gave comfort and hope to the bereaved in such measure that it drained him physically. He never brushed aside the sadness of those to whom he ministered but entered into it with empathy and consolation. His tears often mingled with those of the immediate family, and they were comforted. In order to sustain himself through the intensity of leading a funeral worship, Preacher surrounded himself with people before the service, and later he exposed himself to happy thought to restore his own spirit. Preacher was not treating circumstances lightly but was keeping himself steadied and completely under control.

An admirer of Preacher's for nearly fifty years remembers his undergraduate days at the University when, like countless others, he stood on a special corner of the downtown square to thumb rides to Jacksonville. He was there bumming when Preacher drove up and signalled for him to get in.

"I'm going to Jacksonville right after I hold this funeral," Preacher told him. "You wait in the car for me; I'll only be about ten minutes and then we'll go." The student got in the car, and Preacher drove around the block and parked in front of a funeral home. After about fifteen minutes, he reappeared assisting two elderly ladies, whom he helped into the back seat of his car. Presently he was signaled to proceed, and they drove off at the head of a funeral procession. The deceased was to be buried in Jacksonville, and the young man found himself a passenger in the lead car with two chief mourners in the back seat. When they got to Jacksonville, Preacher stopped his car and let the student out at a corner near the young man's home. Holding up the entire funeral procession, Preacher thanked the student for his good company and told him to come to breakfast with him when he got back. Then he drove away with the two mourners and all the other funeral cars in slow pursuit.

Preacher always did the things that came natural to him and never stood on ceremony. He could fit in with almost every situation or make the situation fit in with him. He always seemed to know the appropriate and tender thing to do and the compassionate words to say.

One time when he buried one of his hunting companions, he was well acquainted with all the deceased's friends and relatives. "On their hunting trips," he told them, "they would build a fire in the evening, sing a little, pray a little, tell jokes, and always wind it up by singing 'In the Sweet Bye and Bye.'"

At graveside, he read the Scripture passages of hope and love.

"Let not your heart be troubled: you believe in God, believe also in me. . . . I am the Way, the Truth, and the life: no man cometh unto the Father but by me."

Then he told the close knit family group about their hunting habits and how much he was going to miss his companion. He ended the service by praying his favorite prayer:

> O Lord, support us all the day long, until the shadows lengthen and the evening comes, and the busy

world is hushed, and the fever of life is over, and our work is done. Then in Thy mercy grant us safe lodging, and a holy rest, and peace at the last; through Jesus Christ our Lord. Amen.
(from Book of Common Worship)

While all were still bowed in prayer and grief, he softly sang, and only faltered once: "In the Sweet Bye and Bye, we will meet on that beautiful shore."

# 21

## "A MAN'S SHADOW"

A SHADOW is said to be only the other side of light, and sorrow is only the other side of glory. How quickly the evening comes to convert daylight into darkness, and how suddenly one's joy in life can become the grief of death. The shadow of a man is almost non-existent at the zenith of his life, but it begins to loom short and heavy in the early afternoon sun. As the shadow lengthens at sundown, it fades into the dark blend of dusk. But the shadow of a fallen loved one should be measured not by the density of the darkness but by the contrasting brilliance of Eternal Light. "God is light; in Him there is no darkness at all." (I John 1:5)

At the peak of Preacher's active pastoring, there was no shadow — only the growing happiness and reflected glory of the heavenly Light of Lights. But, as he started walking into the setting sun, his shadow appeared and ominously lengthened. To look upon Preacher as if he were a wayfarer walking falteringly into the sun leaving behind only his shadow-side, would be a gloomy outlook indeed; his friends rejected contemplation of life without Preacher.

As he grew older, it became important for his followers to position themselves between him and the setting sun; by doing this, they could experience the joys of his life even till the day of dusk, and witness the reflection of his countenance.

On the day of his funeral, Preacher was to have given a sermon in Archer at the Bethlehem Presbyterian Church entitled, "A Man's Shadow." That message was never delivered, nor did it need to be. Preacher's life, itself, was the sermon, and his death weighed heavily on hearts everywhere. The burden of his shadow was borne, not only by his immediate family, but by close friends who now had to face the reality of their loss.

For eighty-two years, he had lived life to the fullest and had given pleasure to all. He kept his sense of humor to the last. He never married, but always quipped about the prospects of marrying. He had enjoyed for many years, the company of a handsome and intelligent lady, who, like Preacher, had never married because she had given her life to her work, that of editing and writing a professional journal. They maintained a long admiration and respect for one another, during the many years she shared a home in Baton Rouge with Preacher's niece. They even teased about being fiances. One time, at a family gathering for a seasonal good time, when both were in their eighties,

Preacher leaned forward with no provocation nor conversational ploy and said to his "fiance," "I don't believe I want any children, do you?"

And so it was that Preacher never let his age dent his zest for fun nor chill his enthusiasm for maintaining centerstage.

But he became plagued by recurring bouts with cancer and was treated in local hospitals to keep it in remission. Even when he was in relentless pain and discomfort, he would not let others know of his suffering for Preacher was never a complainer. Instead, he would allay all concern by saying, "I am so lucky to have all this excellent medical attention right here in town; I don't have to drive fifty miles to receive the best possible care. God has been so good." There is no question but that his courage—his meek and uncomplaining spirit—has given countless others the strength to bear their own burdens.

During his various illnesses, he gave doctors the same instructions he had given his family many years earlier: "I don't want to be kept alive by those life-sustaining machines. Whenever the doctors say there is no way for me to recover, *just give me one spear-thrust!*" As the time apparently was approaching for his terminal attack, he reiterated to his doctors that he didn't want the process of dying to be prolonged beyond the point where they could restore his health. He understood and trusted God's clock so implicitly that he could accept the inevitable whenever it was to come. When he was admitted to the hospital for what turned out to be the last time, there was no surcease from the ravaging pain, and an emergency operation had to be performed.

Just before he went into the operating room, Preacher remembered that he was supposed to perform a wedding for a congressman the next day and said he didn't think he could make it for the ceremony. "Please tell him to postpone it, Les, or get you to do it," he said, as they pulled him out of the room on a transport.

While he was post-operatively in the surgical intensive care unit, the doctors became increasingly aware that a final decision would soon have to be made. As they gathered to evaluate his condition, his surgeon friend came out of his room and said with sad relief, "We don't have to make the decision; the Lord and Preacher have made it for us. He is gone."

Preacher seemed to sense the Lord was telling him it was time to go. He had pressed toward the goal to win the prize for which God had called him heavenward in Christ Jesus. (Philippians 4:14)

This departure was so like Preacher; he had always known when it was time to go. He had started church on time and stopped on time—when the big hand and the little hand were both straight up on the clock. He arrived at parties and at meetings on time and left on time, if not a little ahead of time.

"When you get up to leave, go! Don't stand up for a half-hour first in the living room and then at the door, then in the yard and at the car." Preacher's motto was, "Relax, enjoy your visit, concentrate on the moment, talk and have a good time until you think it is time to leave; then, get up and go!"

Now that he is gone, the very thought of Preacher always brings a smile. Tears are only for those left behind who sorrow for themselves, but smiles are for the memory of this genuine folk-hero. It has been said of him that he was at once a Billy Graham, a Benjamin Franklin, a Will Rogers, a Tom Sawyer, and a Knute Rockne. He will stand the test of time as much as any one of them.

A grieving friend of Preacher wrote what might be considered a modern parable of a lasting human impression: "All who were close to him, whose babies were baptized by him, whose children were married by him, whose loved ones buried by him, feel he is now closer to them than ever before: he lives in our hearts." Certainly, this thought is akin to St. Paul's statement to the Galatians: "I have been crucified with Christ and I no longer live, but *Christ lives in me.*" (Galatians 2:20)

On the Sunday morning of his funeral, the minister of the First Presbyterian Church of Gainesville and the one, who for several years had been Preacher's successor in that pastorate, said in his morning sermon, "This is both a sad and a glorious Sunday for this congregation. There is a tremendous void left in our church and community with the death of Preacher Gordon. But as his niece put it to me Saturday morning, 'Don't you know that Unkie is having a good time this morning negotiating with St. Peter as to where is the best place for bream fishing?' Hallelujah! The Lord reigns!"

From Atlanta, the pastor emeritus of the First Presbyterian Church there wrote of Preacher, "He was one of the greatest friends, one of the finest teachers, the grandest preachers I have ever known. The things he did made everyone love him. Somehow, I felt that the Master walked with him wherever he went!"

"He was truly unique," wrote another son of a church family. "His humor and practical approach to religion were inspirations for many, including three generations of our family. He helped me to grow up and, when his own health was failing, his inspiration and unfailing good humor helped ease the fear of death for my own son who was undergoing treatment for cancer. I like to think that both my father and my son are continuing now to enjoy Preacher's presence."

That his greatest sermon was his own life is demonstrated by this testimony: "Preacher Gordon has unquestionably influenced my life for Jesus Christ not only in his preaching ministry but especially through his daily example of Christian faith and discipline and through his love and concern for people — especially me."

Preacher's death prompted many reminiscences in the form of letters to the editor of local newspapers. One person wrote: "I remember sitting in my great grandmother's dark, green, velvet-draped parlor and piping, *Jesus loves me this I know*. My great grandmother thumped the parlor organ and sang alto to my three-year old soprano. Preacher carried the joyous bass. I also remember seeing Preacher's tears and clenched fists as he conducted the funeral of a young ministerial student who was killed in a freak and terrible car accident. And I remember how the fists, resting on the closed coffin, quietly came unclenched as he said, 'Not my will, but Thine, O Lord.' "

The Baptist preacher, whose church was next door, wrote this tribute to Preacher: "He was a man at ease with saint and sinner alike, with rich and poor, with educated and uneducated. He was married to the church, to a high calling of which he was proud. His sermons and prayers were not built as an architect builds a tower; they were born. When they were delivered, it was obvious that he had been with Jesus. He loved us Baptists. He often said that the only thing separating us from the Presbyterians was a parking lot. When asked, 'Are you behaving yourself?' he replied, 'At my age, that's all you can do.' His voice is now silenced on earth but not in heaven. Somehow, I think he must be spinning some good yarn with fishermen like Peter, James, and John."

To the business world his passing also left a great emptiness. "Preacher leaves a void that no other man could possibly fill," said the chairman of the board of a leading financial institution. "A void so enormous that, in retrospect, it can be filled only by the memory of the great and good will and love that he shared with every man and woman at every walk of life in our community. Those who knew him well understood that there existed no barrier of race, creed, or color in his mission. I would hope that by his passing it would bring men and women together to achieve without malice, without prejudice, and without personal ambition those things he represented and which are paramount to the best interest of mankind."

A tribute prepared by a Rotarian and unanimously approved by the club to which Preacher belonged said in part:

"For virtually a half-century, Preacher Gordon made old things new, as he lived the ancient faith of hope and charity in our midst, and we, in turn, lived in the lustre of his joy and service. Preacher understood the implications of the words, 'to err is human, to forgive is divine.' He knew that no man is as good as he may think he is, nor as bad as either his foes or friends may believe; that all fall short of perfection but that in spite of this, none are beyond the concern of the servant of God. Hence, he was ever quick to forgive and accept men for what they are and lent to all the joy of one who, himself, ran and did not grow weary, who walked and did not faint." (See Appendix C.)

Preacher unwittingly wrote his own epitaph in answer to a newspaper reporter's prodding. "I knew a lot more sixty years ago than I know now. I haven't accomplished all I've wanted to in the ministry; nobody ever does. 'A man's grasp must exceed his reach; else what is heaven for!'"

But Preacher reached further than most and profoundly changed the lives of more than he ever imagined. His giant footprints were not made just in Florida sand where time and tide dissolve. No, his image was printed in the hearts and lives of all kinds of sinners—complacent, intentional, and the self-righteous—all of whom saw and heard the testimony of his Christian faith.

He changed people by reaching into their inner natures—exposing them to no icy piety, no rigid rules, no fiery threats of eternal furnaces. He lived a steady, happy life of kindness, love and forgiveness. His influence was like a balance wheel governing the spiritual movement of human experience. He changed the direction of the wayward by turning them toward their highest calling. Few could resist doing their utmost or striving to do their best after walking in the shadow of a man like Preacher Gordon.

\* \* \* \* \* \*

On his tombstone are engraved the words of the 40th chapter of Isaiah: *He shall feed his flock like a shepherd.* And because his flock had realized he had been one of the great shepherds of Christendom, with grateful hearts it turned even more dependently to the One whose life Preacher had reflected—the Great Shepherd of the sheep, Jesus Christ, the Risen Lord.

# 22

## STILL THE LIFE OF THE PARTY

As people walk in his lingering shadow, which seems to grow taller and broader as the years go by, hearts continue to be uplifted by the brightness of his life. His umbra envelopes people who know him only by reputation or have come under his covering through the actions, the words, the love of the hundreds who continue to reflect the sunny side of his life.

An alumnus, who had been on the varsity baseball team, returned for a reunion with other athletes and fraternity brothers several years after Preacher's death. As they recalled the good old days, the center of attention came to rest on Preacher. One of them said:

"Preacher Gordon seemed to transcend all generations by saying the same thing and holding to the same truths from his early ministry up to his last days. As a result, he touched the lives of vast numbers of people of all ages. One can walk into almost any place of leadership and *Preacher Gordon* becomes the magic word. He put religion into practice."

To this day, many a party, funeral, wedding rehearsal, public gathering, and private affair of almost any kind — happy, sad, or awkward — can be spruced up simply by the mention of the name of Preacher Gordon. His stories are laced like Christmas ornaments through fellowship almost anywhere. If a person has ever heard of Preacher Gordon, there is an anecdote he wants to relate about him or some joke he wants to tell that he heard from Preacher. Mention of Preacher Gordon's name is still an open sesame to the success of a conversation, the cultivation of a new acquaintance, or an entree into a group where one might otherwise be a stranger. Preacher was the life of a party, and he still is. Just recalling his name will bring laughter, tears, or tales wherever he was known. As one lifelong friend told his doctor, "I know no elixir peddled by you pill rollers that so gladdens the heart as swapping memories of our pal, Preacher."

"Were you there at Jack and Jane's house the night he came in late and had an urgent need to use a rest room?" Someone started the swap. "He came quickly through the front door, speaking to no one, but asked the host in his characteristically loud stage whisper, 'Where is your room for ministerial relief?'" There had been no mistaking the nature of that "calling."

The dinner party had been making a slow start. The guests had just gotten past the "how are you getting along" stage. Orders for drinks had been taken, and family friends were helping the host with the serving. But there was no life in the party. Finally someone said, "Now if Preacher Gordon were here, he would say, 'Make mine a small one; just two jiggers!" or 'Just give me a little sacramental wine.'"

If one had asked him how he felt, he would weakly reply in a voice of recuperation, "I am able to set up and take a little weak nourishment."

"Why, Preacher, have you been sick?" would come the distressed reaction.

"No! I'm doing just fine—fer me. Better than I de-serve!"

"I really pulled a good one on Preacher," said another. "Preacher would always say that he had one of the finest remedies for a cold: sheep-pill tea. So when I was in the mountains, I got some well-aged sheep manure and pulverized it and put it in a medicine bottle labelled "Instant Sheep-pill Tea."

Someone else will remember how he protected his head from the hot sun. If he got caught outside without a cap or hat, whether it was a fishing boat or a crowded stadium, he would take out his handkerchief and unfold it. Then, he would tie a knot in each of the four ends so the handkerchief would be pulled into the shape of a skull-cap. This he would put securely on his head without any concern over how it made him look. That act was not for a laugh; it was for self-preservation, and it made practical sense.

Another favorite use of his handkerchief was for naps. When he got sleepy, not just in his own home but any place where it was at all possible, he would fold his handkerchief over his eyes and lean back to doze. Ten minutes of this disappearing act and he was fresh and ready to go again.

Many families remember his flashlight. He loved a flashlight and seldom went out at night without one. As he approached a home, he got out of his car and threw that beam back and forth like a train-engine's oscillating light as he came along the walk. He would throw the light all around his own porch before he stepped through the screen door. He needed the light as his eyesight became less dependable, and he was afraid of snakes and marauders.

\* \* \* \* \* \*

Preacher served during the period of major growth of the church, the city of Gainesville, the University of Florida, and the state. He contributed to that growth by his affect upon people. The city, church and State of Florida are now all "big business" but the size only amplifies the remembrances of Preacher Gordon.

"He told me one time," a troubled friend joked, "that if everything else failed, I could always take up preaching. He was something else, that man was."

## Still the Life of the Party 217

Each will have a different memory of a way in which Preacher had touched his life. He never forgot anyone and none will ever forget him. He had his own way of greeting each person for whom that greeting remains a cherished thought.

"Ain't that my baptized child?"

"Have you been a reasonably good boy? Good, but not too good?"

"Have you been living a righteous and upright life?"

"Are you believing in Salvation by Grace through faith and that not of yourself but by the gift of God?"

"Ain't that my most main and principal deacon?"

"Is that my pal, my podnah?"

"My friend and lodgebrother?"

One of the very first dinners after his death, to which Preacher would have been invited, could have turned out to be an excruciatingly sad affair since he would normally have been there. But because of the legacy he left for his friends, they were bound and determined to carry on for him and in his style. The prayer at dinner, after a social hour of forced merriment, went something like this:

"O Lord, we laugh, because Preacher laughed. We love and cry because he loved and cried and lived a life of devotion to Thee. We thank Thee for the mercy of memory and for the comfort of shared sorrow. Help us to temper our tears with laughter and to control our grief with good fellowship of the faithful. Bless these loved ones and this food as we remember one whom we have loved and lost for a while, but with whom we hope to share eternity because of the promises of our Lord and Saviour, Jesus Christ, in whose Name we pray. AMEN"

An academic scholar of unusual insight captured a concise perception of Preacher Gordon:

"*Sui generis*;
We shall not look upon his like again!"

# Appendix A

## Biographical Sketch

### ULYSSES SHORT GORDON
### 1893-1976

Ulysses Short Gordon was born in Sardis, Mississippi, on December 3, 1893, and as his ministry unfolded, he became affectionately known as "Preacher" Gordon.

He received the Bachelor of Arts degree from Southwestern Presbyterian University at Clarksville, Tennessee, and went on to Southwestern Presbyterian Seminary before obtaining his Bachelor of Divinity from Louisville Presbyterian Theological Seminary in 1915. He pursued postgraduate studies at the University of Florida, the Biblical Seminary of New York City, and Union Theological Seminary of New York.

His first pastorate was in Charleston, Mississippi, from 1918 to 1922, during which time he served a two year duty in the United States Army. In 1922 he became pastor of the First Presbyterian Church in Starkville, Mississippi, from which he was called in 1926 to be the assistant pastor of Second Presbyterian Church of Memphis. He began his forty year ministry at First Presbyterian Church in Gainesville, Florida in 1928, retiring in December of 1968. After that, he was the stated supply pastor of Bethlehem Presbyterian Church in Archer, Florida, where he remained active until two days before his death, April 30, 1976.

Honors that have come to Preacher Gordon are almost too numerous to mention. Outstanding among them are his Doctor of Divinity degree from Southwestern University at Memphis in 1930 and his honorary degree of Doctor of Humane Letters from the University of Florida in 1963.

He was Moderator of the Synod of Florida in 1940, and in 1967 the Synod honored him with a resolution spread upon the minutes recording his long and useful service. He served as a director of Columbia

Theological Seminary and Montreat College. He was National Chaplain of the Pi Kappa Alpha fraternity and an honorary member of Florida Blue Key. Four presidents of the University of Florida revered and recognized him for his service to the students and faculty.

While in Starkville, he inaugurated the South's first student religious program related to a state school campus and, from the outset of his Florida ministry, he closely associated himself with students. He was directly responsible for the building of what was then called the Presbyterian Student Center. He was a pioneer, founder, and builder of student work in Suwanee Presbytery, the Synod of Florida, and the General Assembly of the Presbyterian Church in the United States.

His unvarnished personality and faithful devotion to friends made him an early favorite as a "man among men." He was an ardent sportsman and lived in field and stream, but was respected as a well-read scholar, historian, and pastor. As a Rotarian and Mason, he had received honors of these and other associations, clubs, governments, and groups of all descriptions.

Preacher was "Unkie" to his nephew and nieces who were his only immediate survivors: William Bradshaw Gordon of Sardis, Mississippi; Helen Bridger Gordon of Baton Rouge, Louisiana; Minnielee Gordon Hale, formerly of Memphis; Jane Elizabeth Miller of Pensacola, Florida; and Charlotte McGee of Leland, Mississippi.

After his death on April 30, funeral services were held for him on Sunday, May 2, 1976 at the First Presbyterian Church of Gainesville. The next afternoon, he was buried from the First Presbyterian Church in Sardis, Mississippi, where interment was in the family plot of the Rosehill Cemetery with his father, Charles Law Gordon and his mother, Alice Monroe Short.

Before his death, a retirement center was named to honor Dr. Gordon, the Gordon Glen Manor in Gainesville.

The first building to be dedicated in his memory was Preacher Gordon Memorial Fellowship Hall at the Bethlehem Presbyterian Church in Archer.

The First Presbyterian Church of Gainesville refurbished and renamed its fellowship hall, the Gordon Memorial Hall.

At the Alachua General Hospital in Gainesville, an interfaith chapel and counseling lounge were created to be used by people of all religions for prayer, worship, and consultation. It is called the Preacher Gordon Memorial Chapel.

# Appendix B

## Sermons and Prayers

*The sermons and prayers compiled here are word for word transcriptions of tape recordings left unedited in order to retain the distinctive flavor of Preacher Gordon's impromptu style.*

### INVOCATION
### LAST MORNING SERVICE OF WORSHIP
### OLD PRESBYTERIAN CHURCH
### February 28, 1954

Oh, almighty God who has been our help in ages past, Thou art also our hope for years to come. Down the long corridors of the past, we remember Thy words to Thy servant of old, "Thou shalt remember all the way that Jehovah thy God hast led thee—to humble thee and to clothe thee and to know what is in thine heart." So now with an overflowing heart of thanksgiving, we come into this place which has been and which still is none other than the house of God and the gate of heaven to our hearts. May this be a service of lift and inspiration to all of our hearts. May holy memories come down like bright angels to strengthen and refresh our work for the days that lie ahead. For we ask it in the name of Jesus Christ Thy son, our Savior. Amen.

### INVOCATION
### FIRST SERVICE OF WORSHIP
### NEW PRESBYTERIAN CHURCH
### March 7, 1954

Let us pray. Awaken our lips, Oh Lord, to praise Thee and inspire our hearts to love Thee and our minds to know Thee, so that in praise and love and consecration we may glorify Thy name. We would enter into Thy gates with thanksgiving and into Thy courts with praise. We would bless Thee with our whole hearts. The heaven of heavens cannot contain Thee, much less this house, which we have builded to Thy glory. May we be in the spirit on the Lord's day and may we hear behind us a great voice, the voice of Jesus Christ Our Lord, who though dead yet liveth evermore. In His name we pray. Amen.

## PASTORAL PRAYER
## OFFERED AT THE LAST MORNING SERVICE
## OF WORSHIP
## THE OLD PRESBYTERIAN CHURCH
### February 28, 1954

Let us pray ... Almighty and eternal God, whose fatherly concern broods over all Thy creatures, descend upon us now in this worshipping congregation in the spirit of quietness that we may be prepared for the work, that we may be renewed in the whole man, that the waste bushes of our lives may be tended, and that we may be enabled more and more to die unto that which is unworthy of us. Take away the film of selfishness from our eyes that we may see how fair and gracious life may become to those who share themselves and what they have with their fellowman. And recreate in us the spirit of Christ who died for our sins and rose again for our justification that we may live in him and through him and for him all the days of our lives.

We pray that as we come with our necessities and our burdens and our difficulties that we may experience a lift and a change of view, that we may be enabled to seek those things afresh which are above, those things which are fair and good and holy, and are of good report. We commend unto Thee all whom we love everywhere. We thank Thee for them and for their unchanging love for us, praying Thee that we may have a sense of oneness in this hour of worship, our parents and loved ones and friends, wherever they may be, may we have a sense of oneness in the great church of the living God, and also a sense of oneness of that great host of men and women who have passed over the shining flood unto the far reaches of Thy kingdom; for those who have built this church and for those who have worked in it, and those who have sacrificed for it, and those who have given us such a wonderful legacy, upon the momentum of their lives and their bequest to us, we still travel on and we are grateful for it and we praise Thee for having made it possible for us to stand upon their shoulders and to garner the harvest which ripens upon their graves.

Now, our Father, we would unfurl the banner of Christ over us as we start a new milestone in the history of this congregation. We pray Thee that we may be humble and teachable and united and loving ... that we may have an eye always to serve our fellow man. And we humbly pray Thee that this service may be a memorable service to all of us that crystallizes in our hearts, our resolve and purposes as we go into the new church. Grant us Thy blessing and Thy peace and because we have worshipped with one another, may we be more considerate and may we be more kind as we travel life's common way. Because we have worshipped Thee, may we walk more confidently amid the difficulties of this complex age in which we live. And because we have praised Thee, may we walk that pilgrimage way more joyfully and more happily until the day shall break and the shadows flee away for us forever. For we ask it in the name of Jesus Christ, Thy son, our Savior. Amen.

## LAST SERMON (OLD PRESBYTERIAN CHURCH)
### Proverbs 10:7
### February 28, 1954

In the 10th chapter of Proverbs, there is a good verse for us to remember today. "The memory of the just is blessed, but the memory of the wicked shall rot." I want to dwell upon the first clause of that verse this morning, "the memory of the just is blessed"! I would like for us to place it over against this Old Testament lesson which was read to you ... the story of the death of Elisha. He had been a great and good man and he had come to the age of his death and he had gathered to his Father at the end of a long and useful life. Indeed, he had led such a long and useful life that when another dead man touched the bones of Elisha, the other dead man came to life and stood upon his feet. You heard that story this morning of the marauding Moabites on one of their periodic forays into the land of Israel; they had come upon a funeral ... That is, a man had died and no doubt preparations had been made that were required for a decent and an orderly funeral. Everything was in readiness when this band of nomads appeared over the horizon and suddenly there wasn't anything for the people to do but to find the first sepulcher that was at hand and that sepulcher happened to be the grave of Elisha. So they threw the body of this nameless neighbor into this grave and ran for their lives. And the Bible says here that when this nameless individual touched the bones of Elisha there in the sepulcher, that he revived, that he came to life again and stood upon his feet.

It is not my purpose this morning to discuss a miracle — the kind of miracle or modern miracles that people say come about because they worship at the shrine of some saint or touch some holy relic or get some handkerchief that has been blessed or maybe annointed by some kind of oil. I am not going to talk about that at all. I would rather suggest to you this morning some thoughts of a very practical nature. That is to say, it is suggested here that the influence of people if they have been good men and good women, will live on a long, long time after they are dead, after they have left the land of the living. Mankind has always found it a good thing to build memorials, to rear up monuments and that has been particularly true after we have had a great war. You know how many monuments have been reared in bronze or in stone and it's an appropriate and beautiful thing that we should do that! After the War Between the States, our south country was covered over with monuments in nearly every courthouse yard. You're familiar with Grant's tomb, and the great monument there at the circle in Indianapolis, and Washington's monument, and the Shrine of the Unknown Soldier, where a light is kept burning always so that men would be reminded that they ought to keep in perpetual memory those who made the supreme sacrifice for their country. You know what I mean by that! And turning back to a clipping out of a magazine (I noted that it was in August, 1944), the dominion of Canada was proposing to do a thing that to some extent we did in this country. Instead of rearing up a monument, they were devoting as memorials a certain plot of ground for a children's playground or maybe for a hospital or maybe for some school. They thought a memorial ought to have a utilitarian value. We did that to a very considerable degree in this country.

Now as appropriate and as beautiful as the monuments are that we have reared here in our own republic and in England and indeed in every country of this earth, there are the invisible monuments. I want you to think about this fact this morning! There are invisible monuments which are far more precious than a beautiful bronze tablet or some shaft of gleaming marble. They are far more beautiful because they too are reared up to the memory of the righteous dead. Oftentimes, the monument is in loving and grateful hearts. I trust that every one of you has such a monument in his heart this morning. The poet Wordsworth has a great line in one of his poems. I think it is in the Prelude; he speaks about "the reanimating influence of memory." Just as this man who touched the bones of Elisha was reanimated, he speaks about the reanimating influence of memory. The writer of the Proverbs took the pithy things that everybody realized to be true and put them into words. He said the memory of the just, the memory of the righteous, the memory of good people is blessed. It is forever true . . . that proverb! It's always true!

Now with that, I would link another statement out of the writings of Shakespeare. If you schoolboys or schoolgirls remember the play, "Marc Anthony", you remember that when a eulogy was being pronounced over the bier of Caesar, that he goes on to say this, "The evil that men do lives after them and the good is often interred with their bones." That is not such a true statement as the one I read to you this morning. There is just a half truth in that. It is true that evil does live after us, and it does become a blight and it does become a shadow and it becomes a bitter memory in people who live a long time after the evil man has passed off this stage of action . . . a long time after the evil man has become nothing but a handful of dust. But the inference in that statement of Shakespeare that a good man has just a temporary sort of influence, that his influence doesn't last so long . . . that statement is not true at all! It is altogether false!

There is a sense in which fame and reputation often pass over good people, nameless people; such as the people who builded this church and who put themselves and their sacrifice and their heart into it. I know the story of this pulpit, I know the sacrifice! I had it from the mouths of two or three persons how it was procured. The good and the righteous oftentimes are not mentioned at all and they are nameless. In the same sense, we have a very undesirable quality, I think, in the public press today . . . that is evil is glorified! The gangster, the man who has committed a terrible murder, the man who has killed his wife, the woman who has shot her husband, they get all of the front pages of the newspapers, without the asking! Oftentimes while crime and violence usually get the big headlines, you do not see anything there about people who are leading decent and helpful lives. You do not see enough about the doctor who goes about from day to day in his faithful work. You don't see enough about the teacher! You see mighty little about the home where love and confidence still reign. You don't see much about that. And in that sense, I suppose you might say that Shakespeare was right. The evil that men do lives on with them. You take a man like Hitler. You take a monster like Stalin or Nero and of course, their infamy will be perpetuated a long time after they are gone from this stage of action.

In the same sense, we have a very undesirable quality, I think, in the public press today . . . that is, evil is glorified! The gangster, the man who has committed a terrible murder, the man who has killed his wife, the woman who has shot her husband, they get all of the front pages of the newspapers, without the asking! Oftentimes while crime and violence usually get the big headlines, you do not see anything there about people who are leading decent and helpful lives. You do not see enough about the doctor who goes about from day to day in his faithful work. You don't see enough about the teacher! You see mighty little about the home where love and confidence still reign. You don't see much about that. And in that sense, I suppose you might say that Shakespeare was right. The evil that men do lives on with them. You take a man like Hitler. You take a monster like Stalin or Nero and of course, their infamy will be perpetuated a long time after they are gone from this stage of action.

The point that I want to make is this. That while that is true about the people who are cast as evil, here are the honorable names who have been hardly ever heard about. You never have heard very much (certainly in speaking after the manner of men) about the fame of people who built all these churches here in Gainesville. You never have heard very much about that. And perhaps their memory has been neglected. History does appear to exalt those who have been a scourge and a curse and does appear to pass by those who are good and worthy. But there isn't any doubt in the world about the lasting influence of the righteous! And that's a constant miracle!

Down here in the Florida straits, we have the great Gulfstream that flows up the eastern seaboard of this country and passes the shores of England and northern Europe . . . countries that would be cold and inhospitable as would be the shores of Greenland or Labrador without the warming influence of that current! So, it is true of the righteous! So it is true of the good! This dead man, this nameless dead man touched the bones of Elisha and immediately he was reanimated! He revived at once! Through the years you and I touch the lives of other people. We have a great debt of gratitude to people who have lived and who have influenced our lives . . . who have gone out of this life. Memory revives and reanimates you and me because they have lived! And you and I are living in them again. Somebody wrote these lines, "And is he dead whose glorious mind lifts thine on high . . . to live in heart, we live behind if not to die."

I wish to make this application on this significant day. There are the days in your life and in my life, when the Moabites, those marauding thieves of long ago, come under another name, into our lives. There are the sordid motives! There are the insincerities of life. There are the lapses. There are the unworthy things in our lives. Oftentimes, we have done this thing or that thing in life which once we would have scorned to practice. Again and again it has been true that quite suddenly without any choice on your part, you touched the life of somebody else and you were reanimated, and you revived! . . . that person maybe was an individual who thought about you . . . maybe your wife who has been dead a long time . . . maybe your husband . . . maybe some little child sleeping out there in God's acre. Maybe some old preacher, some old pastor; maybe some Sunday school teacher . . . some faithful teacher down here in J. J. Finley or Kirby-Smith school when you were a little boy; maybe someone who thought about you in terms of love and truth and honor. And that quite unexpected contact that you had with them in memory brought you back to yourself.

I have been in one other location where we built a new church. And in that pastorate back in Mississippi, the old church was built as a result of the labors of the Haystack prayer meeting. You may know something about that; in 1806 in Massachusetts, Congregationalists were there who came down when the Presbyterians came into the South. There was an old elder in the church who prayed for the generations unborn. We had a record of his prayer. And he took five bottles of wine, as I remember, and he put them in the cornerstone of that church; it was built in 1849. And we found there his prayer and we found that wine when that old colonial church was demolished. We used the wine in the first communion service that we had in the new church. But the significant thing is this. He envisioned people who came on after him. And he said, "Lord, make this a vine of Thine own planting" . . . that was in the prayer. "And let there be good fruit for the generations unborn!" He thought about people who were coming after him.

I wonder if you have ever been drifting rapidly towards the rocks and there came the gleam of some beacon and you were saved just in time because of somebody who lived a long time ago. It wasn't very much; maybe it was the stanza of that hymn; I chose that hymn in the beginning purposely. What a connection it has with our fathers . . . that old hymn immortal . . . "Mighty God, while angels bless Thee. May a mortal sing Thy name?" Generation after generation of people in our particular communion have sung that old hymn. And maybe it was just the memory of a hymn that when the peril came, you were steadied and fortified. By what? By father, mother, brother, sister, wife, child, pastor, Sunday school teacher, doctor, and where did that light burn? I'll tell you. Maybe in a portrait, maybe in some old letter; maybe in some book which was lovingly inscribed to you, maybe in some story which was given you out of the long past, and the past became a sort of whispering gallery to you. And those who lived back there in Gainesville's early days, maybe they have been speaking to you far more loudly than I have been speaking in audible comments this morning upon this passage . . . that people being dead are still speaking to you and you have been reanimated and you have been revived by contact with the long past!

Then there is that other time in life and not a few people know about this . . . all of the stars dropped out of your sky. They were blotted out by the clouds of doubt and gloom and bitterness and sorrow or cynicism as the case may be. Life's trials and life's sorrows . . . life's hardships swept over you just like those Moabites who came in there a long time ago and swept over that little funeral cortege that went out to the cemetery. In that hour, the memory of the just is your salvation! Because people have lived and because they have bequeathed something to you and me! Maybe you took up an old Bible and the eyes that looked at that page in the Bible no longer see dimly through the glasses, but they see face to face! . . . but there is that old Bible and you took it up because of somebody who loved and honored and worshipped God and whose influence is upon your life, and they helped you in your life and faith to have hope and courage in order to triumph over doubt and gloom. There is a hymn in the book, "Fall on the ears the distant triumph song and arms are strong and hearts are brave again!" I do not know of any faculty that the Bible takes and makes such great use of as this faculty. The Bible speaks about imagination and about thought and recollection, but it takes the faculty of memory . . . and even if in this holy hour there has been started in the heart of any of you a train of recollection of a remembrance from the past . . . some old home embowed by the trees back yonder in Massachusetts or Pennsylvania or Indiana or Kentucky or maybe to some church pew, maybe to a church pew right here in this church, or to some quiet spot out there in Evergreen Cemetery, or wherever it may be . . . memory if it says anything to you this morning, and I would say this to you . . . I have said it so many times in these past twenty-five years . . . if ever you have a good impulse, act on it. Don't act on a bad impulse. But regardless of the embarrassment, financial or otherwise, that a good impulse may cause you, act on your good impulse! Memory is saying that to you! Do it! Do it now and be worthy of it. And believe me, my friends, that is the voice of God!

In conclusion, there is this practical consideration, I think, this morning for all of us in this church and for all of you friends . . . I've looked into your dear faces for a long, long time here. There is a practical consideration for you and for others who have come here most recently, and brought a tide of fresh blood into the life of this congregation. We ought to live so that we will be worthy of being remembered! I do not remember much Latin! But I do remember some fine things in Latin, one of them from Tacitus. Tacitus says this. He says, "It's the duty and obligation of everybody to leave behind him a pleasant memory of himself!" What do you think of that? Isn't it? It is the duty of everybody to leave behind him a pleasant memory of himself! That is to say, there are the times when maybe we are tempted to be depressed and cynical. Everybody feels that way. Sometimes, your physical make-up has a lot to do with it. Maybe you need to go and see a doctor. Maybe you're run down. Maybe you're tired . . . you're depressed and you're cynical. And you say sometimes (I have heard people say this and I think I've said it myself) what difference does it make what people think about me when I am gone from this stage of action? At best or at worst in a few short years . . . why my name won't be remembered and your name will not be remembered. There won't be any Grant's tomb and there won't be any Washington monument, and there won't be any Tomb of the Unknown Soldier, and my name will be sunk down into forgetfulness and oblivion. Now that's just a passing mood! I don't believe any of you folks believe that . . . even if you have said it! A man knows and a woman knows that he or she will be remembered by somebody! And most of you will be remembered by a great many people. And I should think that all of us want to leave behind a pleasant memory of ourselves!!

And so, beloved in Christ, as we leave this fine old structure with so many wonderful memories, let us remember that we are standing on the shoulders of those who went before us . . . their sacrifices and labors . . . We are building on the foundation which they have laid. Let us strive to do our work well so that those who come after us will have a worthy heritage and a good memory of us all.

## PASTORAL PRAYER
## LAST PRAYER MEETING
## OLD FIRST PRESBYTERIAN CHURCH
### March, 1954

Let us pray. Our Father, we thank Thee tonight for all of the holy and blessed associations through the years which cluster around this church; for all of the heavenly aspirations which have been started here in our hearts and minds and for the memory of those who have been with us and who have gone on to be in the church triumphant, the general assembly and church of the first born whose names are written in heaven. We thank Thee for the inspiration that we have been sometimes unconsciously to one another. We bless Thy name that through the years there has been the spirit of unity and concord, harmony and love among the people of this flock. We are grateful for all of these things. We do not take them for granted, but from full and overflowing hearts, we say, "Bless the Lord, O my soul and all that is within me, bless His Holy Name!"

Appendix 229

We thank Thee for the milestones that come along the journey of life and all of our experiences in the homes of this congregation . . . for birth and anniversary and for the comfort that comes when some are taken as they have slipped away into the nearer presence of God, into the other rooms of the Father's house, and we remember that we are traveling that way and that is not a melancholy thought, but a comforting thought that we shall be with them forever and praise Thee without ceasing.

And now, our Father, accept our gratitude in this prayer meeting hour in this old church which we are soon to leave for another. Help us to take with us always the right spirit and the right attitude. Make us good within . . . sincere and honest, true and loyal, generous and forgiving. Fill our hearts with loving kindness and tender mercy toward all men, especially to them which are of the household of faith. Now we would all pray together from the heart the prayer that Jesus taught us!

## PASTORAL PRAYER OFFERED BY DR. U. S. GORDON
## WEDDING OF JUDY AND PERRY FOOTE
### September 25, 1965

Eternal and ever blessed God, whose presence is the happiness of every earthly condition and whose favor sweetens every relationship in life, in whom we live and move and have our being, who is the author of our life with all of its wonder and mystery, with its interests and joys, and with its friendships and fellowships, look down into the hearts of these, Thy dear children, Perry and Judy, whom we now bless in Thy name. And unite their lives, we pray Thee, with a pure and steadfast affection the one toward the other! Bless them now, Oh Lord, as they start the journey of life hand in hand together. Bless them in life's sunshine and bless them in life's shadows. Bless them in the rough places of the going and in the smooth. Bless them with great and continuing devotion and loyalty the one towards the other and crown their lives with Thy loving kindness and tender mercy. And enable them so to live together in this life that in the world to come they may have life everlasting through Jesus Christ Our Lord.  Amen.

## LAST BAPTISMAL SERVICE
## IN THE OLD PRESBYTERIAN CHURCH
## BAPTISM OF BENMONT TENCH, III
### February 28, 1954

The mercy of the Lord is from everlasting to everlasting upon them that fear Him and His righteousness is unto children's children. For He shall feed His flock like a shepherd and carry the lambs in His bosom and tenderly lead them that art with young. Benmont and Catherine, the promise is unto you and your children and all that are afar off even as many as the Lord, our God, shall call. Here in the church of your fathers, this child is the fourth generation. Now you come to dedicate this little one in the service of God. Do you promise to pray with and for this child and to teach him the scriptures and catechisms of the church and do you promise to set before him a Christian example and to bring him up in the nurture and admonition of the Lord? And do you, the sponsors that stand with them, also join together with these parents in these promises?

Let us pray. Grant, Oh Lord, grace to these Thy servants to perform that which they have promised to set aside this little boy in our common supplication for Thy service through Jesus Christ Our Lord. Amen.

Benmont, will you name this child? Benjamin Montmorency Tench, III. Benjamin Montmorency Tench, III, child of the covenant, I baptize you in the name of the Father, and of the Son, and of the Holy Ghost. Amen. This little child is now acknowledged as a member of Christ's church. Whosoever receiveth one such little child in my name receiveth me.

Let us pray. Let him grow up, Oh Lord, like Jesus grew from a little boy increasing daily in wisdom and in stature and in favor with God and man. And let his parents be ever faithful to the vows which they have taken here as this little one becomes a member of the household of faith. And now may the Lord bless you and keep you, the Lord make his face to shine upon you and be gracious unto you, the Lord lift up his countenance upon you and give you peace through Jesus Christ Our Lord. Amen.

## COMMUNION MEDITATION
### Text: Luke 24-Verse 35
### October 1, 1961

What a moving chapter this is. "He was known to them in the breaking of bread!" The name God that we use sometimes in profanity and that we take again and again on our lips in prayer. The name God! It's the most mysterious and it's the profoundest word in all of our vocabulary. When you get down to pray at night, do your thoughts ever flounder and do you find yourself in deep water trying to visualize something which sometimes seems nothing but an abstraction? Such an abstraction indeed that the heathen around about Israel made it real to themselves in making images! There were the fertility cults . . . and Paul goes on to make an indictment of all of that . . . He said, "They," speaking of the world before Christ and the world that was contemporary with Christ, he said, "They change the image of the incorruptible God to a corruptible image, like unto beasts, birds, four footed animals and creeping things." It was not a sin certainly contrary to the craving of the human heart. Neither is statuary or objects that we do not find in our own plain meeting house here. Symbols are alright . . . not too many symbols! The Jews wanted images. The prophets said, "No! You have words, that's all you have. Words!" And yet again and again they went out after images until the idea of idol worship, image worship was ironed out of their souls forever in the 70 years of captivity. Never again did they have images after that. And had you been in the Old Testament Church, you would have found beautiful architecture and you would have found symbols. Even had you gone into the Holy of Holies (whose veil was rent at the crucifixion of Jesus), you would have found it empty. Nothing but a chest there, a chest that had the tables of the law in it and Aaron's rod . . . only it was in the fullness of time that God sent forth his own Son, made of woman and made under a law . . . and then there were no more words . . . no more words! The Word became flesh! And the Christians didn't have an idol, they had a man. They had a real man of flesh and blood, like themselves, Jesus Christ Our Lord. We call that the incarnation and John goes on to say this, he says that which we have heard, that which we have seen with our eyes and our hands have held of the word of life. Thomas said, "Lord, let me reach and touch your wound prints, let me thrust my hand into your side." And Jesus said, "Thomas, because thou hast seen, thou hast believed. Blessed are they that have never seen, and yet believe." We don't see, do we? That's been a long, long time ago. When we get down on our knees, we think about a man, we think about Jesus. We think about what he said. "He that hath seen me, hath seen God, hath seen the Father." The Word became flesh!

Now to you and me, because we cannot go back through the silent centuries of 1900 years, because we cannot go back and literally touch and see him, The Word becomes something else. The Word becomes sacrament. The children used to sing this song. I, as a child, have sung it. "I wish that his hand had been placed on my head and that his arms had been thrown around me, that I might have seen his kind look when He said let the little ones come unto me." That isn't possible. But we have the sacrament. Jesus said, "This is my body, which is broken for you." Something that's so common, something that's so ordinary; you see it there on the table; you handle it in your fingers. I doubt that they understood it anymore than we would have understood it. Jesus was always teaching by parables. One time, he said in setting forth the value of the kingdom, he said, "Here's a precious pearl" incomparably valuable. Or when he told us how we ought to live, he said, "You are the light of the world, you are a lamp." And then when he spoke to anxious and worried people, he said, "Consider the lilies of the field." Now here he doesn't talk about a pearl. And he doesn't talk about a lamp. And he doesn't talk about a lily. He says, "Here is the bread." Something that's right on your table. Something that's so ordinary. Something that everybody sees every day. And I do not think those disciples took it in just then . . . He said, "I am with you always." And here we read in this moving story, "He was known to them in the breaking of the bread." So it has been ever since that time beloved!

This morning, if we had a table long enough it would stretch all the way around the world. Black men, brown men, yellow men, all kinds of men and women would be sitting down and breaking the bread of this holy sacrament, because all that Jesus did and all that He said and all that He suffered and all that God said and did and suffered in and through him, his death and his resurrection, is remembered here in the common bread. God so loved the world that He gave his only begotten son. It is a faithful saying and worthy of all acceptation that Christ Jesus came into the world to save sinners. What great words these are! These are the words of the gospel! But at the table of Communion, the Word becomes a sacrament! The Word that became flesh, the Word becomes a piece of bread ... That on which we live day after day. We can see it with our eyes and we can touch it with our hands.

It may be that some of you have come to church this morning without very much faith and without very much hope and without very much love. But God is waiting to be gracious to you this morning in the sacraments, in the bread and wine. And as we do celebrate it, may our faith be kindled and may we realize that the grace of our Lord Jesus Christ is just as real as that bread ... that we see with our eyes and that we touch with our hands.

Let us pray. Almighty God, who by the blood of Thy dear son, has consecrated for us a new and living way into the holiest of all, grant us now, we beseech Thee, the assurance of Thy presence here! And sanctify us that we approaching with singleness of heart and cleansed consciences, may offer unto Thee, the sacrifice of righteousness ... through Jesus Christ Our Lord.   Amen.

## INVOCATION
## NORTH FLORIDA REGIONAL HOSPITAL
## DEDICATION CEREMONY
### February 4, 1973

Almighty and Eternal God who madest all things in earth and Heaven and who lovest all that Thou hast made; who hast called us to be fellow workers with Thee in healing the hurts and woes of our Human Kind, we now dedicate in our common supplications this hospital to Thy glory, and for the comfort and well being of all people.

Let the foundation of this building be strong and lasting; Let the walls and the roof be firm and sturdy to shut out the tempest and the storm; Let each room be a sanctuary from the pressure and anxieties of life. May all who enter these doors leave behind the discords of life and find this place a haven of Serenity and Peace.

Lord Jesus, Divine Physician of body, soul, and spirit, come to all sick people in our hospital and show them Thy love and compassion and Thy healing touch as of long ago. Give patience and courage, endurance and cheerfulness, to bear all weakness and pain; and please save us from whining and self-pity.

Give to all doctors, surgeons and nurses skill in their hands, wisdom and common sense in their minds, and gentleness and understanding sympathy in their hearts; and let them even have appreciation and gratitude from those to whom they give so much.

In the name of Him who came not to be ministered unto but to minister, and to give his life a ransom for many.   Amen.

# Appendix C

## Tributes and Citations

### PLAQUE PRESENTED BY CHAMBER OF COMMERCE
### Gainesville, Florida
### September 18, 1963

In 1928 a young preacher came to Gainesville and throughout the intervening years he has given unstintingly of himself, not only to his church and its members, but to every person, regardless of faith or creed.

Perhaps no other person in the life of our university community has so influenced the lives of townspeople and students alike. His ministrations have transcended every formal barrier. By sheer dent of kindness and genuine concern for others he has brought himself into the hearts and lives of thousands of persons in this community and into the hearts and lives of hosts of university students who deeply feel that he symbolizes all that is good in Gainesville.

All of us while traveling in other parts of Florida, and to wherever Florida men have migrated, are met with the common inquiry of, "How's Preacher?", attesting to the fact that the warm image of his influence never fades from the minds of those who—even so briefly—come to know and love him.

He is an avid sportsman—a lover of dogs and dove and quail—and perhaps knows more places where good fish bite than any other six men in the county. When all other remedies fail, he can conjure a cure with a "buck eye" that is just short of a miracle.

For 35 years he has given of himself generously, consistently and unselfishly. His contributions of service and devotion to this community and its people are indelible upon the minds and hearts of all who know him.

As a tangible expression of recognition and appreciation from a grateful Chamber of Commerce, this plaque is presented to—Preacher Gordon.

## THE UNIVERSITY OF FLORIDA

## PRESENTATION

Mr. President:

It is with great personal pride and satisfaction that I present Ulysses Short Gordon for the honorary degree of Doctor of Humane Letters.

Born in Mississippi in 1893, he graduated from Southwestern College in 1915, and received the Bachelor of Divinity Degree in 1918 from Presbyterian Theological Seminary, Louisville, Kentucky. He was ordained in the same year and then served in the United States Army during World War I. His early pastorates were in Charleston and Starkville, Mississippi and in Memphis, Tennessee. In 1930, he was honored by his Alma Mater with the degree, Doctor of Divinity.

While in Starkville, he inaugurated the South's first student religious program related to a state school campus, and in accepting the call to Florida in 1928, he was eager to take up again this vital work. From the outset of his Florida ministry, he closely associated himself with the students at the University and was directly responsible for the building of the present Presbyterian University Center. His unique and warm personality and faithful devotion to friends made him an early favorite as a man among men in the all-male student body. An ardent sportsman, he lived in field and stream; he engaged athletes in strenuous games of handball and prayed with them in the simple sanctuary of his study. A scholar respected for his simplicity, goodwill, and good humor, he became known by countless numbers as "Preacher" Gordon. He has challenged students in their thinking, understood them in their weaknesses, and encouraged them in their academic, professional and spiritual pursuits. There is no way of estimating the breadth nor depth of his influence upon those fortunate enough to have found him.

Mr. President, I am proud to present for the honorary degree of Doctor of Humane Letters, one of the best-loved men in Florida, "Preacher Gordon."

May 4, 1963

LESTER L. HALE
Dean of Student Affairs

## CITATION

ULYSSES SHORT GORDON, distinguished pastor, teacher, public servant, and friend.

You have endeared yourself to thousands of University of Florida students and faculty members over a period of thirty-five years.

You have recognized and exemplified how scholarly achievement best serves the public good when embodied with a spirit of compassion, forgiveness and forbearance.

It is a real pleasure, by virtue of the authority vested in me by the Board of Control of this state, to confer upon you the degree, Doctor of Humane Letters, *honoris causa*, with all of the rights, privileges and emoluments thereunto appertaining. As a token thereof, I now present you with this diploma and cause the appropriate hood to be placed upon your shoulders.

May 4, 1963

J. WAYNE REITZ
President

## RESOLUTION
### SYNOD OF FLORIDA

That Synod approve the following CITATION with a *standing* vote:

THE SYNOD OF FLORIDA, Presbyterian Church in the United States, recognizes and pays tribute to "PREACHER" GORDON.

WHEREAS, *Ulysses Short* "Preacher" *Gordon* has served as the pastor to thousands of University of Florida students and faculty members over a period of thirty-nine years with understanding and compassion, and

WHEREAS, his contributions to his fellowmen have made him a highly respected and esteemed shepherd of men, and

WHEREAS, his warm personality, his untiring devotion to duty, his quick wit, and his love for his fellowmen have resulted in his being loved by all of those who have had the benefit of his ministry, and

WHEREAS, he has challenged students and faculty alike in their thinking, understood them in their weaknesses, and encouraged them in their academic, professional and spiritual pursuits, and

WHEREAS, he has enriched the lives of many, provided leadership and challenge when it was needed, aided in shouldering the burdens of misfortune and sorrow, and always stood ready with understanding, forbearance and forgiveness, and

WHEREAS, he has served as a pillar of strength for justice and moral integrity in his community and is regarded with deep esteem and affection by all Presbyterians in Florida, and

WHEREAS, the University of Florida recognized him with the honorary degree Doctorate of Humane Letters in 1963 in recognition of the constructive influence he has exerted over the many faculty and students with whom he has had contact and who have, in turn, carried this influence and spirit into all walks of life and into every corner of the world, and

WHEREAS, there is no way of estimating the breadth nor depth of his good influence,

THEREFORE, may all men know that the SYNOD OF FLORIDA, Presbyterian Church in the United States considers it a distinct honor and privilege to recognize and pay special tribute to this distinguished pastor, teacher, public servant, and friend for the many contributions he has made through his life of service to the needs of his academic community and thereby to his Lord and his Church, his state, his nation, and the world.

Gainesville, Florida  
June 21, 1967

HUGH C. HAMILTON  
Moderator

## SESSION, FIRST PRESBYTERIAN CHURCH MEMORIAL RESOLUTION

WHEREAS, the Reverend Ulysses S. Gordon, a native son of Sardis, Mississippi, served this church as its minister from 1928 until his retirement on December 3, 1968, and

WHEREAS, during his ministry the church built a new sanctuary and educational building and assisted in establishing three other Presbyterian churches in this community, and

WHEREAS, particularly during his early years here, he developed an enduring relationship with numerous students at the University of Florida. He led many to the faith and to Christian service and acquired the beloved title of "Preacher", and

WHEREAS, he was the prime mover in establishing the Presbyterian Student Center at the University of Florida, and

WHEREAS, while in retirement, he served the Archer Presbyterian Church as its preacher for over five years, and

WHEREAS, he was a greatly beloved pastor to the members of the First Presbyterian Church as well as to a wide range of citizens of Gainesville, and

WHEREAS, he was at ease with the lowly as well as the great and among them his name was blessed. By his manner and actions he taught the refinement of simplicity and extolled the good and the beautiful wherever he went, and

WHEREAS, he displayed great intellectual ability as well as a deep human understanding in his sermons and public utterances — holding that the scriptures were an inviolate guide to right living. His knowledge of the scriptures was of unusual breadth and his memory of Biblical passages was phenomenal, and

WHEREAS, in recognizing the frailties of man, he did not bemoan the past, but rather acted positively in the present and looked forward to the future, and

WHEREAS, he was a good athlete and in his younger days a great competitor on the handball courts. He was a lover of nature, of hunting and fishing, and of birds and dogs, and

WHEREAS, along with his many rare qualities and attributes, he possessed a delightful sense of humor,

Now, THEREFORE, this Session of the First Presbyterian Church extends its sympathy to the family of the Reverend Ulysses S. Gordon and expresses its deep sorrow over the loss of our beloved "Preacher." At the same time we give thanks to Almighty God for the life of this His great servant. This we do in the faith that he is now in the presence of his Heavenly Father and enjoying the life eternal.

HENRY G. HAMILTON
J. WAYNE REITZ
H. PHILIP CONSTANS

## The City of Gainesville Florida
### Office of the Mayor

### PROCLAMATION

WHEREAS, occasionally in the history of a community a man or woman will live an exemplary life that leaves a deep spiritual imprint upon the minds and hearts of its people; and

WHEREAS, the Reverend Ulysses S. Gordon lived such a life in our town for almost half a century as he ministered to the religious and bodily needs of the members of his congregation and of anyone else who had need of his loving care; and

WHEREAS, Preacher Gordon's humor and charm radiated moments of happiness and good cheer into the lives of countless people throughout this community as he went about his daily toils; and

WHEREAS, while the deep sorrow of Preacher Gordon's death is still upon us, we nevertheless rejoice that this kind and compassionate man passed our way.

Now, THEREFORE, I, Joseph W. Little, by the authority vested in me as Mayor-Commissioner of the City of Gainesville, Florida do hereby proclaim the month of May, 1976, as

### PREACHER GORDON MONTH

in the City of Gainesville and urge that all of us celebrate the works of this good man and remember him forever.

IN WITNESS WHEREOF, I have hereunto set my hand and caused to be affixed the official seal of the City of Gainesville, Florida, this 3rd day of May, A. D., 1976.

JOSEPH W. LITTLE
Mayor-Commissioner

# Board of County Commissioners
## of Alachua County

### RESOLUTION

WHEREAS, with the untimely death on April 30, 1976 of Ulysses Short Gordon, Gainesville and Alachua County lost a revered and dedicated minister, and

WHEREAS, his services as pastor of the First Presbyterian Church spanned forty years and touched countless lives and souls, and

WHEREAS, this community will feel his loss for many years to come;

NOW THEREFORE BE IT RESOLVED BY THE BOARD OF COUNTY COMMISSIONERS OF ALACHUA COUNTY, FLORIDA, that the great contributions made by Reverend U. S. Gordon to this community will never be forgotten, and that the Reverend Gordon shall be forever in the memories of the citizens of Alachua County.

DULY ADOPTED in regular session this 18th day of May, 1976, A.D.

JOHNATHAN F. WERSHOW
Chairman

## MEMORIAL TRIBUTE
## to
## U. S. "Preacher" Gordon
## May 4, 1976

It has been well-said that "Time which makes all things old doeth ever make some old things new."

For virtually a half-century, Preacher Gordon made old things new, as he lived the ancient faith of hope and charity in our midst, and we, in turn, lived in the lustre of his joy and service.

Preacher understood the implications of the words, "to err is human, to forgive is divine." He knew that no man is as good as he may think he is, nor as bad as either his foes or friends may believe; that all fall short of perfection but that, in spite of this, none are beyond the concern of the servant of God. Hence he was ever quick to forgive and to accept men for what they are and lent to all the joy of one who himself ran and did not grow weary, who walked and did not faint.

Preacher Gordon made new some other very old things. He realized that nothing broadly worthwhile can be done by one person alone; that man is saved by love. He knew that no great task can be completed in one lifetime of three score and ten; that man is saved by hope. He understood that complete goodness can not be found in the immediate, temporal scene nor in any one specific age; that men are saved by faith.

He believed—that faith, hope, and love are the necessities of the spirit yesterday, today, and forever.

Men such as Preacher Gordon do not pass life's way often, although, perhaps, they come more often than we know or deserve. We rejoice indeed that so many in this part of the land had him with them for so long. Truly his good deeds were numberless and his influence superb. Our hearts are full of sorrow and wonder. We have had a glimpse at how fine a man can be on this earth and we are very pleased with what we have seen.

Prepared by: Delton L. Scudder, Ph.D.

Approved unanimously by the Gainesville Rotary Club, May 4, 1976.

## TRIBUTE TO U. S. "PREACHER" GORDON

With a buckeye in his pocket, a sheepish grin on his face, and a mischievous twinkle in his eye, he walked erect and stood tall.

He was a man at ease with saint and sinner alike, with rich and poor, with educated and uneducated—one who knew no strangers. His ready wit provided him with an answer for every occasion—some humorous, some barbed, some bold, but all provided windows through which we peeked into the soul of a saint.

He never married, so he never knew the pleasure of having a wife and children. But he *was* married—married to a church, to a city, to a high calling of which he was proud.

His sermons and prayers were not built as a constructionist builds a tower; they were born. When they were delivered, it was obvious to his hearers that he had been with Jesus.

Hundreds of blushing brides found themselves pronounced as wives to husbands by his raspy voice, and through the years thousands of mourners found comfort from his well-chosen words of faith, and hope and love.

He was a real man who loved life, who laughed, who wept, who cheered, and who could get a little angry when the occasion warranted.

He loved us Baptists. He often said that the only difference between us and the Presbyterians was a parking lot. I can hear him now: "Are you still preaching the gospel—salvation by grace through faith and that not of yourselves, it is the gift of God"? "It's the only way," he would say. And he was right.

"Are you behaving yourself?" he was recently asked, and he said in response, "At my age, that's all you can do. And if you could do anything else, you've got a right to."

If you knew him you loved him. If you ever met him, you will never forget him. He grew with a city and somewhere through the passage of time, a city came to know him as their "Preacher".

His voice is now silenced on earth, but not in heaven. Somehow I think he must be spinning some good yarn with fishermen like Peter, James and John.

"Preacher Gordon, we loved you and on this Sunday when you would have been preaching somewhere, we miss you. But you fought a good fight. You finished your course. You kept the faith. Put your crown on—it fits you well!"

May 2, 1976

JERRY HAYNER, Pastor
First Baptist Church
Gainesville, Florida

## DEDICATION ADDRESS
U. S. Gordon Memorial Hall
Bethlehem Presbyterian Church
Archer, Florida
April 24, 1977

*(Also delivered in modified form at the dedication of the Preacher Gordon Memorial Chapel, Alachua General Hospital, Gainesville, Florida, March 25, 1979.)*

It is a high privilege to participate in this dedication ceremony and I am most grateful for the invitation. This building is dedicated to the glory of God in memory of Ulysses Short Gordon known to all of us as "Preacher". It is a miracle of love and Christian devotion to behold this building here today exactly one year after Preacher ended his earthly journey. Again and again I heard people remark, there is no way that little church, that handful of people, can put up that building, and yet, here we are in this fine structure today. What a great testimony it is to the power of faith and Christian determination and to the love this congregation had for Preacher Gordon.

Like so many great Americans he was born in a little town—Sardis, Mississippi. He inherited a sound, strong body and was felt intellectually to be a child prodigy. He was educated at Southwestern College where he excelled academically and athletically. He received his formal theological education at Louisville Presbyterian Seminary and Union Seminary in New York City. He served many pastorates including ones in Mississippi, Tennessee, and Florida. As you know, he was pastor of the First Presbyterian Church in Gainesville for forty years, from 1928 to 1968. The last six years of his ministry were spent serving in the Archer Bethlehem Presbyterian Church. I often heard him remark that those weeks and months were some of the happiest of his life.

This building is dedicated to God in memory of Preacher because people loved him. We loved him for what he was and for what he stood for. Most of all he loved Christ and brought us all closer to the Master. He was always there to meet you just where you stood, to help you carry your load and bear the burden. Rarely did he sit in judgement. He understood peoples' shortcomings and found some good in everyone no matter how low they had slipped. His was a heart filled with love, kindness, and compassion, always ready to lend a helping hand. His ministry knew no bounds. We were all considered to be part of the Lord's flock. He had a great zest for life and loved being a pastor to all manner and conditions of men regardless of their race, denomination, or status. Preacher was a plain-spoken man and yet when the occasion demanded he could and did wax eloquently. He meant what he said and he said what he meant. People always knew where he stood and more often than not it was on high and holy ground.

His sermons were brilliant in their subject matter, yet filled with good, basic common sense. His spiritual depth was revealed in his moving prayers which were spontaneous creations of beauty – prayers which led us all to the Throne of Grace.

He loved to heist a tune and frequently did so after breakfast or while driving his car. His powerful voice often drowned out the choir. Most hymns he had committed to memory. Preacher believed in common courtesy, good manners, a good name, and respect for your parents and elders.

He had a profound influence on others and God worked through the life of this man in wondrous ways. Many souls, including hundreds of university students, were started on the Christian path by Preacher's guiding hand.

About forty-five years ago, former United States Senator, George Smathers, John Stembler, and Jack Beckwith, were on their way to the First Presbyterian Church in Gainesville early one Sunday morning. Along the way they saw a big, blond-headed kid sitting on the curb all by himself looking real lonesome. They stopped in front of him and asked if he wanted a lift to which he replied, "No thanks". They introduced themselves and recognized him as one of the freshmen football players. "Come on", again they said, "and go to church with us and meet Preacher Gordon who is a real all-round, regular guy who makes going to church worthwhile." The athlete said that he was not interested in going to church, but that he would go to town just for the ride. On the way to town they convinced the big guy to take an hour off and go to church. After listening to one of Preacher Gordon's down-to-earth personalized sermons he said he would like to meet the "Preacher". This was easily accomplished and the "Preacher" and the athlete became real good friends. The inspiration of the Holy Spirit working through Preacher transformed the life of that big football player and he later went on and became a Presbyterian minister.

His life was lived entirely for others – a kind and reassuring word when one was needed, always present in times of adversity, an extensive correspondence with the lonely and troubled, baby shoes for the newborn, flowers and cards for the sick and infirmed, always at the hospital or visiting shut-ins, gifts for the newlyweds, telegrams and Bibles for the high school graduates, candy and gum for the children after church. His generosity knew no end. His salary was given away as fast as he received it.

From about 1950 to 1960, Preacher held an early morning chapel service every other Sunday for the prisoners at a local road camp outside of Gainesville. Now those boys would kill snakes along the road as they worked during the week and would convert the hides into billfolds. Sunday after Sunday I would see Preacher buy four or five wallets in order to give those prisoners a little spending money. In a year's time his purchases amounted to five hundred dollars and during that ten year period he bought about five thousand dollars worth of billfolds from his own meager income. In those days every Presbyterian male in Gainesville carried a snakehide billfold given to him by the "Preacher".

God gave him a wonderful sense of humor; his wit and earthy wisdom were known far and wide. This seemed to keep his life in balance, because in his work he was always around so much sorrow. People loved to be with him for he had a way of giving you a lift with a warm story or perhaps some keen insight or observation about the world in which we live. During the Depression years he would say when the collection plate was passed, "If you can't afford to put a little in, take a little out".

In the days when the Roman Catholic church frowned on intermarriage between their members and members of other churches they required people who were marrying across church lines to be married in the Roman church and for the non-Roman Catholics to sign a pledge that all the children would be raised in the Roman church. A citizen of Gainesville who was a Roman Catholic wanted to breed his dog with one of Preacher's. When approached about this possibility, Preacher thought for a long time and finally said, "I will agree to this alliance, provided that you sign a statement that all the dogs from this litter will be raised Presbyterian."

A good many years ago he was attending a church meeting away from Gainesville and one of the good ladies greeted him in what she thought an appropriate manner and not knowing of his confirmed bachelorhood, asked him, "And where is Mrs. Gordon?" Preacher replied with a straight face and without hesitating, "Thank you, she is with her mother".

Preacher had a great fondness for animals, especially dogs, and over the years had a number of pets. His first cocker spaniels, Deacon and Elder, accompanied him everywhere. Later spaniels were named Noah and Nicodemus. He then raised a Weimaraner whom he called Joseph. This great big gentle animal was particularly close to Preacher's heart and was noted to be a good retriever. One day a little old lady looked at "Joe" and said, "Preacher, what kind of dog is that?" He replied, "A carpenter dog!" The little old lady bit down hard on the hook and said, "A carpenter dog?" Preacher chuckled, "Yes, he likes to do odd jobs around the house . . ." His dogs were always present at mealtime and would frequently catch a morsel tossed from the table. At the end of the meal the plates would go on the floor and the dogs would lick them clean. Preacher would laugh and say, "Now we don't have to wash them." His last pet "Dicki", a Chihuahua, was proclaimed an "imitation" because he was so tiny and was termed, "the world's most spoiled dog." Dicki slept at the foot of the bed and if the night was really cold he frequently turned up the next morning on the pillow next to Preacher.

In his latter days he was beset by all manner of physical ills – the terrible pains of arthritis, failing eyesight, and cancer, but his mind and spirit simply did not decline as did his body. His flesh grew frail and weakened, but his mind remained alert and his spirit embraced the world. In the twilight of his life his spirit grew larger and people were nourished and strengthened by his wonderful, vibrant presence. He was an extraordinary man – God's man – one of the great men of our church and day. We were privileged to know him and we are all better people because we journeyed with him. Throughout history at sundry times and in diverse places, God sees fit to grant us a fleeting glimpse of That Ultimate Glory which shone in the face of Christ. A reflection of That Glory was revealed in the life of Preacher Gordon.

This church was founded in 1866 in Wacahoota as the Bethlehem Presbyterian Church. The founding pastor was Dr. W. J. McCormick who also founded the Kanapaha Church and the First Presbyterian Church in Gainesville. In 1875, the church was moved to Archer. In 1908, it was renamed the Archer Presbyterian Church and in 1976, at the urging of Preacher Gordon the name was changed back to the Bethlehem Presbyterian Church in Archer. Looking back over the years we can see that Almighty God has rewarded the faith and determination of the founders of this church and richly blessed its members. And so we come to another milestone in the history of this congregation – the dedication of this Ulysses Short Gordon Memorial Hall. During his last few years of life, Preacher was a great supporter of the idea to construct this building. He believed in Christian education. He was a great student and teacher of the Bible, most of which he had committed to memory. I know he is with us here today! And so we join the name Gordon to this building; the name to the building and the building to the name; the word to the stone and the stone to the word; spirit to spirit and life to life, in the earnest expectation that all who enter this building will be transformed and will go forth better able to serve in Christ's kingdom. In dedicating this hall I think Preacher would want us to remember Paul's advice to Timothy of old, "Study to show thyself approved unto God". May this be a building where truth illumines minds and causes people to grow in grace. May it be a place where men discover their own Christian obligation, where people commit themselves to the task of making a life in Christ Jesus as well as a living. Let this building be a place wherein the minds of men seek actively after the will of God. Let it be a place of instruction where age speaks to youth out of the depths of learning and experience. Let it be a place of thoughtfulness where people speak honestly with each other as friend to friend, man to man, and Christian to Christian. Let this building be our resolution to carry on in Preacher's name and in his spirit. And in this building may we always find a vision of the truth that is revealed in Christ our Lord and that was exemplified in the life of our beloved friend and pastor Preacher Gordon.

PERRY A. FOOTE, JR., M.D.

# PRAYER OF DEDICATION AND CONSECRATION

U. S. "Preacher" Gordon Memorial Chapel
Alachua General Hospital
Gainesville, Florida
March 25, 1979, and April 8, 1979

Almighty and eternal God, whom the heaven of heavens cannot contain, we stop now to worship Thee and to ask for Thy blessing on this ceremony and to thank Thee for all whose contributions of time, artistry, architectural, building and administrative genius are wrought here this day. Sanctify this chapel and counseling chamber as a holy place, Oh God, in which those who call upon Thy name can feel the comfort and power of Thy Presence.

Just as Thou didst in the beginning divide out of chaos the land and sea, day and night, and cause a beautiful garden to grow of exquisite beauty yet of tempting dangers, so unto all generations hast Thou preserved Thy bounty but required of us responsible stewardship. Thou hast given us the brain-power to unlock a few of Thy secrets of growth, re-creation, and energy, yet, having also created us in Thine own image, Thou hast given us a spiritual-power capable of communing with Thee and transcending the limits of time and space into the everlasting dimensions of life.

We thank Thee; we seek to glorify Thee; we worship Thee in this quiet moment of prayer. As we see the beauty of life through the ages reflected here in this chapel on this beautiful Palm Sunday, we contemplate the cup of living water given to the desperate one fallen by the wayside, the hands ministering to the cripple lowered for a touch of Thy healing hands. We pray Thee, that this place of prayer, meditation, and counsel will serve the intended purpose of providing comfort and courage to the spirits of those who tarry here. "Comfort ye My people," saith the Lord God of Israel. May the skill and care of doctors and nurses in this house of healing minister to Thy hurting children as Thou hast given them the talent to be Thy agents of mercy.

And now, O God, we consecrate this holy sanctuary to Thy Glory and in memory of Thy beloved servant, Ulysses Short Gordon, and cause it to bear his name. We do so, not so much to reflect the personality of the man, as much as to do him honor. He loved his Lord, Jesus Christ, accepted him fully as his personal Savior, and devoted his life to ministering in His name to persons of all faiths or of no discernible faith at all. He led them, each one, to a better understanding of Thee, O God, and blest and comforted them in the name of Thy Son who said, "If you have done it unto the least of these my brethren you have done it unto me."

As the Bible was a lamp unto his feet and a light unto his pathway, Preacher Gordon walked these halls and lighted a candle in the hearts of patients in every room of this hospital and gave encouragement and appreciation to every employee. He was a friend to all and his smile and cheerful greeting was an antibody for gloom. The corridors have echoed his certain but slowing step as the years hampered him physically but never stunted the twinkle in his eye. He died almost three years ago on April 30, 1976, and within a few feet of this very spot. His jokes, laughter, and prayers no longer linger on his lips, but remain engraved in the hearts and lives of countless patients, anxious and grieving families, devoted physicians, nurses, aides, friends, and relatives. His influence has already hallowed these walls, so we pause now only to thank Thee, O God for his life and to consecrate in his memory this chapel as a place where people of any and all faiths can put their problems into the perspective of Thine own Everlasting Truth.

"Open now the crystal fountain whence the healing streams doth flow" and make this Preacher Gordon Memorial Chapel a haven of rest for those who are weary but grateful, or who are desperate and alone. May there be a blessing here for all who enter in faith, and who will "be still and know that Thou art God." Let them depart with a deeper awareness of their spirits' having communed with Thee. As the sands flow slowly but surely through the hour glass of time for all of us, O God, "support us all the day long, until the shadows lengthen and the evening comes, and the busy world is hushed, and the fever of life is over, and our work is done. Then in Thy mercy grant us a safe lodging and holy rest, and peace at the last, "Oh God, our Refuge and our Strength." Amen.

LESTER L. HALE, PH.D.

## IN MEMORIAM

### DR. U. S. 'PREACHER' GORDON

When Dr. U. S. "Preacher" Gordon died last spring, he left a memory of service and dedication to others that will live on as part of the heritage of Southwestern.

The 82-year-old "Preacher," as he was known to all, was a 1915 graduate of Southwestern. He spent his life in the ministry, retiring in 1968 after 40 years as pastor of First Presbyterian Church in Gainesville, Florida.

Throughout his life, he was the college's unofficial representative wherever he went, and any effort of Southwestern from attracting qualified students to raising funds, became a responsibility he shared with enthusiasm.

His many friends remember him as a kind, generous man, quick to find the bright side and always ready to bear the brunt of his own jokes. But he was equally ready to listen to problems and to do whatever he could to help others.

He was a familiar figure in Gainesville area hospitals as he made his rounds comforting people of all faiths. He once said of his ministry that he "liked to throw hay where even the smallest goat can nibble."

One of the many who were influenced by Gordon was Southwestern trustee William C. Rasberry of Shreveport, Louisiana who worked for "Preacher" in the 1920s. Rasberry remembers the dedication of his friend to the work of the church, and his genuine interest in the young Rasberry, whom he called his "assistant pastor."

"Preacher Gordon was like a father to me," Rasberry said recently. It was through him that Rasberry learning of Southwestern, and with his help and urging that Rasberry came north from Mississippi to take a job with Southwestern and complete his college education.

Funeral services in Gainesville for "Preacher" Gordon saw more than 1,500 people gather to pay their last respects. In a tribute to Gordon, Lester L. Hale recalled the preacher who had touched the lives of so many:

"He would answer the phone by saying, 'Ain't that my most main and principal baptized child?' To Preacher, we have *all* been his most main and principal friends. He has loved us all and has been loved by all of us. He will forever live in our hearts, as indeed he will have everlasting life with his Lord and Savior."

(From *SOUTHWESTERN TODAY,* October 1976)

## A TRIBUTE TO "PREACHER" GORDON
### Remarks by the Rev. Lester L. Hale at the Funeral

A Christian giant has fallen!
> Nay, has been lifted up and glorified by the Holy Spirit of Christ, Our Lord. Let us pray.

O, Lord, we have dreaded the coming of this day, but we have known from the beginning that it would have to be, for there are "ends that were in the beginning and beginnings which lie concealed in the end." "That which Thou sowest is not quickened except it die, and yet, to die in Christ is gain!"

And so we cry out, unashamedly, in sorrow because the natural body and happy voice of our beloved "Preacher" Gordon will be absent from us; but we rejoice in the faith that his spirit will forever be real to us.

"Though we live in a world of change, it is not a world of chance," as "Preacher" has so often prayed, and the time now has been fulfilled when his work on earth is done and his new work in heaven's begun.

"Come, Holy Spirit, Heavenly Dove, with all Thy quickening powers; kindle a flame of sacred love in these cold hearts of ours."

We pray in Jesus' name, Amen.

It seems that my whole life has been lived to bring me to this moment. How unworthy one can feel to say anything that has not already been said or that you do not already know about "our pal," "your partner," who, all along, has been our "most main and principal" pastor and friend.

He would answer the phone by saying, "Ain't that my most main and principal baptized child?" To Preacher we have *all* been his most main and principal friends. He has loved us all and been loved by all of us. He will forever live in our hearts, as indeed he will have everlasting life with his Lord and Savior.

His life was lived completely for others. Years ago, women of the church quit giving him a warm, winter coat each fall because he kept giving the coats away to those he considered to need them more than he did. On the day he was taken to the hospital, he gave instructions carefully concerning the carrying out of commitments he had made.

During his day of travail, in his disorientation because of pain, he kept looking at his hospital bracelet and asking me what time it was. When I told him, he would say, "My goodness, let's call it a day — we've been here long enough," and he would try to get out of bed.

"Preacher," I said, "you can't get up, you've got too many tubes — you've got everything but an inner tube."

"Lesterbell," he said, "you're right — I've got too many tubes. Tell them to give some of them to the poor and needy."

Always thinking of someone else! Always trying to find the twinkle of laughter in the tear of tragedy.

Why did we love him? Let me count the ways:
> Because he understood people's weaknesses and forgave them!
> Because he found some good in everyone, and revealed the mischief in himself.
> Because he was empathetic with those in trouble and could become involved emotionally without losing his own composure.
> Because he could break tensions with an appropriate anecdote, or a "Well, sister?"
> Because his influence has reached from the low places of life to the leadership of state and nation.
> Because his friendship knew no bounds of church, denomination, social status, race, nor creed.
> Because he could walk with kings and not lose the common touch.
> Because he met you where you were and walked with you to help carry the load.

> Because, when he "cut the fool," his wit was tempered by goodwill and a profound human kindness.
> Because he was *good*, but not too good, and people could identify with him: rich men, poor men, beggar men, thieves—doctors, lawyers, merchants, chiefs.
> Because he had the divine gift to be our "spiritual advisor."
> Because he loved his church and served the body of believers whether they were in or out of the sanctuary.
> Because he was natural and had a deep down reverence, and was revered, but had no superficial piety . . . he was just "Preacher."
> Because, above all else, he loved his Lord and, by precept and example, brought us all closer to Jesus because we were close to "Preacher." To love "Preacher" was to love what he stood for most in life!

To him, we were all sons in the Gospel and daughters in the love of Jesus. To us, he was our father in the faith—the nearest and dearest disciple of our day.

How Christlike was his personality, his love, his life. He tended his Master's sheep and kept His flock by night. He was first and foremost a pastor—a good shepherd.

How much like the Apostle Paul was his lack of concern for his own comfort and welfare, and were his warm greetings to all.

"Man, don't give me that . . . I don't need nothin'."

"I'm feeling just fine . . . much better than I deserve."

"Ain't that my baptized child? My lodge brother?"

He prayed with and for prisoners, students, the aged, firemen, policemen and all who "wait upon the public good." He wrote letters without ceasing.

His "Muscle Deacons" rise up and call him "blessed." His buckeye talismen are a national institution: "Here, you carry this; it will help what ails you. If you don't get better, there's no telling how bad things might have been if you didn't have it."

In Paul's letter to the Philippians, he said what I think Preacher would like for me to say to you today.

> "This I pray, that your love may abound yet more and more in knowledge and in all judgment . . . Fulfill ye my joy, that ye be likeminded, having the same love, being of one accord, of one mind . . . Look not every man on his own things, but every man also on the things of others. Let this mind be in you, which was also in Christ Jesus . . ."

So Preacher lived out his life to the end observing the Great Commission Jesus gave to his disciples: that they go teach all nations, baptizing them in the name of the Father, Son and Holy Ghost, and teaching them to observe all things whatsoever Jesus had commanded—feed the poor, comfort the disconsolate, help the needy, stand fast in the faith, love the Lord.

"And, now, unto Him that is able to keep *us all* from falling, and to present us faultless before the presence of His glory with exceeding joy – To the only wise God, our Savior, be glory and majesty, dominion and power, both now and forever."

LET US PRAY.

"O, God, our Father, from whom we come, unto whom we return, and in whom we live and move and have our being: We praise Thee for Thy good gift of life; for its wonder and mystery, its friendships and fellowships. We thank Thee for the ties that bind us one to another. We bless Thee for Thy loving and patient dealings with us, whereby Thou dost ever teach us Thy way; for the meaning that lies hidden in the heart of sorrow, disappointment, and grief; and for Thy guiding hand along the way of our pilgrimage.

"We give Thee thanks for Thy servant, Preacher Gordon, recalling in him all that made others love him. We thank Thee for the goodness and truth that have passed from his life into the lives of others, and have made the world richer for his presence . . .

"O, Lord, support us all the day long, until the shadows lengthen and the evening comes, and the busy world is hushed, and the fever of life is over, and our work is done. Then in Thy mercy grant us a safe lodging, and a holy rest, and peace at the last; through Jesus Christ our Lord. Amen." (from *The Book of Common Worship)*